CloudDancer's Alaskan Chronicles

CloudDancer's Alaskan Chronicles

Volume II

CloudDancer

iUniverse, Inc.
New York Bloomington Shanghai

CloudDancer's Alaskan Chronicles
Volume II

iUniverse books may be ordered through booksellers or by contacting:

iUniverse
1663 Liberty Drive
Bloomington, IN 47403
www.iuniverse.com
1-800-Authors (1-800-288-4677)

Because of the dynamic nature of the Internet, any Web addresses or links contained in this book may have changed since publication and may no longer be valid.

The views expressed in this work are solely those of the author and do not necessarily reflect the views of the publisher, and the publisher hereby disclaims any responsibility for them.

ISBN: 978-0-595-48770-7 (pbk)
ISBN: 978-0-595-60838-6 (ebk)

Printed in the United States of America

Dedication

Eighty-four years now. That's how long it's been since a flimsy open cockpit wood and fabric biplane first soared aloft over the frozen tundra of Alaska in 1924. Bush Pilot Carl Ben Eielson was the first to haul the mail. The first I'm sure to do so many things with an airplane over the Great Land. Hot on his trail came the Wein brothers, Harold Gillam, Joe Crosson and the rest of the REAL Alaskan aviation pioneers.

I am often asked "Hey Cloudy. What's with that goofy paper bag over your head alla' time? Why don't you want us to know who you are?" And the answer is as remarkably simple as it is complex. It truly started as a gag. But it grew into a creed I will swear by.

After the very first flying adventurers came, the following decades saw more pilots trickle north. Most of them were pretty well known, if not famous too. Then the trickle became a small stream. By the late 1970's, a few years after I had arrived, the stream flowed smooth, steady and mostly anonymously. Young pilots came up from the Lower 48 to places like Barrow, Bethel, Nome, Kotzebue, Juneau, and Dillingham. All over the state. Every month almost a new pilot would show up and one who'd been here for a while would leave.

"A while." Ha! I went to Alaska for "only six months" I promised Mom and Pop CloudDancer. I stayed for twenty years and left my heart there forever. Many showed up and didn't last three days. By now there have been hundreds if not thousands of pilots plying the Arctic skies.

The stories in the first book and this one as well are all true and really happened to me or my closest friends. But folks, my biggest joy now in life is when a current or former "bush pilot" writes, Emails or calls and says "Hey Cloudy! You got it so right on!" And I came to understand that "CloudDancer's" stories are OUR stories. CloudDancer could be any pilot you see at Gwennie's chowing down on some reindeer sausage and sourdough hotcakes. CloudDancer could be any pilot you see hanging around Lake Hood longing for just one short "little airplane" ride over Alaska again. CloudDancer could be any airline pilot you see getting off an Airbus A320 who looks just a little uncomfortable in his uniform.

This book then, is dedicated to all of us. The one's who came before me. The one's who followed. And to the new generation who do the job today.

CloudDancer

Contents

Foreword. xi

Author's Acknowledgments. xiii

Handy-Dandy List of Acronym Meanings xv

"GOOD! ... We're VFR"

CHAPTER 1	The Sun Also Rises 3
CHAPTER 2	Pants on Fire!! 5
CHAPTER 3	And Then Along Comes Penny. 12
CHAPTER 4	Seldom Seen Cedrick. 15
CHAPTER 5	The Pepsi Generation 23
CHAPTER 6	No Business Like Snow Business 28
CHAPTER 7	Hi Ho, Hi Ho, It's OFF to Work We Go 31
CHAPTER 8	Chitty-Chitty Bang BANG!! 35
CHAPTER 9	Just How DARK is Dark?? 40
CHAPTER 10	"Good! We're VFR!!" 44

"Hi. I'm From the F.A.A., and I'm Here to Help."

CHAPTER 1	Is That One STUFFS or Two? 55
CHAPTER 2	Remember the Alamo 57
CHAPTER 3	Blue Propellor Thingy. 60

CHAPTER 4   You In a HEAP'o Trouble Boy 68

CHAPTER 5   Pilot Police. 71

CHAPTER 6   The Death Penalty. 73

CHAPTER 7   Keep the Change 82

CHAPTER 8   Buy Ya Books 'n Send Ya' to School 86

CHAPTER 9   Bless Me Rod, for I Have Sinned 89

CHAPTER 10   A Few Well Placed Words 91

The Jeremy Newton GCA

CHAPTER 1   Meow, Meow, Meow. 97

CHAPTER 2   East is ODD (+) 500, Right? 101

CHAPTER 3   The "State Flower" Approach. 103

CHAPTER 4   With Apologies to Charles Shultz & Snoopy 108

CHAPTER 5   Can You Hear Me NOW? 110

CHAPTER 6   Every Which Way but ... UP! 113

CHAPTER 7   Oh Say Can You See 116

Epilogue 126

PostScript—One Pilot and a Dog 133

"Weren't Nobody SHOOTIN' at Me?!"

CHAPTER 1   Gotta' Know When to Hold 'em 139

CHAPTER 2   Mercenary Pilot ... or Novelist?? 145

CHAPTER 3   Groundschool, On the Rocks Please 152

CHAPTER 4   "Maintain Visual Separation". 157

CHAPTER 5   The Faith of our ForeFathers 161

CHAPTER 6   "Weren't Nobody SHOOTin' At Me!!" 165

CHAPTER 7   Two Kinds of Legends......................171

CHAPTER 8   A Man of Few Words 173

CHAPTER 9   The Golden Triangle......................176

CHAPTER 10   Share and Share Alike 183

CHAPTER 11   "... AND If Ya' Ask Me AGAIN" 190

CHAPTER 12   How LONG Can You Hold YOUR Breath?......193

CHAPTER 13   Cumulus Ganitus INTERRUPTUS!! 196

CHAPTER 14   "Hey. Spill a Little of That Over Here." 199

What Could POSSIBLY Go Wrong?

Prologue 205

CHAPTER 1   Washed Up at Twenty-Seven 206

CHAPTER 2   He USED to be a PILOT 211

CHAPTER 3   A Day about ... NOTHING 213

CHAPTER 4   An Offer I Can't Refuse....................216

CHAPTER 5   On Converting Kerosene to NOISE!..........219

CHAPTER 6   Coming to America...................222

CHAPTER 7   A Place For Everything 226

CHAPTER 8   Back in the Saddle ... Almost 229

CHAPTER 9   It's a Done Deal 232

CHAPTER 10   RIDE That Bronc Cowboy!................235

CHAPTER 11   Over or Under.........................239

CHAPTER 12   What Could POSSIBLY Go Wrong?..........244

CHAPTER 13   When Good Guys Wore White Hats..........252

CHAPTER 14   You In a Heap o' Trouble Boy 256

CHAPTER 15   Carmel Sue Somebody 261

Epilogue 266

In the Beginning 269

Closing Comments 275

Foreword

The Kotzebue of the 1970s, where I first met CloudDancer, was a village on the edge of the world. It was closer to Russia than to the continental U.S. There were more huskies than humans, more snow machines and three-wheeler ATVs than cars. The main medium of communications was the the Tundra Telegraph message service on public radio station KOTZ, where CloudDancer and I both did volunteer shows.

Kotzebue is surrounded on three sides by salt water, so a trip of any distance meant a ride in a Bush plane. Bush planes served as taxis, ambulances, and grocery vans for the people of Northwest Alaska. It was pilots like CloudDancer who made the system work.

I was a private pilot myself at the time, doing for fun what he and his fellow Bush pilots did for a living. I was also an air traffic controller at the FAA station in Kotzebue. So I had a front-row seat for the work these men—all the Kotzebue Bush pilots were men in that day—did under conditions of remarkable difficulty: howling winds, bitter cold, blinding fogs and blizzards, and primitive village airstrips or, at times, no airstrip at all, just a gravel bar on a remote river bend.

CloudDancer and I both left Kotzebue and went on to other things. He worked his way up through the airline system and now flies an Airbus jetliner for a living. I had a career in journalism and now work as external affairs director for an organization dedicated to preventing oil spills like the Exxon Valdez.

As a journalist and amateur Bush pilot, I've seen a lot of Alaska. But Kotzebue is the most interesting place I ever lived, and it's a hard place to get out of your system. A few years after I left, I began writing mystery novels starring an Eskimo cop in a fictional village modeled on Kotzebue. And CloudDancer eventually began posting his memories of the place online, which led to the book you hold in your hands.

I get back to Kotzebue a couple of times a year. In some ways, it's changed a lot. A few of the streets are paved now and the bars where CloudDancer and I used to hang out have closed. There's a pretty good espresso stand near the airport where you'll find kids updating their MySpace pages over high-speed Internet connections. Finally, cars outnumber the snowmachines.

In other ways, though, Kotzebue is still its old self. The men still go out and hunt seals along the ice edge in front of town and KOTZ still beams out the Tundra Telegraph messages. Pilots like CloudDancer still run Bush planes in and out of tiny village strips in all kinds of weather.

I've read a lot of Alaska flying books, and very few them qualify as great. Those few include CloudDancer's chronicles of his time and adventures in a remarkable little town on the edge of the world. I'm glad he's bothered to write it all down and I'm wowed by how good he is at it. Enjoy.

Stan Jones, Anchorage
Fellow aviator and author of the Nathan Active mystery series: "White Sky, Black Ice," "Shaman Pass," and "Frozen Sun."
www.sjbooks.com

Author's Acknowledgments

First and foremost comes my thanks to the legions of "CloudDancer's Alaskan Chronicles" readers and supporters. Without your constant encouragement and prodding, your patience during the "dry spells" and your enthusiastic response on the internet, there would've been no book, much less the Volume II you currently hold in your hands.

Much credit must go to my primary literary mentor as well, Mr. Stan Jones of Anchorage. A fellow author and pilot himself, he was kind enough to write the foreword for this book. But since the beginning, he has been generous to a fault. His sound counsel on all facets of the literary process have been invaluable.

Finally, assisting me in one of my most challenging aspects, is Ms. Noel Lindner. As a result of her long hours of volunteered personal time, you shall find this book to be far easier reading than the first. Noel's editing and formatting skills are to be praised for that. Once I convinced her that "breasticles" and everbody were really words irregardless of what SpellCheck says, things went swimmingly. Thank You Noel.

Handy-Dandy List of Acronym Meanings

ADF—Automatic Direction Finder (a low frequency navigation radio)

AGL—Above Ground Level

ANC—Anchorage

A/S—Airspeed

BRW—Pt. Barrow

BS—Sometimes it means Blowing Snow

CDI—Course Deviation Indicator

CHT—(Engine) Cylinder Head(s) Temperature

DG—Directional Gyro (think electric or vacuum operated gyro compass)

FAI—Fairbanks

FED/FEDS—F.A.A. Flight or Maintenance Inspectors (O.K. guys ... mostly)
FSS—Flight Service Station (a division of the F.A.A.)

GCA—Ground Controlled Approach (radar operator "talks" you down)

HF—High Frequency communications radio

IAS—indicated airspeed

IFR—Instrument Flight Rules

KIAS—indicated airspeed in knots

MAG/mag—Magneto (Think distributor on your car's engine)

MAYDAY—International radio distress call

MSL—Mean (above) Sea Level

NM—Nautical Mile(s) (About 7/8's of a "regular" mile)

NWS—National Weather Service

OAT—Outside Air Temperature

OME—Nome

OTZ—Kotzebue

RPM—Revolutions Per Minute

TAL—Tanana

SLED/sled—Sometimes Author's disrespectful term for a Cessna 207

VFR—Visual Flight Rules

VHF—Very High Frequency

VOR—Very high Omni Range (a high frequency navigation radio)

"GOOD! ... We're VFR"

1

The Sun Also Rises

It's the middle of December and the days just don't get much shorter than they are right now. Here, 37 miles above the Arctic Circle the old "sun rises in the East and sets in the West" that kids Outside are taught from grade school just don't cut it.

I always have to laugh when people ask Alaskans "How do you stand being in the darkness for six months?" But, I guess until someone explains it to you and you think about it for a little while you just accept it like ... well, like "the sun rises in ... etc".

So for you "outsiders" do this for fun one day if you think of it. To be more specific, mark the calender for Dec 21st and June 21st the summer and winter equinox and solstice. If you live in the northern half of our great nation, on those two specific days, compare the time between sunset and sunrise from your newspaper's weather page and say Miami.

And you southern tier folks do the same thing for your town and say Bangor, Maine. The further north or south you live in the 48 contiguous states the greater will be the difference. And the further you get from the equator the more drastic will be the change. You can see it on a daily basis too. Simply do the same thing on either March or September 21st. You will find that while Kotzebue is gaining or losing nine or ten minutes of sunlight a day Miami may only be changing by a two or three at most.

This explains why in Kotzebue, on the day of this story the sun came up in the (almost) due south around 11:15 AM or so . Actually it rose vertically straight up about five degrees east of due south. After rising in a straight line to about 10 or 12 degrees above the southern horizon it then moved horizontally to the right about ten degrees. Finally it then dropped vertically straight down below the horizon about five degrees west of due south. It disappeared completely by about12:45 PM. Add on about 25 to 30 minutes or so of workable "civil twilight" before and after and you've got about two-and-a-half hours of "daytime" flying, even on the shortest winter day in Kotzebue.

Of course, all this only applies on a clear day. (... you can see forever! ... oops!) If it's cloudy and snowy, you are lucky to get about 1:45 of early morning type "workable" daylight. This explains why, when one of the town's other part-time "gun-for-hire to the highest bidder" charter pilots and full time ops agent for Wien Jerry Knickerbauer used to joke ... "Boy I had a tough day. I flew from 'cain't see' 'til CAIN'T see" it was pretty funny. At least in December.

2

Pants on Fire!!

Well I've been around Kotzebue for almost five full months now. And nearly every day is some sort of new adventure; a new village (rarely) or maybe a new "off-airport" landing strip. Most of the time it may just be a new customer I've never met before. Or once in a while it's finding yet another prominent or subtle landmark I can add to the mental rolodex file I keep in my brain for locating village runways in less than ideal VFR conditions.

I've memorized every runway heading and field elevation for every village in our region and a few on the Seward Peninsula too. And for each village I now have memorized as well what heading must be flown immediately off either end of the one runway for how many second or minutes at my approximate sixty MPH projected groundspeed during the climb ... just in CASE!

Taking off from Kiana's runway six is an immediate climbing right hand turn to a heading of 210 degrees for at least eight minutes before turning to a heading of 256 degrees. That should put you just about over Noorvik. At most you'll be no more than a mile to the northeast of the village when you make your turn towards Kotzebue. And you'll be within reception range of both the VOR or NDB at any altitude of 700 feet or higher. Now you can verify a bearing to or from Kotzebue to confirm that you are indeed a safe four or five miles to the south of the hills immediately west of Kiana.

Now taking off on 24 on the other hand requires an immediate LEFT hand turn to about a south heading. Hold it for at least sixty seconds to avoid the ridgeline no more than a half mile to the west of the runway. It's about 800 feet higher. But don't get distracted and forget to make a turn to the 210 heading because the Waring mountains which run east/westerly between Kiana and Selawik are rapidly approaching your slowly climbing little ChickenHawk. Lying ahead invisible in the dark, they will be intent upon swatting you out of the sky if'n you're where you don't belong. Some villages easier and some a little harder. Pay attention and make sure you wear a good watch!!

5

But some of the newness was starting to wear off. While my job was far, far from becoming routine I was sort of settling in. I had some level of comfort and confidence both on and off the job. But, much to my dismay and the absolute delight of the Gunderson brothers, while I wasn't looking, someone was settling in with young CloudDancer.

I'd been introduced to Kotzebue's chief form of year round entertainment, which is consuming alcoholic beverages by the friggin' boatload apparently. I was now a well known figure and good tipping favorite of the bartenders in three of Kotzebue's four gin joints. Unfortunately for the piggy banks of the hard workers at Leroy's Arctic Lounge on Front street, having only a beer and wine license, prevented me from spreading some of my growing wealth in their direction. Seems my sensitive pallette was unable to handle such unrefined swill as mere beer and wine.

I had NO problem whatsoever though pickling my internal organs with daily overdoses of the cheapest gins and rums, some aged I imagine for purt near a week or two.

Aside from owning the Arctic Lounge, Leroy also just happened to be the Gunderson's number one competitor, often stealing a Gunderson trip. "I stoled 'em fair 'n square" Leroy was oft heard to say. A common method of which was, upon arriving in his parking lot and alighting from one of his planes 50 yards to the east of our lot, Leroy would spot a good load of Gunderson's passengers next door. They were awaiting Dan's return from the trip he was on.

Whereupon Leroy would casually holler over "Hey. Did you guys miss Dan?" and the people would reply "Oh no. We're supposed to leave at three."

Now Leroy glances at his watch and sees it is 2:55, and goes "Huh. Well geee. That's kinda' strange. (Lying now) I just passed Dan on my way in, about five miles out. He said he was going to Kobuk (or Shungnak, or Pt. Hope ... any-place far away). I guess he must've forgotten you." This is doubly devastating as Dan, unlike Leroy, is very likely related by some blood to the passengers. This would leave the passengers somewhere between frustrated, slightly wounded pride, or downright mad.

Now Leroy could occasionally be VERY unreliable himself. Most likely he doesn't have a damn thing to do for the rest of the day anyway. He has been slowly taking a couple of steps every few seconds toward the passengers, and would now make a big show of looking at his watch again.

He would then announce initially somewhat reluctantly it appeared that, "We-e-ell. I DO have another trip at four (liar liar), but if I hustle I can get you guys over to Noorvik and get back in time. Uh, that is as long as you guys are paying cash." The Gundersons were know as real soft touches and extended way too much credit to far too many people. This would eventually lead to their business failures.

Usually the passengers would agree and begin dragging their stuff over to Leroy's yard. And once Leroy had their cash in his pocket, trust me, it wasn't coming back out. There are no refunds here or at the Arctic Lounge. The objective then became to load the passengers and baggage as quickly as possible and beat feet outta' town. See Dan might actually well have been calling in at the west shore of Kobuk lake for advisories with Flight Service as Leroy was touching down on runway 26 while listening to Dan on the radio.

This scenario would result in Dan taxying in passing Leroy taxying out with Dan's load, any one or two of whom Dan would probably recognize across the short distance. Much the same as the chivalrous and glorious dogfighting of World War One would result in mid-air salute from the victor to the vanquished foe, an episode such as this often ended in a mutual salute (of sorts) between these two old foes as well. They were fewer fingers involved though. Between the two of them, the passing salute(s) used less fingers total that one good boy Scout salute. So when I met Leroy on my very first trip to the bar, on my second week in town, I knew by then who he was. I'd been warned to be wary of the man.

Imagine then my surprise when the man, instead of treating me like "the enemy", welcomed me by name and called me over to the empty barstool next to him. He even offered to buy me a "welcome to town" drink. But I, never having consumed alcohol in any form other than communion wine was clueless as to what to order. So I just told the gorgeous Eskimo girl behind the bar at the Drift Inn (the town's ONLY thirty or so room hotel) "Gimme' what he's having", which turned out to be a Tom Collins. Over some following still (to me) unknown period of time, Leroy plied me with both friendly conversation and many, still (to me) unknown number of adult beverages.

Although I was technically "the competition" Leroy willingly offered a few scattered tips about some of the traps to be found in Arctic flying. Where the summertime fog banks hung, and which village runways were nastier and more dangerous when rain soaked; that sort of thing. Also, upon learning that it was new to this drinking business, he kindly offered me the benefits of his years of overindulging experience as well.

When I allowed that the Tom Collins (gin) was actually a little too sweet when I finished it, Leroy suggested I try a ScrewDriver (vodka) as that had the added benefit of being healthy, containing orange juice 'n all. Well, I'd always since childhood drank freshly squeezed sweet orange juice and the bar mixed with canned unsweetened so that really kinda' tasted bad. But not wanting to offend Leroy who'd been generous enough to buy that drink as well I made sure to drain the glass as a sincere show of appreciation before commenting that the drink was just a Li-i-ittle too TART! (Expecting the three bears to show up any time now).

I had expected Leroy to show a little disgust or slight impatience at my obvious youthful inexperience, as I struggled to come up with just the right drink to order. But, surprisingly to me, the man appeared genuinely concerned that his two suggestions had fallen short of the mark. Further, he insisted that he buy the next round as well in recompense. He assured me that it was quite important for a man to find just the right drink that appeals to his taste buds. I believe he said something about it being one of the inalienable rights guaranteed by the Declaration of Independence, and then suggested that possibly I should try a Scotch 'n Soda (whiskey). Always loved the song, but as it turned out the Kingston Trio knew more about good harmony than good cocktails, this one being definitely too SOUR.

Again, manfully, I worked my way through this drink still basking in the warm glow of my new found friendship with this nice fella' Leroy, who was obviously just grossly misunderstood by my employer.

I'd been eyeing Sheila the bartender, A good looking little Eskimo cupcake, she had LONG eyelashes and long hair down to her heart-shaped little Levi labeled butt. I'm tickled pink to find out that this is a part time job for her as she is a full time ticket agent for Wien and loves pilots it seems. The fact that she has a really … no I mean REALLY nice set of naturally tan love melons prominently displayed by the deep vee neck of her tight contrastingly virginal white cashmere sweater had absolutely NO influence on my firm decision to make her my first future ex-wife.

Things were warming up in more ways than one, by the time I had finished my fourth drink, a RUM 'n Coke. This drink had also been bought for me by Leroy. Having decided that since I was so new I hadn't even gotten my first paycheck yet; the VERY least he could do was spring for one more. He generously said he'd gladly wait for me to make it up to him on my payday.

By the time I had knocked back the Rum 'n coke, which was good but still not perfect, a whole hour had passed already. My, my. How time just flew by with good company!

As Leroy suggested I might like to try something blended, like, oh … say … a GRASSHOPPER Sheila was at that moment once again bending down over the ice bin to load up another glass with ice. Alas, nearing the bottom of the bin the ice cubes were starting to melt together, This necessitated a vigorous assault on the offending lump with the hand held ice scoop. That had the possibly unintended effect of setting Sheila's (barely) and loosely holstered love puppies to swaying and bashing to and fro against each other and … (chorus of heavenly angels) … HA-A-A-A-LELIUJAH!! Well, that cashmere sweater reminded ol' CloudDancer of couple of large kitty cats fighting in a small burlap sack. Cue angels again!

So focused was I on this vision of what I was now sure must indeed be heaven; (I mean I knew I wanted to spend eternity there …), so focused was I that not seeing above the neckline I missed the dirty looks that for some reason Sheila was laying on Leroy. The rest of that night, however long it was (the sun's up all night and the bar's open 'til five AM) gets fuzzier than Sheila's sweater after that.

According to news reports received on the other end of town the following morning Gunderson's new kid pilot from Texas was apparently seen staggering wild-eyed down Second Avenue sometime after midnight singing the theme song from the musical western comedy movie starring Burt Lancaster, Brian Keith and Maureen O'Hara … something called Hallelujah Trail at the top of his lungs. The second chorus was interrupted mid-Hallelujah, it is further reported, by a rather sudden and violent beet-blowing frenzy which brought the poor boy literally to his (hands and) knees. Several eye-witnesses all seemed to agree that our intrepid airman then resumed his wobbly journey home in a much subdued manner, gait noticeably unimproved by the episode.

So. That was the first time I remember going out as an adult to a bar. Coincidentally it was also the first, though certainly not the last time, I was unclear as to the details of my departure. Nor was it the first time I uttered the now all too familiar words upon first opening my eyes in the morning and rolling over … "Oh God! Where AM I?!" At 11 A.M. the next morning I awaken to a POUNDING! on the door, which meshes perfectly with the POUNDING! in my head! I fling open the door to my apartment, owned and provided by the company as part of my compensation to find the quite irate face of you guessed it. the owner.

"What the HELL are you doin' boy!? You're wastin' daylight!" I open my mouth to speak, but instead quite powerfully and unintentionally BELCH out the word "Well.…" I begin. Dan reels backward against the opposite hallway wall, knocked almost on his ass by the offending odors emanating from within my abused innards. He'd already heard the reports. Being one of the not too many Eskimo-drinkers, he was therefore very unhappy with his new boy blunder.

"Get your butt dressed and out to the airport now!" he says heatedly and turns to leave as he continues to fan the air with his hands.

In less than 20 minutes I sheepishly walk into the one room office to find Dan behind his desk, considerably cooled down, thankfully for me. Dan has kids only three years younger than me and has decided to approach this problem in a "fatherly" sort of counseling manner one time, at least.

Talking to me gently, he counsels me about overindulgence, forgives me. And offers me some fresh coffee which I gratefully accept. Everything seems to be going swimmingly and I am not going to lose my job it appears. That is, until Dan asks me what provoked such behavior anyway.

Like any good sinner, I welcomed the opportunity to shift as much of the blame as I could, and realized that it would also give me the opportunity to share with Dan my perception of his misperception of my new friend Leroy. But, the instant I mentioned Leroy's name Dan tensed up. And for some reason, as I explained the earlier part of the evening (the part I could remember) Dan's face got visibly redder and redder. And I continued talking about how nice, how generous, how pleasant.... KAAAH ... BOOM!

"Youuuuuuu DUMMY!" Dan screamed at me. "He spent all of 40 dollars getting you drunk last night and has already stolen three of our cash trips this morning worth five hundred bucks! Get OUT! Get out and GO FIND US A TRIP!" Man, I skeedaddled right back out the office door. I went to my ChickenHawk and began furiously polishing my windshield. Reaching in my shirt pocket I pulled out my cigarette pack and a piece of paper fell out of my pocket onto the gravel below. Quickly I leapt off the step and landed with my size twelve right boot squarely on the small scrap of paper before the ever present Kotzebue breeze could blow it away. At the same time I struck then quickly cupped withing my rolled up hands a Fire Chief match. Into the flame I buried the tip of my Malboro sucking deeply.

With the throbbing in my head gradually subsiding, the nicotine rush was further unwinding the tenseness inside from the morning's abrupt and unpleasant start. As I started to bend down, the whining of a nearby engine starter stopped me. I turned around just as the individual blades on the front of Leroy's Cessna 206 turned into a blurred disc. Immediately he gunned his engine and was rolling down the property line that separates our yard from his toward the paved asphalt taxiway. As he was passing, he leaned forward over the dash so I could see him clearly. With a big "cat ate the canary" grin on his face he tossed off a friendly wave in my direction. In my somewhat weakened condition, I responded as best I could, but it was a few fingers short.

I continued to watch and within seconds he was roaring over the gravel strip southbound leaving only a trail of sideways blowing dust behind. I bent down, moved my foot and picked up the scrap of paper. With very beautiful penmanship was written only a name and four digits. It read "Penny 2271".

3

And Then Along Comes Penny

As previously noted, much to the delight of my employers, the Gunderson brothers, I had somehow, with no real effort on my part acquired my first live-in girlfriend. I fact, I clearly remember doing my darndest to dissuade this girl from moving in. No, really, I mean it.

Four numbers. That's all you needed to dial in Kotzebue in those days to make a local phone call, as it was all one exchange. It operated only slightly better than the party line in Petticoat Junction's mythical Hooterville. And seeing the name Penny and the four digit phone number prompted some brief flashbacks to the previous evening.

One can only imagine the depths of my despair upon learning at some point the previous evening that while Sheila did indeed like pilots and was not herself averse to occasionally demonstrating it, she was married. I'm sure I must've, at least momentarily, wondered if A.) Her husband had a sense of humor, and B.) If not, how big a guy is he. What must of sealed the deal for me, sending me in search of greener pastures, was the added knowledge that her husband was one of the State's finest Trooper's. While short on humor he had plenty of ammo, not to mention ways to make it look like a righteous shoot! Therefore, with a heavy heart not to mention I'm sure, a woodie not even a cat could scratch, I was off in search of other game. Which led me to Penny.

Now, when you think of words like possessive, stalking, domestic disputes a certain picture comes to mind. And I'm here (all of me still, thankfully) to tell you. Man, when one of those cute little village girls starts to think your bed is HER bed, it is pretty hard to change her mind!

Unbeknownst to me just yet there is some sort of unwritten law apparently. Yes, Eskimo girls too, like all women of the world have a Book of Rules for Men.

Apparently it was first written by Eve during idle time in the Garden, when she tired of toying with the old man. This handy reference has been passed down through subsequent generations of females. No male has ever seen it. A female clerk at a Barnes and Nobles once even tried to tell me it didn't even exist! But I know better. And furthermore, I can tell you that the Eskimo (village) version contains a tenant that reads something like the following.

If randy, young pilot with promising future takes you home from the bar on three consecutive nights for stchupping this is a clear indication that he loves you. An Addendum to this rule apparently goes that "If at least two out of the three stchuppings are well above average, this is a clear indication of an intended long-term relationship."

In order to avert being saddled and "busted" it is quite necessary and acceptable to insert another girl into the equation. Doesn't matter if she comes between the first and second, or second and third time. Just make sure the first gal is aware of it! This resets the "stchupp counter" to zero, allowing you … allowing you … whatever. But this alone is all that can save you.

And so it was that having called Penny and invited her out for dinner and a drink the following night (which of course led to … you know … boinking!), I was feeling quite "relieved". Well, the next night I was back in the bar again (never sensing that a pattern was starting to develop here) and to my surprise, so was Penny. Well we chatted, but not wishing to deprive any of Kotzebue's other fair young maidens the opportunity of a lifetime, I stayed for only one or two before moving on to a bar at the north end of town. I needed room to operate, y'know?

Now there are only so many really, really good looking girls in a town of 2500 people. What with sharing being out of the question ol' CloudDancer was coming up scoreless after still another two or three hours. Then, lo and behold, who else but Penny walks into the second bar. Yada. Yada … drink drink … Follow me home follow me home … WHAPPATTA! WHAPPATTA! … Smoke smoke. I'll spare you the details of the next day other than to say it was like GroundHog Day the movie. Woke up with Penny by my side and fell asleep after a couple more … (um … amazing what you can do when your nineteen … smoke smoke) with Penny in my arms yet again.

Now imagine my surprise when on the following evening, done flying early, I return to my apartment. I was determined that tonight I was coming home either alone or (preferably) with a different girl. For I'd seen a good dozen or so deserving of my attentions. Penny was nice. But I mean hey, let's give it a little break here, right?

I open my apartment door to find curtains hung I didn't know I had and food cooking on the stove. I hadn't even known if it worked 'til then. Quickly, certain I had accidently entered the wrong apartment, I backed out the door and checked the number. No. This is my apartment. Or at least it was when we left for work this morning. I mean, Penny was nice enough to drop me off in her Dad's car, which he let's her use mostly.

So I slowly walked back in, surveying the scene in the front room when I hear a very feminine humming coming from the back (or) MY bedroom. Creeping very slowing toward the back I see Penny. She is unpacking a few suitcases and stowing things here, there, everywhere!

Again, I'll spare you the minutia of the long, long discussion we had in which I attempted to dissuade her without hurting. But, the lesson for me was summed up when I finally did recover my ability so speak. I walked into what 'til then had been MY bedroom and casually asked. "Hi. Whatcha' doin?" I received a one sentence response along with a look that I would soon come to know means "Why you silly man, it's so OBVIOUS!" Her answer was … "Well, I thought if I was going to be staying here, I should have some of my stuff here too." It would be many years before I repeated this error, but I was roped in now. Much to Dan and Rod's amusement it appeared I was going to be around for a long, long time maybe.

Alcohol is addicting and makes you do sometimes funny, sometimes stupid things. Sex is also addicting and makes men do mostly stupid things. It is how Penny, tired of my long discussion trying to talk her into repacking her suitcases and returning to her parents home, ended all further discussion of the matter. It hadn't taken a month from my arrival in Kotzebue and my new addictions had me in deep doo-doo. But at least my addictions hadn't put me in the hospital. Dan Gunderson had been hospitalized for almost eight weeks as Christmas '73 approached for illnesses brought on by his devastating addiction.

4

Seldom Seen Cedrick

Most any pilot regardless of their age when they start flying are generally working towards flying bigger, higher, and faster airsheens and I was certainly no exception. I had every intention when I started to be in at least a 737 or DC-9 withing a matter of a few years. That was another benefit of going to work for the Gunderson family. They were already operating both a Baron and a Twin Bonanza from the Beech family, but also a 1959 Dornier SkyServant STOL twin piston.

Added to the family's already eclectic (even for the 1970's) collection shortly after my arrival was a 1960 model Aero Commander 560E. This high wing twin mounted two Lycoming GO-480-C's putting out 295HP at 3400RPM to lift it's legal gross load limit of about 6600 lbs as I remember.

One of the earlier aircraft built with an eye toward passenger comfort, it's plush interior seated five to seven in a cozy rear cabin in seats with armrests! The true sense of "cockpit" was added with floor to ceiling dark wooden panels behind the two pilot's seats extending outward to the cabin walls. The plane featured a front office totally cluttered with internally lit big rocker style switches, knobs, clocks and dials everywhere you looked. Man, now THIS was some big time heavy iron. Yeah!

But the way Dan flew the thing you'da thought it was an ag truck! Standard practice for Dan when departing any runway was JAM! the throttles forward bringing a howling scream from both engines and practically warping the propellor tips forward. They waited only a few milliseconds for the rest of the attached blade/hub/engine-bolted-to-the-airframe to catch the rest of the assemblage up with them. As noted previously in other CloudDancer epics, Dan wasn't exactly renowned for ... uh ... finesse.

As a matter o' fact; I knew a dozen or so Eskimo pilots in those days. There was Dan and Rod of course. Then there was Smelly Henry down in Nome and Jack Fredricks outta' Barrow along with ol' Barney Huntley from Bethel. Some more Eskimo pilots were another set of brothers Geoffrey and Randell Rheinertz.

Among their many offspring, male and female, are numbered Captains for multiple Major US airlines and a couple of ATC controllers to boot.

In fact only in Alaska would you ever hear the following exchange between a 121 Air Carrier Captain and a enroute center controller. I was privy to it only because Randell had allowed me the rare treat and privilege of riding in the jumpseat of his Wein 737-200 combi that night.

Capt. Rheinhertz; (CR) ANC center, Wien 53 checking on, offa' Galena at four-seven climbing to two-five-zero.

Center: (Sweet feminine voice) Well! Lookie whose here, wouldja' now!! Hello Wien 53. You're cleared to climb to flight Level 310 and don't forget to tell me when you GET THERE this time.

Capt. (CR): Okay little girlie. (Obviously LONG before sexual harassment and sensitivity training) Hey! What do you think about me heading straight home?

Center: Wien 53 you are cleared present position direct to Anchorage. But as for going straight home, Mom called and said to tell you to stop at the store on the way home. Get some eggs and milk. Contact ANC center abeam McGrath on 128.9 Goodnight Daddy

Capt. (CR): Okay. 128 decimal niner. Goodnight Kitten!!

There was ol' James Vandergriff in Aniak and more flying native families in Golovin and Unalakeet

But while they all were good and most of them GREAT or superb pilots (none has ever been killed that I know of to date in an accident up there yet) their flying styles fell into one of two drastically different formats.

The airline trained guys, like Rod were as comfortable and relaxed on the gauges as they were in clear skies. And they usually flew with a sense of style and grace that eluded the others. They had more patience in general while in the air.

The others fell into Dan's "camp" (so to speak). They could get TO anywhere FROM anywhere within three hundred NM of their home base with a quarter mile visibility. They'd fly visually at the lowest possible altitudes without breaking a sweat! And these guys were as comfortable and relaxed that way as the other guys were thousands of feet above them in the soup (flying VFR, of course). And these guys were cowboys among cowboys. They purely reveled in making airplanes do what other pilots, even manufacturer's said they couldn't.

As I was saying about Dan's takeoffs in the Commander ... (I get sidetracked easily) once all the parts of the airplane had sufficient (in Dan's mind) airspeed flowing about them, Dan would (obviously) haul back on the yoke and get the nosewheel offa' the runway. Now. Which main wheel left the ground first was most often governed by the direction to the destination moreso than the direction of the prevailing wind.

If the destination was a left turn out then invariably a good solid full deflection thumping roll of the control wheel combined with a little more back pressure would result in the right main parting company with the runway first. Of course, vice-versa, for the other direction. As to the one remaining wheel still in contact with terra firma, I was never quite sure when watching one of Dan's take-offs, whether it left the ground before or after the gear retraction sequence started., Dan was a firm believer in reducing drag ASAP in an effort to get there faster.

Dan's natural tendency toward exuberance in operating his machinery assured that there was always plenty of work around our hangar for the town's only two wrench slingers Dudley and Clark. However, poor Dudley and Clark were in high demand constantly from the east to west end of the ramp. These resulted in a quite predictable and repetitive cycle wherein the mechanical dynamic duo would work exhausting hours for days or weeks on end. After getting all the operator's flying machines back to an airworthy status and having ascertained that all the really important work had been completed, they have worked themselves out of a job so to speak. One would help the other cowl up the last airplane, and pockets now bulging with cash, they would repair post haste to the hotel bar and commence the second half of the cycle.

The second half of the cycle they became the Drunken Duo far more concerned with wenches than wrenches. These fella's worked had and played hard as well, and sometimes they played for a l-o-n-g, LONG time. This would invariably result in some aircraft reaching the point where they just had to be fixed or a 100 hour had come and gone. That's when either the operators did their own wrenching or, as one of my bosses enjoyed telling me (in later years) knowing I was not a mechanic.... "Hey kid, go out there 'n 100 hour your 206."

There was an understood procedure for me at that command. I uncovered the engine, pulled, sandblasted, gapped and then replaced all 12 plugs. This because we never hardly had any new ones. Following that, I drained the old oil, pulled the oil screen and ran a magnet around the screen checking for any metal shavings or residue. Assuming there were none to be found I would replace the oil filter and throw in 12 quart cans of oil. If any important lights were burned out (like nav or landing or taxi lights) and we happened to have any spares on our part ledge at the time ... I would also attend to that major chore.

Thus, having completed the required "100 hour", it now became my obligation and duty to take 50 bucks from the cash drawer and proceed with the aircraft logbook down to the Pondu or the Whale in hopes of finding at least one of our mechanical miscreants able to focus well enough to legibly scrawl his name in aforesaid logbook. For the aforesaid 50 bucks, of course! And while this often "kept our boys in the air", it also had the unintended effect of prolonging Dudley and Clark's "out of service" portion of their two-cycle lives. Especially if too many 100 hours came due within a few short days.

In later years this would lead to one of Kotzebue's operators, having finally lost patience with the "now you see us, now you don't" hometown wrench benders; to actually importing a pair of A&I's from the big village of Anchorage. These two guys, whose names escape me, would generally knock back a couple every night, but would work every day. Reliably. Dependably, and most of all…. CONSISTENTLY. And after a couple of weeks, the operators planes were good as new. All of 'em. And the boys from Anchorage got on the big Wien bird and headed back from whence they came.

Well, the following week a big old Alaska International Air Hercumles drops outta' the sky and deposits on Kotzebue's ramp two Ford Econoline vans driving by none other than … you guessed it … the same two fella what left town last week. Now having formed a company with "Have SocketWrench, Will Travel" and "Parts is Parts" emblazoned on each side of both trucks; the boys were back to make their fortune. And a fortune they did make, having the forethought to load up the inside of their vans with (beside a small cot and LARGE toolboxes) durn near every conceivable Cessna and Piper single-engine part you could think of except actual airframe pieces. They charged a premium for the parts as well as their labor too.

But this was years later and demand for travel had risen so much that operators could not afford any down time on the air machines. It was just too costly. So they paid the "mercenaries" as the operators liked to call them, the premium rate. And they were darn good mechanics to boot. But that was years in the future. Meanwhile back in (present day) 1973….

Many of the children in the villages all over Alaska, like kids all over the world, were drawn to aviation and airplanes. Also just like elsewhere in the world there were some who were not so interested in flying the darn machines as they were in figuring out what MADE them fly (work). Some folks are born pilots, and some folks are born take-it-apart-and-put-it-back-together people.

Young Cedrick Seevaak from Buckland was just one such young man.

Fortunately for all concerned there was a program available for native Eskimo and Indian kids from all over the state that would pay for their education in certain fields, aviation being one.

So Cedrick, whose mechanical aptitude was noted as a youngster, had gone off to school to get his A&P license in the big village on the banks of the Chena River, Fairbanks.

Now quite often when folks from the smaller villages in the bush travel to either Fairbanks or Anchorage they usually do have a specific purpose in doing so. Such as, go to school, the hospital, National Guard drills, or shopping for Christmas at Diamond Center. Generally they bid their friends in Kiana or Kwethluk or Venetie goodbye at the airstrip and promise to be back on such-and-such a date. I know. I've seen it a bazillion times. (And done it a few dozen times myself.)

Invariably though, regardless of age, gender, or ethnicity; many of our big city visitors or temporary residents become confused finding their way back to Anchorage or Fairbanks International Airport(s) from whence they are (repeatedly) scheduled to depart for home.

Most often the source of all this "confusion" and lack of proper navigational abilities was not so much the lack of a good hand held GPS in those days, but rather a 12 to 20 oz. container being firmly hand held and repeatedly drained of it's contents, until the only thing left to hold onto was the floor! So it was always with some amount of trepidation that village parents sent their children off on these excursions.

However, in the case of Cedrick of Buckland, son of a minister; there were no such worries. Surely given his staunch fundamentalist Christian upbringing in a teetotaling environment, to worry about Cedrick succumbing to the temptations of the Big City was nonsensical. And . . . that was correct! Cedrick came home almost a year later, on schedule to the day, and without having picked up any bad habits, it seems. He was intent on succeeding. He'd been warned to avoid the pitfalls that would sidetrack him from a promising future. Ergo, our young Cedrick kept his nose to the grindstone day and night and took NO time to stop and smell the roses. So he arrived back in Buckland with a newly minted A&P license sober as a judge still. But, with no airplanes based in the tiny village of Buckland, our new wrench bender had to go out into the world to practice his newly acquired skills.

The Gundersons hired Cedrick just a few short weeks after bringing me to the country and he and I, both being about the same age (19 or 20) hit it right off from the beginning. Being summer then, with round the clock daylight and flying there was no shortage of work in our hangar for ol' Cedrick and he took to bending wrenches day and night on the Gunderson 's hodgepodge fleet of workhorse air machines. He wuz living the dream. He swapped out cylinders, ran up engines, filed props, checked cable tensions and got good money for doing it.

Now Cedrick had also arrived in town during Dudley and Clark's "work cycle" as I liked to call it. And Cedrick worshiped the ground the old timers walked on just as I worshiped the ground under the Gunderson brother's feet. Ergo, whenever the young mechanic was stumped by a particular problem he was able to seek out one of the two elders not only for verbal counsel, but much "hands on" demonstrated help. Sort of like graduate level mechanic's training so to speak.

Then came "the fall", and I don't mean the season, although it did coincide.

Having brought all the operator's various airplanes back to airworthiness, Dudley and Clark, as was their custom sashayed back down to the a.) Golden Whale, b.) Pondu or c.) the hotel bar (pick one) to recover and rest up from their most recent bout of mechanical ministrations.

This had a couple of unanticipated effects. First of all, now when Cedrick got stumped with his hands buried in some engine's innards, with "Google" not to arrive for another couple of decades or so; his sole source(s) of practical knowledge were not there to stand over his shoulder and provide guidance. They were down at the bar. Ergo, for the first time in his life, Cedrick was confronted with the new experience of having to actually enter a drinking establishment. In search of knowledge, no less.

Now, I have often entered a bar in search of ... of ... oh, any number of things. But I can truly say I have never gone into a BAR in search of knowledge. Although I will admit that I've had many of my most Divine Revelations in a bar.

Nonetheless, our quite naive young mechanical marvel-to-be, covered in grease to his elbows would oft jump in the company truck and set off in search of "the wise ones". This brought young Cedrick a quickly gained familiarity with the comforting feeling of a solid but slightly padded barstool comfortably supporting your buttcheeks, being as how both Dudley and Clark disdain table service. As do I, they both much preferred the last stool at the end of the bar, next to a wall preferably.

In addition to offering a comfortable leaning or even semi-reclining position for later in the evening (or morning, the bars opening at 7 AM) as the effects of a prolonged thirst-slaying adventure take their toll; it also prevents unwanted person with questionable intent from coming up behind you. Just as well it offers a full view of the "working" side of the bar. This being of critical importance as we all know, both for an unobstructed view of any cute female barkeeps, as well as enabling you to monitor all barkeeps to assure that you are not being "short-poured"!

This desire for preferential seating often lead to yet another squabble between Dudley and Clark as to who gets the very end seat THIS time. Sometimes watching these two stagger into the bar and argue over who had which seat last time could best be compared to watching Lucy and Ricky in an old "I Love Lucy" episode. Usually this oft seen routine debate was settled by the mixmaster-in-residence slamming down a screwdriver (Dudley's drink) and a Jack and Coke (Clark's preferred poison). Setting one in front of each of the two stools, and hollering "Shut up and sit DOWN!" usually worked. Whereupon the two would sit down and commence to argue about something else ... for hours! This dog and pony show, while mildly amusing and sometimes downright hilarious was known to all and invariably got on anyone's nerves after the first two or three hours or so. Hence one could almost always expect to find at least one empty barstool next to the two old grease monkeys, if not a couple.

So Cedrick always had a stool to park on for the period of time it took to explain his problem to the old pelicans and obtain the necessary advice and instructions. These "training sessions" as Dudley liked to refer to them, could last from two minutes to an hour depending not only on the complexity of the mechanical problem, but whether or not Dudley and Clark were in agreement as to the best approach to resolve same. Exactly how early in the day's (or night's) outing Cedrick had shown up for guidance had a large bearing on the outcome as well. Just because it's 10:30 AM doesn't mean these guys were downing a morning eye-opener.

Inevitably, as you might have guessed, after two or three months, Cedrick broke down. At the repeated prodding of both his revered mentors young Ced had his first beer which apparently tasted pretty good. For it was followed by a second, and a thi ... well, alot of beers. See, Dudley and Clark had taken note of the fact that young Cedrick, overflowing with youthful enthusiasm and passion for working on airplanes, was actually being hired to work on other folk's airsheens whenever the Gunderson's fleet was all in the air or fully operational. This had made a dent in their "sign off a 100 hr at the bar for 50 bucks" market, which of course made the two fellows feel a little threatened. The obvious solution being (ala' Leroy) we gotta' teach this boy how to drink!

Subsequently any time Cedrick headed out to the bars to get some "technical assistance", upon arriving Dudley and/or Clark would demand alcoholic compensation for their "tech support" insisting the younger mechanic join them for "just one". Invariably this would result in Cedrick's absence from the hangar for the remainder of that day, as well as most probably the following day as well. As time passed, Cedricks fondness for Olympia beer frequently outweighed his desire to further his career and sometimes he would go a week and be seldom seen at the hangar.

As the middle of December approached we had been calling him "Seldom Seen Cedrick the Mechanic" for a number of weeks now, as he had really earned the sobriquet, often going on two to four day binges. Seldom Seen Cedrick the Mechanic was quite a lot to wrap your tongue around at one time so, as to be expected it was shortened to just Seldom Seen, as in "Hey. Where's Seldom Seen?" or just plain Seldom as in "Hey. Anybody seen Seldom??".

But this day in December, we were lucky. (Sort of). Seldom was not only here but clear-headed as Dan roused us way before dawn this frigid winter's morning and announced "I want to fly the Commander today!" Which was a total shock as both the Commander and Dan had been hors d' combat for about four months, and while Dan was now fit as a fiddle; our baby AeroCommander had been sitting unused and unattended for the last sixteen weeks. It was in fact, BURIED under massive snowdrifts, unheated, and uncovered. Somehow I just knew this was gonna' be one interesting day!

5

The Pepsi Generation

I've always been kind of a morning person. If not in "recovery mode" from a previous night's assault on one or more of Kotzebue's adult beverage vendors, it was most common for me to wake up, even without an alarm clock within one or two minutes (usually) of exactly eight hours from when I went to bed. And while I didn't exactly bound out of bed full of vim and vigor (if not hungover); getting out of bed was not unpleasant. I generally was in the shower within a matter of minutes having prepared the coffee pot the night before as do so many of us.

Also I am very much a "creature of habit" as the saying goes. 'Til now I had lived most of my life as an unattached bachelor. Possessing all the natural kitchen skills of oh, say a mountain yak; after three days of nothing but cold milk on Frosted Mini-Wheats and toast for breakfast I knew I had to come up with a better plan. Much like the character "Hannibal" on the television show "A-Team" I loved then, and still do, using the line "I LOVE it when a plan comes together!"

Momma CloudDancer had impressed upon me as a little tad that a hearty, healthy and preferably hot breakfast was important. So on my fourth morning in Kotzebue I arrived at the Drift Inn Hotel and went to the top (fourth) floor restaurant. From that day forward for oh, the next twenty-five years or so almost every day started with some sort of either Denver 'n Cheddar cheese (extra CHEESE please!) or Ham 'n Cheddar cheese omelette (extra CHEESE please!). Either omelette would be consistently accompanied by a good pile of hash browns, slightly crisp, but still chewy. Nothing aggravated me more that crunchy hash browns! Except maybe hash whites! Two biscuits slathered in butter and strawberry jelly, a half gallon of coffee and a large glass of good orange juice complete this culinary ensemble.

Over twenty-five years only the slightest of variations was allowed whether dining at home in OTZ (I mean at the Drift Inn, later Nu-luk-vik Hotel facilities) or at the Denny's where I met Dan Gunderson in Fort Worth on the occasions when I went back to visit my parents and old friends. Grape jam or even jelly was the only possible acceptable substitute for strawberry and if neither were available the biscuits were eaten with just butter. Also, occasionally additional shredded real Cheddar CHEESE might be thrown on top of the hash browns.

The only real major variance first occurred in the 1980's when I spent a substantial period of time in the Interior and discovered the Fairbanks Denny's-style restaurant then called Jeffrey's. These guys had a shrimp 'n DOUBLE Cheddar omelette. What's not to like about that! So it appears that, for decades, I have consumed every month, the probable annual output of a herd of Guernseys in cheddar cheese and butter, not to mention half the contents of one of Juan Valdez's coffee bean laden burros. Therefore it should come as a surprise to absolutely no one (but me of course), that aside from old Juan and America's dairy farmers, the happiest man on earth is the CEO of the pharmaceutical company from which I currently purchase my high blood pressure medication! My new medico seems somewhat concerned that possibly even Roto-Rooter will be unable to clean out my blood veins effectively (sigh). But, yet again I digress.

So, I bebop brightly into the dining room to be greeted somewhat reluctantly by Elsie, the very matronly Eskimo women who would in the coming months become a good and lifelong friend. This only after though I accustomed myself to Kotzebue's rather laid-back attitude versus where I'd come from. This morning though was not to give any indication of how I would enjoy the experience in the future.

Seems the newest young local boy, freshly graduated from cooking school and hired because he was local, did not place the same priority on my breakfast as did Momma CloudDancer and I. Yet again he has failed to appear on the property anywhere even close to the appointed opening hour.

Although by the time fifteen years went by, having quit a dozen times and been fired just as many, Derwood did finally achieve a level of consistency routinely showing UP at opening time. This meant you could expect the first hot food of off the grill at about 6:30 AM, thirty minutes after official "opening" time. Seeking to both keep Derwood and the morning customers placated, management changed the opening to what it perceived was "required" by Derwood to get things going in the morning. (Apparently 6:30 AM) No surprise here. As you might suspect this immediately resulted in an ADDITIONAL 30 min. delay in receiving hot food. The following week we were back on the original schedule, and just came to understand "the rules".

Now on a daily basis in the summer there would be half "outsiders" tourists from Long Island to the Bahamas. Which created quite a dilemma for 55 year old (or so) Elise the waitress. See, Elise treated everybody exactly the same. Regardless of where they were from she treated both locals and tourists as she would guest(s) in her own home for breakfast. In my mind's eyes I could easily visualize "Elise's Rule" lovingly crocheted into a framed doily and hung carefully at eye level to the entrance to her kitchen at home. "If you don't LIKE something … either LEAVE or serve yourself!" In a dining room that seated 48 at tables of four each, Elise operated day in and day out at just one speed, and it wasn't hyper.

Now I'm sure as a twenty-something gal hired when the hotel opened in the mid 1950's, Elise had full command over the entire dining room and hummed along at a good clip, but over the years, her speed had diminished in inverse proportion to her increasingly ample girth. By the time we met, Elise was down to fairly capable handling no more than four full tables of locals (who understood her "system") only! Most tourists expecting silly things like second served cups of coffee. This "operating limitation" as it were, was further predicated on 1.) A cook being present along with 2.) one or two of the eight to ten high school girls constantly employed as maids and waitresses during the summer. They are all scheduled to work daily in hopes that actually two may show up to assist Elise. These girls though charming and mostly cute, must've bought their alarm clocks at the same store as Derwood and were generally drawn from among the dozens of Elise's nieces and granddaughters so she could boss them about with impunity.

This morning, sans any help whatsoever, Elise mostly just contented herself with supervising the customers. We made our own toast and coffee and selected which of the two available brands of cold cereal we wanted. Elise sometimes frowned rather severely at the tourists as she silently took their money at the register having noted with her still sharp eagle eyes that most were failing to leave a tip. This actually shamed half of them into returning to the table and throwing a buck down. Elise would approach a table of locals and ask if they needed anything (that she could have the busboy bring out).

After leaving a healthy two dollar tip (after all, I did have two of everything) and introducing myself to Elise as "the Gunderson's new kid pilot from the States" I am wishing of course to clearly establish that, while not quite yet a local, I did not wish to be mistaken for a tourist, just in case any future service opportunities became available. After graciously pocketing my change (minus pennies because "Oh no! Ahhh-deeeee!! Noooooo pen-nies!!") and undergoing the "Whose your NAME" ritual, I was off to the airdrome, all of 200 yards away.

As I rounded the corner and mounted the three rickety wooden steps of the ramshackle and dilapidated old 10 x 14 structure that served as the Gunderson's "office" I noticed movement through the small portion of the hangar side window that wasn't completely frosted over and covered by a large snowbank that had accumulated in the narrow, three foot opening between the two structures.

Poking my head in the side entry door revealed that Cedrick had beaten me to work this morning, a rarity indeed. Bundled from head to foot in a parka and snowsuit only his neck face and hands were bare, with his ski-type goggles slid upward onto the top of his head pushing his jet black hair back and off to the sides in a style I can only call a Dagwood (Bumstead). Not hearing the door open over the roar of the fans from the oil fired heaters, Cedrick stood with his back to me examining a tear in one of the hoses for our Herman Nelson.

Now, if ya'll don't know what a Herman Nelson is, picture this. A 55 gallon steel drum sized main metal combustion chamber laying on it's side on a "carrier" with wheels. On one end is a control box, an electric cord for plug in and handles to move the thing around with, kinda' like to drive a wheelbarrow. And on the other end of the drum is one large exhaust opening over which you fit a cap with two or three smaller diameter hoses attached to the cap.

When you light the sucker off, with a big WHOOSH, you have a large, large volume flow of 250 degree or so air coming out the other end. Thanks to the splitter cap you can now direct this heated air to three different places which may be quite far apart from each other. Indeed your choices are only governed by the number and length of hoses available. Ergo you can run one hose to each engine on a twin and one to inside the cabin, a quite common configuration when using "the herman" at the time.

I'm not sure who invented the darn thing. I know it cost alotta' dough, but almost no operator anywhere was without at least one of those suckers. Yeah, the pre-herman nelson and Carter heaters days were a REEEEAALLL pain in the ol'keister, what with having to drain the oil every night and put it on the stove til you were ready to fly again. Then you'd carry it back out to the plane it the morning and dump it back in the engine which you have already thoughtfully preheated also, probably with what is known as a "smudge" pot. But each and every time you got to use the darn thing you thanked your lucky stars you hand it. I backed out into the bitter cold from the warmth of the hangar's side entry. It was only 15 degrees above zero, but the damn wind was blowing it's usual 15 knots as well outta' the east making the cold feel much worse.

Turning again toward the office so I could get completely inside and warm up for a few minutes I took a quick glance at the Aero Commander. It was firmly anchored to the frozen solid ground, each wing being tied to two drums of (frozen) water and one for the tail as well. It was facing into the usually prevailing easterly winds. The front end was absolutely buried under a ten foot snow drift that was the result of the half dozen two, three, and even four day Arctic blizzards which had occurred so far this winter.

The Commander was Dan's personal plane and nobody got to fly it but him. It had been sitting idle for over three months now as Dan had been in Anchorage for over three months as a result of his addiction. To Pepsi-Cola.

I've never seen anyone, anywhere, before or since, drink as much Pepsi as Dan put away. If the man didn't go through two cases of four six packs a day, each day, seven days a week, I'm a monkey's uncle. I mean, a three hour round trip to Kobuk, and the guy would come back with one can out of a full six pack! I mean I like soda too but … Holy Liver a'Quiver Batman!!

After decades of swilling that much Pepsi, one day a few weeks after I had come to work for the Gunderson's Dan took ill. He went to the PHS Hospital and was subsequently sent to Anchorage for more intensive care. The details of the illness escaped me, but I remember he was in the hospital for a solid month before doing better. Then came two months of outpatient treatments. And now, at doctors orders, being "Pepsi Free" so to speak, he has returned from the Big Village much healthier, but much grouchier than I'd first known him.

His mood was not improved one iota when he caught sight of his neglected pride and joy the Commander. I guess Rod had been telling him his "bird" was just fine and would be ready to fly upon Dan's return home. Only Dan hadn't given us any warning he was coming back a few days early. Hence, this morning's early rousting for Cedrick and I. Time to put on the coffee pot, enjoy a last couple of cups o' java and another smoke before going out to begin what was quite obviously going to be a long and hard day's work. No trips on the board yet for today, and it looked to be slow, flying-wise, as it was a Saturday.

6

No Business Like Snow Business

We'd pushed the Commander nose first into an area behind our fuel tanks. The two five hundred gallon steel cylinders were mounted in twelve foot tall wooden cradles made of six by six heavy timbers. Given their height, they allowed us to gravity feed almost all of the fleet without ever having to use the electric pumps which were ancient and crapped out constantly.

Underneath the cradles in the open spaces below gathered every sort of junk (for lack of a better word) that is normally associated with bush flying. Blazo boxes, a 55 gallon drum (the State Flower of Alaska), and multiple wooden pallets. You know ... junk!

When we rolled the baby Commander nose first into the space behind the tanks in early September Dan had only been gone to the hospital a couple of days. The first nip of frost was in the air and we pushed on the struts as Rod guided the plane with the nose-wheel attached tow bar rolling over the gravel pad that constituted the ramp area in OTZ in those days. Only where the Alaska jet pulled in at the far west end of the ramp was paved. All else was gravel, except for the parallel taxiway that spanned all the operator's lots. Now the gravel, along with a lot of other stuff (including the forward third of the Commander) was buried under the snow and ice.

The Commander squatted forlornly. It was buried aft and upward to the midpoint on both sides, with the engine nacelles completely packed with snow. From the leading edge of the wings aft she was fairly well free, although the snowdrift on the left side continued rearward to bury the entire left landing gear assembly before petering out halfway to the tail. The propellers were absolutely immobilized having not moved so much as a quarter inch in the last three months or so. I could quite literally do chin-ups with my 165 lb frame on the horizontally parked blade of the 3-bladed Hartzell mounted to the right engine. Frozen SOLID this baby was. And Dan wants to fly this thing today!?

Cursing and slipping on the snowpacked ramp, Cedrick and I wheel the Herman Nelson out of the hangar with the hoses dragging behind. It's a little before eight AM just as Dan comes pulling in front of the office in his pickup. He leaps out and rushes over to help as Ced and I are trying to plow, push, and manhandle the unwieldy piece of equipment through the last small foot-and-a-half foot high snowdrift between us and the rear of the aircraft.

Dan is positively giddy as a child on Christmas morning, a beaming grin on his face as he throws himself at the opposite end of the bulky machine. Laughing and chiding, he exhorts us "kids" to "PULL ... PULL ... PUUUUUULL!!" as he lifts and pushes the heavy end over in a burst of pure muscle power. As we break through the berm Cedrick and I pull the machine right out from Dan's body and, tripping over the berm he goes down hard it appears.

But before we can even recover from stopping the momentum of the big machine and drop our end, the boss-man is up like a jack-in-a-box. Big grin none the worse for the fall he is chanting excitedly ... "ohboyohboyohboyohboy ... I get to fly my plane today!" Like a kid! And he races over to pick up the hoses as Cedrick and I swing the machine through a 180 degree turn to get it lined up with the hoses facing the airplane. Dan scampers over and grabs the electric cord male end, throws the remaining coil on the ground and races hurriedly over to the hangar wall to get the big fire breathing monstrosity a power source.

In less than two minutes hot dry air has softened the freezing yellow thick plastic hoses that are intended to begin resurrecting Dan's frozen bird from it's "suspended animation". But first, both Cedrick and I grab one hose each and tucking the hose under one arm, we extend our mittened hands down between our knees. The clasping our knees tightly together slide our cold wet-with-sweat hands out of our mittens into the frigid air. But the cold disappears immediately, if only for a few moments, as we bathe our faces and hands in the hot air taking turns holding the hose for each other. Then quick as a bunny dive back into out mittens and facemasks to finish the first part of the job.

Cedrick grabs the longest of the three hoses, which has already melted its way through two of the three to four inches of the packed snow and ice on the ramp. Stretching it out he crawls under the low aft fuselage portion of the plane to fix the hose to the aft end of the right rear cowling. As he does so the hose leaves behind the thawed portion of the ground where it had been, and given the ridges in the hose, [formed by the thick elongated (sort of Slinky-like) coil that gives the hose both rigidity and flexibility) it appeared as though some pre-historic snake-lizard fossil had been recovered there.

My first choice was to get a hose into the passenger cabin through the aft left side cabin boarding door. But like everything else, it too was frozen solid. I mean there was no way this handle and it's associated levers, pinions, ball joints and other hardware were going to move. I couldn't help but think that the plane was no more enthusiastic about this morning's rude awakening than I had been only a scant two hours or so earlier. But hey! "If I gotta' work under these conditions so do you!" I muttered to myself. Meanwhile I directed the stream of hot air directly onto the handle itself and the center of the door where I estimated the inner workings to be.

In a matter of a couple of minutes the door opening mechanism had thawed and was moving smoothly and freely, but yet the door itself was still immoveable! One more minute it took to slo-o-o-wly outline the doorframe with the hot air and "OPEN SESAME" she popped open of her own volition, the door handle being already in the open position.

I hadn't even so much as peeked in the cabin in the last two months since the first big storm, and I had forgotten how pretty it was, an all dark brown and gold interior. I pulled about five feet of hose into the aft cabin. It was more than enough to make the turn around the three passenger couch on the left side of the cabin and, laying on the center floor, the business end of the thing was just a couple of feel short of the cockpit, which is exactly where we wanted it. Even when the heat was moderated to 150 degree output, you really don't need it blowing right on anything for too long, especially delicate aircraft instruments.

Leaving the rapidly rising temperatures in the small passenger cabin I returned outside to help Cedrick get the last hose wedged into the lower outboard rear portion of the engine nacelle. Then we quickly untied the engine cover from around the belly of the engine and double-checked to ensure that the front of the cover WAS tied securely. This ensured the melting snow inside the packed cowlings could melt and escape freely. Meanwhile the front end and topside remained sealed and covered to facilitate heat causing a quick reduction in snow packed in the cowlings.

All totaled we had been outside no more than 20 minutes, but already I was one whipped puppy. Yet, only one small initial step of today's project was completed. Cedrick and I headed for the coffeepot simultaneously.

7

Hi Ho, Hi Ho, It's OFF to Work We Go

Banging my boots against the side of the doorjamb to knock off most of the excess snow I push open the wooden door expecting to be greeted with a rush of warm air escaping the tiny room at face level as the cold air from outside is sucked in to fill the void left behind. Instead I am disappointed to note that, while still much warmer than outside it is relatively fairly cool inside the office. Damn!

I note the 30 cup cafeteria-style upright tin and black plastic coffee maker is making it's last few perks. The boiling coffee spews volcano-like upward from the bottom of the urn through the central tube. It erupts against the glass knob on the top of the cover and explodes out horizontally in all directions to drain down through the grounds one last time. At least the coffee is going to be hot I note as I jerk my mittens off and place one hand on top of the oil burning stove type heater. No surprise. Cold as a stone.

Picking up the heavy black plastic receiver out of the cradle of the late 1950's style phone (the darn receiver alone is almost as long as a football and must weigh four pounds all by itself) I dial the four digit phone number of Arctic Lighterage. I hope for a quick commitment for an early delivery of stove oil. As I press the cold plastic receiver against my ear I reach out to gratefully accept the steaming heavy porcelain mug of java proffered by Cedrick. It feels really good in my hand as I cup it without using the finger hole. While I wait for someone to answer the phone I raise the mug and hold it first against one cold cheek and then the other. The spreading warmth of the cup permeates my face.

With the call completed and stove oil on the way (sometime before lunch PROBABLY we are told), Ced and I enjoy two more cups of coffee apiece before reluctantly acknowledging that we "ain't gonna' get no warmer sitting here in the office". We've been inside for about twenty minutes now and the residual snow hasn't even melted off our boots yet. Must be all of plus forty in here and dropping as the dilapidated old building leaks air in and heat out at a steady rate.

We have barely scratched the surface of getting the Commander in flying condition today. As Dan has gone back home to help get his kids off to school, Cedrick and I are left to our own devices to get this project well under way.

We decide our next priority should be readying the aircraft for movement into the hangar as we wait for the snow to melt out of the engine nacelles, the engines to dry out, and the oil to thaw. So after slipping back into the upper portion of our snowsuits and zipping up, we head back outside and grab two of the snow shovels leaning against the side of the building. Still it is completely dark as the clock shows 9:30 AM. Our goal is to have the airplane basically dug out and ready to roll rearward in about an hour and a half by the time we have some decent daylight.

That should be plenty of time, well over two hours of heating, for the aircraft to be ready. It will also give Ced and I enough time to remove the majority of the massive snowdrifts burying the landing gears assemblies on both sides of the airplane. Then we'll shovel a path through two more three foot snowdrifts wide enough to accommodate the airplane's retreat into the sanctuary of the hangar. If we're really lucky, maybe Rod will get out of bed sometime before noon and show up with his brand spankin' new Dodge Ram pick-em-up truck. The plow mounted on the front end would come in handy about now. I'm not plannin' on it though as Rod never gets up (or out of the house anyway) before noon and nobody, not even Dan is allowed to touch that truck!

As we approach the plane, just barely illuminated by the porch light from the office at this distance, Cedrick and I are pleased to see that the underside of the left engine appears as though a rain forest area. Water is pouring out of every available seal gap, cowling hole, and drain port. A quick check confirms the scene is the same on the other side of the fuselage as well. This had the added, unanticipated benefit of melting away the snowdrift portion that is under the engines as well. That will save two or three minutes of shoveling hard packed snow. Probably at least another dozen shovelsful we won't have to heave.

Over the course of the next hour and a half, minus a couple of ten minute coffee breaks which we enjoy in the warmth of the hangar, Cedrick and I must've shoveled a small dump truck loadful of snow. Over what had to be about our tenth cup of coffee apiece for the day thus far [isn't it amazing what healthy young internal organs can handle in the way of daily abuse? Although after three and a half decades of repetitive caffeine and alcohol overdoses I don't think there is even a medical school that could make any use out of my kidneys and liver at this point. Except maybe to use photos of them as the "after" portion of one of those "before and after" picture posters intended to shock and scare impressionable youth out of various (mis)behaviors. But which never, in reality work because ALL kids know that these are pictures of really old people's organs and I'll never get THAT old anyway, so why worry!] ... but I digress.

So, Cedrick muses as we take a warm-up in the hangar, over his coffee; that his mechanic's training school did not really put a lot of emphasis on all the manual labor that was involved with his career choice. Specifically, no one mentioned shoveling humongous piles of snow! This seemingly was all too frequently a part of his mechanic's job. And of course, I allowed as how my pilot training hadn't ever bought out that particular unpleasant aspect of my career choice either. However that it wasn't too much of a surprise as, shoveling out of large snow-drifts was not a even an annual occurrence in my part of Texas from whence I had arrived. In fact, I loved the snow almost all the time. But I could see my enthusiasm level for snow sliding down somewhat after days like today.

Along about 11:15 AM, just as we moved the very last of the snow by hand; sunrise, the Arctic Lighterage stove oil delivery trunk, and Dan all pretty much arrived simultaneously. Even Rod had gotten hisself up and out early so he could come over and help on this momentous occasion. His contribution though was pretty much limited to a supervisory level although, to his credit, he did get the stove fired up immediately.

After that, with coffee in hand he spent an hour trying to talk his brother Dan out of what he considered to be a dumb, ill-conceived, and poorly planned flight. But Dan could easily be the most stubborn man I've ever known when he sets his mind to it. Ergo, Rod did not succeed, and then turned his attention to pitching in with all of us to ensure that (dammit) if his crazy brother insisted on fly the machine it should be as near perfect as possible.

By eleven-thirty AM, in the weak daylight of the just risen sun, we were ready to haul the Commander out of her hibernation position. As we were unable, without moving a HUGE amount of snow by hand, to access the nose area of the airplane; this would be a two stage operation. First we finally made some use of Rod's brand new Dodge Ram by attaching it to the rear tie down of the baby Commander using a sixteen foot length of 3/4 inch nylon rope to make the connection between the two vehicles.

Ced and I got on opposite sides of the airplane throwing our limited weight against the respective landing gear assemblies. The puddles of water that had come out of the nacelles had fallen to the ground and immediately froze into BIG puddles of glare ice on the ground just where we needed to get some traction with our feet to support the effort. No joy.

We then hit upon th idea of first doubling then quadrupling the rope usage. Finding three more of the ropes, we first untied from the tail to Rod's bumper. Then we added another rope and made the connection from the outermost portion of Rod's rear bumper to the right main landing gear strut. The same was done on the other side. Now the Commander was bound to move. And in fact, she did! She popped out of the remaining snowbank like a cork out of a champagne bottle before stopping her rearward motion after only a roll of about a dozen feet or so. But that was all we needed. From here it was a matter of only a few short minutes before the Commander rolled backwards into her hangar berthing spot as the doors were slammed closed behind her. Incredibly, outdoors, where the airplane had been parked; there remained behind an absolutely perfect detailed life-sized cave-like indentation in the snow bank.

Now the hangar heaters poured out BTUs at a furious rate and volume to replace what had been the indoor warmth. Opening the hangar doors in those days, even thirty-three years ago, was said to cost the operator upwards of fifty dollars in heating fuel. All of us stripped out of our snowsuits completely. Even though at the moment the temperature was almost the same as the outside air, within a matter of four or five minutes the heaters will have raised the temperature to about twenty above inside. And with no wind to suck the warmth out of your body, working in the hangar in just flannel shirtsleeves and your jeans is quite comfortable. Snowmachine suits are great for keeping you warm while you work outside or roar across the landscape at fifty MPH on a snow machine but they are much to bulky, for me at least. So I am the first to dress down any chance I get. Finally now we can really get to work on this machine.

8

Chitty-Chitty Bang BANG!!

Sliding the engine covers off, (these babies are HOT still) we hurriedly begin popping the various butterfly latches, zeuss fasteners and plain old phillips head screws that make the cowling whole. In moments the still hot to the touch engines are fully exposed. Over the next few hours Dan, Rod, Cedrick and I, along with one of our ramp boys labor studiously. We perform every sort of revitalizing check and procedure we know of to bring the Commander back to a state of readiness she hadn't seen since joining the company months before.

Stevie, our ramper was an airplane crazy sixteen year old second (or maybe third) cousin of Dan and Rod from Selawik . Like me, he was just so happy to be in his position working around real airplanes at his age, that he would've (and sometimes did wind up) doing it for free. Of course, as neither of us were mechanics, anything we did was at Cedrick's direction and under his supervision. The first chore he assigned us was to drain the oil

Buckets on Blazo boxes, snip the safety wire holding the plug, a couple of quick turns with the wrench and (ouch!) the burning hot oil is spilling down the (as yet) unremoved plug onto my hand. This of course surprises me to the extent I jerk my hand back and, yes, drop the damn plug into the gathering hot oil in the bottom of the five gallon plastic bucket. Diving back into the hot oil (better now and only burn the tips of my fingers than wait and burn more, or wait until it is cold and have to dunk my whole hand and wrist in the black sludge to fish for it) I retrieve the plug and throw it into the shop towel in my left hand to dry.

As I am about to come out from under my engine and go check to see how Stevie is doing, I note that the oil flow has dropped off dramatically after only the first thirty seconds or so. I peer into the plastic bucket and stick my pointer finger straight down into the hot oil 'till I touch the bottom of the bucket and quickly jerk it out. The sludge mark level is barely at my knuckle and confirms for me that nowhere near the expected twelve to fourteen quarts of oil has come out of the engine. More likely only four or so.

Unbelievably, after almost three full hours of preheating, we still have most of the oil in the pan frozen in a solid lump. I confirm this by rapping on the bottom of the oil pan with the end of a box end wrench. Sure enough I am rewarded not with a nice metallic clanging, but more of a dull metallic THUNK!

About this time Dan returns from Rod's house where he had gone to retrieve the aircraft's battery which Rod had thoughtfully remembered to remove and kept stored indoors where it is warm. Also to get Rod's wife Millie to make a dozen fresh sandwiches (roast beef and cheese and ham 'n cheese) for the hard worker's lunch.

Upon learning of the oil situation, Dan blows up, starts chewing on Rod in particular, and everybody in general for letting this happen to his airplane. Long story short? Let's do lunch! But first, we roll the airplane forward until the nose is almost against the doors. We crack the doors, and pull in the Herman Nelson heater hoses and safety wire them to hold and blow directly on the bottom of the oil pan(s). While this allows a little heat to be sucked out the hangar door openings it is necessary. This way the body of the heater with the exhaust stack remains outside. We then throw the engine covers back over the bare engines and adjourn to the office coffee pot for some fresh stuff to wash our sandwiches down with.

After lunch it back to the hangar where the rest of the day passes in a blur of draining fuel sumps over and over and over. Man I couldn't believe how much water we got out of those tanks. I helped with compression checks (good), pulling and replacing plugs, filing props, and polishing plexiglass. And finally, at seven PM, with the sun long gone and inky black moonless night skies overhead we are ready to roll her out and try an engine run. Amazingly, but not totally unprecedented, the entire day has gone by without one lousy trip. No good for my pocketbook, but I did learn a lot today. Cedrick and Dan climb into the front and I ask Dan if I can sit back in the cabin and watch the proceedings over their shoulders.

Dan flips on the master switch and the warm glow of the white post lights and internally lighted overhead switches bathes the cockpit. From there ... well, things just didn't manage to go so good. As Dan was firing up the second (right) engine, the first begins to cough, sputter, and die. Cedrick starts working cross-armed with Dan from the right seat trying to keep the left engine running with shots of boost, leaning then enriching the sliding mixture control knob and, and pumping the throttle.

Then engine number two catches with a roar for about two seconds. Then joins it's left side mate in belching, backfiring, roaring and then dying in a repetitive cycle. At least number two had a rhythm. ROOOAR ... BLAM! ... cough-COUGH ... SILENCE ... ROOOOAR ...

BLAM! ... coughCOUGH ... SILENCE ... ETC. The number one engine meanwhile has no such program. It roars for a few seconds then maybe it quits altogether or not. Maybe it backfires. Then it roars happily for a whole ten seconds before backfiring three or five times in a row.

Manifold pressure gauges, fuel flow and RPM needles are in constant motion swinging wildly about their instrumental arcs. Hey, at least you know they are working, right? The needles are matched by the four arms frantically flailing about the small cockpit from lever to lever to high boost pump to magneto switches. Dan and Cedrick look like two competing conductors on the same podium trying to direct an orchestra composed of kazoos, moonshine jugs and a guy with only one cymbal and a ball peen hammer, to play Handel's Messiah.

Finally, after about three minutes of this barely harnessed pandemonium, just as both seem ready to give it up and shut 'em down the two engines begin to smooth out, the wild swings of the engines gauges start to dampen, and over the next two minutes are reduced to just an occasional every fifteen or twenty second minor hiccup from one side or the other. Dan seems much pleased by this and now reaches out to flick the silver switch that controls the ... duum-de-dumdum ... dadadadada ... JANITROL HEATER! Now, for those of you who have had the pleasure of using these things, you know what I mean when I say ... you just never know. Will it work today or not?

Particularly the early models of this heater came soon to be cursed by pilots and mechanics alike. In addition, early on the pilots would quite often curse the mechanics as well as the heater. We assumed that there was something basically lacking with a certificated mechanic who couldn't keep a lousy simple combustion motor going. Only later after we talked it out amongst our fellow pilots did it come to pass that we learned that nobody else's mechanics could keep the damn things running consistently either.

Well, of course the damn thing didn't come on. Heard the motor fire up but that was all. The FIRE didn't fire up. And now there was the three of us just frosting up the windows after having been in the plane for over seven or eight minutes. As the engines settled down the windows frosted over on the inside.

Over the next few minutes as the frost created by our warm moist exhalations built on the insides of the windows, Dan and Cedrick checked out the engines and other systems. Cycling the props numerous times gave all the appropriate indications and noise; the flaps went up and down and stopped where it seems they were supposed to. Even the external lighting produced a glow in the frost covered windows. Seems only the heater was uncooperative as now the left engine continued to purr evenly at all RPM settings and gave a good mag check as well. So did it's partner on the right wing although it did still give just the very briefest, almost instantaneously there and gone little hiccup.

Surely another closer examination of the fuel feed system and a few more swipes at the sumps would resolve that problem I thought. Dan asked Cedrick if there was an ice scrapper somewhere but a search of the airplane found none, so Dan was about to shut it down there and said we would pull it back to the hangar from there. But this idea did not appeal to me at all as the wind was now up to about 20 knots out of the west and the plane was over 100 yards from the hangar. So fortunately as he was reaching for the mixture controls, I remembered I had my wallet in my pocket and hollered "Wait a minute Dan!"

Sure enough my drivers license had just enough rigidity to serve as an effective frost scraper and Dan first cleared his forward windshield and then passed it to Ced so he could clear the right side as well. This worked just long enough to taxi the plane right up into the glare of the lights from the open hangar doors, whacking the mixtures about 10 feet out and allowing the plane to bump over the lip of the hangar floor and drive itself nose first into the hangar on momentum alone. As the plane came to a complete stop with only a little of the tail feathers still sticking outside we were once again "flying blind" behind the frosted windows. Flipping off the mags and the master switch now left the winding down of the gyros the loudest noise in the universe it seemed.

Cedrick was ready to call it a night but Dan badgered him mercilessly until he agreed to uncowl just the right engine again and check the fuel filter and injectors and any other fuel related stuff he could think of so Dan could give it one more good run at least tonight. Apparently he had given up on the idea of flying her, at least until tomorrow. Meanwhile Stevie was sumping the fuel tanks and coming up with a little more water. He reported that after five more of the big plastic jar sumps that there was no more water to be found. That job was considered done.

Meanwhile as I sought to remove the access panels for the Janitrol, Rod and Dan poured over the Janitrol manual and the Commander books trying to come up with stuff to check on that.

In another hour and a half, Cedrick had determined that the right engine fuel supply was clean and functioning properly. Dan and Rod had come to the same conclusion on the Janitrol heater. They found that the fuel supply was what was not functioning properly for the Janitrol; having ascertained that the igniter was working fine and producing plenty of spark, but finding absolutely no trace of fuel. It seemed not even a fuel vapor was getting to the Janitrol when commanded.

By now it was around nine o'clock and we'd been at it for the better part of 13 hours more or less. No further amount of pleading or cajoling on Dan's part was going to sway Cedrick's decision to go home!

Dan decided that he and I would take it out one more time and run it up again to see if the hiccup on the number 2 engine had been corrected and also top off the gas tanks before rolling her back into the hangar to prevent any more condensation in the tanks in the hangar overnight. So, as bone weary tired and hungry as I was, I was not about to pass up the chance to get some right seat twin time … even taxying around!!

Once again another 50 bucks in stove oil goes rushing out into the atmosphere as the hangar doors are thrown open. With Rod on the nosewheel towbar, Dan pushing on the nose right beside him and Stevie and I on the props we get a running start and launch the Commander backwards out of the hangar with enough momentum to carry it through a 90 degree turn and as we start pulling backwards to bring her to stop I holler at Dan that I'll get the fuel hose. But he hollers back that we'll do it after the runup as he wants to really fill 'er up for the night. I don't know it yet, but before too long I will be very, VERY grateful for THAT decision.

As tired as I am, inwardly I am excited that I get to occupy the co-pilots chair on this test and I clamber up to the cockpit crawling across the various loose seats that have been laying in the cabin for months. This is gonna' be so-o-o cool I think! You know, it's a good thing that you can't really see the future sometimes.

9

Just How DARK is Dark??

Dan opens the small door under the left wing and jumps in to scamper forward into the cockpit with me close on his heels after firmly securing the cabin door behind us. I am tired of crawling and twisting among the four or five seats laying haphazardly every which way about the small cabin. I stop and stack them to one side, noting that we have all five. The bench seat on the left wall holds two seats as well. As I shoe-horn my lanky 6'2" frame through the narrow "doorway" and into the right seat of the cockpit Dan already has the left engine at a rumbling low idle. The three blades of the right engine are rotating in a jerky manner through each individual compression stroke of the six cylinders of the Lycoming on the right wing. As my seat belt snaps locked a moment later, the right engine finds a couple of consecutive compression strokes it likes for ignition. The number two engine joins into a smooth harmony with it's partner.

Just for nothing, Dan reaches down and hits the switch for the Janitrol. The fan whines, the cold air rushes about the cabin and … nothing else happens. But, noting that even the cold air blowing through the defrost vents somewhat slows the accrual rate of the internal frosting from our warm breathing Dan decides to leave it run anyway. He asks me to take out my license and scrap the windows clear again. I do this, noting that indeed the frost thickness is greatly reduced. I practically peels off the insides of the windows in paper thin shavings instead of the heavier type hoarfrost that had been caked on the insides earlier.

Having decided that he wants to do a full throttle runup for a couple of minutes Dan taxis over to the west end of the ramp well clear of all the other airplanes and firmly locks the brakes. The thin frost has already rebuilt on the inside of the windows and is thickening. Since we intend to remain static for a few minutes Dan tells me to give the scraping a break for a while and just sit back and hold the toe brakes as a backup to the parking break.

Then, as Dan begins advancing the throttles and the Lycomings dull rumble outside gradually begins shifting to a higher pitched defiant roar … we hear a

WHOOOOOSH … and almost immediately feel a rush of warm air in our faces! Amazingly … somehow fuel has now found it's way through the empty feed line to the combustion chamber of the Janitrol and is blazing merrily away within. Life is getting better as both engines scream in the cold night air. The tips of the propellor blades cut through the frigid air outside less than a foot or two aft and outboard of my head.

After a full two minutes straining against the brakes at full power the engines haven't missed so much as a beat. Everything is looking pretty rosy when I hear Dan holler at me over the roar of the engines … "Well. As long as she's running so fine and we are warming up and all … we may as well go FLY, huh?!"

And as he pulls the throttles slowly toward close and he stops about 2200 RPM for a quick mag check and to cycle the props; the Janitrol loses either fuel or fire or … who knows?! But the damn thing quit again after only having run for about two minutes and clearing only half the forward windscreen. Within a matter of less than 10 seconds from the time we noticed the heater quit, it is already pumping out icy cold air again. In another minute or two, the inner plexiglass had cooled sufficiently so as to allow the frost to begin coating the inner side of the windows.

The fact that the Janitrol had crapped out on us after running for only a couple of minutes and that the windows were now fully frosted over again on the inside; made up really only a small portion of the total feeling of apprehension brought on by Don's suggestion that we go aviating.

Granted the engines had been running smoothly for all of about five minutes now. And other than the Janitrol it appeared that the other systems were functioning normally … but … but … still! I mean this bird had been sitting for weeks … no … MONTHS absolutely lifeless. It was dark out. No. I mean really dark. Blacker than the ace of spades dark. Darker than Ol' Hailey's EIGHT ball dark! Meaning Dan, with his lack of comfort on instruments will have his hands fairly full just flying this big beast if all goes well.

Not to mention that he only has about 25 hour total time in this critter which is a FAR different machine than the Aztecs and Twin Bonanzas that he is used to flying. And then there is me! With my sum total multi-engine time at this point of about 25 hours. Seven of which I got in a Beech TravelAire a couple of months ago to get my rating and the other big eighteen hours spent riding shotgun for Rod in his Dornier SkyServant! So I should be about as useful on this ill-advised "test flight" as … oh … say … A third TIT for chrissake.

What I don't know is that Dan had been talking to Rod. And Rod, based on his observations of my performances in the right seat of the DoorKnob; (ONCE

… Rod even distracted my vision outside as he let me climb us out on the gauges in a snowstorm, and then WHACKED a mixture control to see how I handled it … I guess I musta' did pretty good) that my instrument flying skills were particularly sharp given my limited total time at this point in my life.

So Dan, figures (I guess) that if worse comes to WORST that I will make sure we stay oily-side down. I am equipped with the only available frost "scraper", so Dan has now decided that these two pieces of good fortune coming together are the last ingredients he needs to conduct a successful "test flight". Accordingly, he now flips on the KX-170 and notifies OTZ Flight Service that "Commander One Red Robin is ready to taxi out". Sure, it's really supposed to be Romeo Romeo, but "the Red Red Robin" has been Dan's favorite song since childhood, and he can often be heard humming it as he goes about his daily business. Ergo, even thought the exterior is Brown, Gold and White 1RR never had a chance of being called Romeo Romeo. At least, not by Dan.

As we listen to "Correction Chris" (so named because he was seldom, if ever, able to complete an entire transmission and release the mike's transmit key without having had to say the word "correction" at least once) feed us the OTZ Advisory; (winds 260 @ 20G25, Clear and minus 10 C. and no other reported traffic) Dan asks me for my license again. Reaching inside my snowsuit to my left breast pocket, I extract the license from what has now become a somewhat damp pocket. Repeated usage has resulted in several small amounts of residual scrapped frost being deposited, along with my license into the shirt pocket.

After initially having the effect of hardening my left nipple (let me guess … more information that you needed, right?) My body heat would melt the shavings into a wee small reservoir of ice water which would then evaporate.

Dan does his side of the plane before turning the slowly deteriorating unit back to me so that I can scrape my side as Dan maneuvers the Aero Commander mostly down the centerline of the runway as we head to the east end of the runway. We make a U-turn and line up faced directly into the wind while the airplane rests squarely "on the numbers" two-six.

Dan prompts me to give both sides of the forward windscreen one last internal scraping to maximize visibility for takeoff. As I am completing the job on my side, Dan starts advancing the throttles, and over the increasing pitch of the hungry propellers, looks sideways to me and says "READY??!!??" with that Alfred E. Newman silly grin plastered on his face.

Any negative response would be at the least fruitless, as Dan was relaxing his feet off the top of the rudder pedals brakes as he spoke the one word question-statement. Forward movement had begun. With forced bravery and cheerfulness,

I responded "Let 'er Rip Danno!" while a little voice in the back of my head (which over then next few decades I would come to know well and learn in retrospect of course to heed) is desperately hollering at me … Hey DUMMY!! You don't know enough about what you are doing! The voice is still screaming in the back of my mind as the airspeed approaches the minimum control red line on the indicator which, to Dan has always meant rotate!

As I take another glance forward through the re-frosting windows, I see the two bright strings of runway lights narrowing into the distance ahead of us. All else is just black. Except for the glow of the runway lights. It remind me of riding in American Airlines first Boeing 707 simulators as a child over ten years earlier. Oh yeah. That's it. This is just like looking out a simulator I think. The airspeed needle touches the bottom of the Vmc red line hand painted (hopefully in the right place) on our lone airspeed indicator on the far upper left of the instrument panel. Oh well. Here goes NUTHIN" …

10

"Good! We're VFR!!"

Sure enough, as the needle touches the Vmc mark ol' Dan starts reefing back on the yoke and lifting the nose. And I will be forever grateful for many things that night. It was cold. We were light with no passengers and only about two hours of fuel. But mostly I will be grateful that Dan was not headed anywhere in particular that night on that takeoff. Ergo his plan was to go straight ahead and stay in the pattern instead of making on of his usual "three-point-takeoffs"! The cold temps and light load assisted both in rapid acceleration and improved flying performance which is going to be coming in REAL handy any moment now. You see ...

Astute readers have probably noted a couple of things by now. One being that the Aero Commander is a retractable landing gear aircraft. It was designed to operate that way. This little bit of info may jog your memory such that one would remember that thus far, this is the first reference to this oh so critical system throughout the story. Not since ol' Red Robin "popped" out of her snow cave after her long winter's nap have I mentioned the landing gear.

That's right. The one system that got absolutely no attention during the resurrection process was ... in a manner to make Murphy (of Murphy's Law) very proud; is now poised to get even with us for snubbing it while administering so much loving care and attention to all the other systems and parts. Now, it's not entirely our fault. Number one, being poor folk, we don't own a set of aircraft jacks.

If we need to fix a flat tire on something, we gather up a couple of 6 x 6 wooden blocks, some two by fours (basically whatever is necessary to hold up the plane, be it a Dornier, Cessna 207 etc. In fact, there are specifically cut and designated pieces of wood and blocking materials in everybody's hangars. I mean ... you DO have to change a TIRE ever now 'n then ... right??) Also gather as many people as necessary to lift the appropriate side off the ground to the appropriate height.

Besides. From what I learned later, you need something other than an engine driven hydraulic pump to generate the appropriate pressure for such an operation. It's called a (electrically operated) hydraulic "mule". But again, being poor, we was short one hydraulic jacka … er … mule! All of which, as we're about to see mattered not one whit to ol' 1 Romeo Romeo. 'Cause meanwhile … back in the cockpit.…

I sense more than feel that the main gear have parted company with the earth and as Dan continues raising the nose somewhat to a good angle, I note the glow of the runway lights edging downward and out of sight through the already frosted over windows again.

As I said, thanks to the conditions, we are accelerating rapidly, and thanks to the lack of visibility Dan is waiting an extra few seconds to assure we have left mother earth quite a few feet below before ordering me to raise the gear, which he now does. At well above minimum control speed, still accelerating and ripping through about 200 feet agl, now solid on the gauges, I move the little gear handle locking pin, grab the plastic wheel and jerk it upwards.

Now in my quite limited experience with retractable gear aircraft, I can recall no other airplane where the gear handle was somehow tied to the continued operation of the right #$%@ING ENGINE! But this night it WAS!

As the handle "sets" into the "Up" position I can clearly hear the hydraulic valves, fluids, gears, gizmos, and whatchamacallits all starting to do their "thing" (however it works) to raise our three wheels. One of the reasons I can hear all the whoziwhatsits so good … is that the roar of the engines at takeoff power has DROPPED BY 50 PER CENT!! At the moment the gear handle hits the up position the right engine craps out!

No. I don't mean it started surging. It didn't back-fire or just run rough. I mean the &^%*er just QUIT!! ZERO! ZIP! NADA!! The damn thing was silent for the full three or four seconds it would take for Dan and I to recognize what had happened. We stared and glared at the offending engine instruments in total disbelief. After evacuating our colons and begin we began to act!

The airplane of course, reacted immediately with absolute disregard for the fact that I was scared poopless. And the function of my SPHINCTER had just as quickly reserved itself while I watched in horror as the airspeed ceased increasing along with the altimeter of course, and we start rolling to the right!!

Dan hollers at me … "You fly! I got the engine! Happy to have anything to divert my attention from my prostate at this point I grab the wheel slamming it against the left stop as Dan lets go and mash the size twelve clodhopper on the end of my skinny (but thankfully long) left leg to the floor! HARD! This stops the roll to the right and commences a left bank thank God and I watch as the directional gyro swings back through 275 degrees headed for 260, the runway heading.

Next I search for the airspeed indicator and see that the needle is hanging just above blue line by a couple of MPH and I ease the yoke gently aft in an attempt to turn that extra 3 or 4 miles per hour into a better climb!! Meanwhile Dan is doing his impersonation of Leonard Bernstien conducting again. The right engine, after the initial interminable silence had come back with a roar for all of two seconds before going silent again for another two.

GODFREY! Why won't this thing climb better and why is it taking damn near full deflection on everything to go straight ahead?! A glance at the gear indicator, (red??? is that good??) followed with a quick one handed, three finger-nailed scrape of my right window confirms it. Despite all the nice noises, the right main gear remains in it's down and locked rosition thereby adding to the drag on the right! Dutifully, in a calm and measured tone, I report this additional bit of slight misfortune to my Captain. "JEEEE-ZUUUS CHRIST! DAN! MY &^%$ING WHEEL IS STILL DOWN!! ^%$#!"

As I have both hands wrapped tightly around my yoke, without saying a word … Dan now reaches out, grabs the gear handle and SHOVES IT BACK TO THE DOWN POSITION!

"There." he exclaims. "That'll help even out the drag!" He continues to push, pump, switch on, and switch off, any and all switches and knobs and levers which may have something to do with getting fuel to the right engine.

Well yes. I suppose evening out the drag is some improvement. And I note as the other two wheels return to their down position that indeed I am able to relax a SMALL amount of left rudder and aileron. Any thought of climbing though is pretty much wishful thinking as now blue line, which WAS giving me about a 200 foot per minute climb is now barely producing a 50 FPM climb with all three wheels back in the slipstream.

It's been at most ninety seconds since we broke ground as I continue westward. I could SWEAR we are in a simulator being solid on the clocks with only absolute blackness ahead. I assume we are about a mile and a half or two miles west of town out over the frozen Kotzebue Sound. Barely able to hang on to the 500 feet of altitude I have, I announce to Dan "Hey Dan! I'm gonna' turn back for town now." As he grunts and mutters to the right engine coaxing it sweetly … "C'mon girl … C'mon girl … be sweet … whatcha' wanna' do this for …" He interrupts his attempted seduction of the right engine for long enough to confirm it's a good idea.

Relaxing a little the pressure I have been holding with both hands to maintain almost full left aileron, I simultaneously ease up the pressure on my now quivering skinny left leg a bit. I allow the sickly twin with the spasmodic right engine to roll into a twelve to fifteen degree right bank. And while I'd surely like to get this thing headed back toward the airport (can the ice below hold us up if we start losing the other one??) I am DEATHLY afraid to allow the bank to increase any further as I am having to give up precious altitude just to hold blue line in the turn! I am concerned that if I let it roll any steeper I may not get the wing back up!

Since I need to turn to the right anyway, I holler at Dan "HEY! I'm gonna' try the gear again. I've GOT to get rid of some drag!" I figure since I need to make at least three right turns again before I can be lined up into the wind for a runway 26 landing, no matter HOW many wheels are participating at the time; I may as well get rid of SOME drag and maybe I can hold on to my altitude. "C'MON Lord! Give us a BREAK here" I pray silently as I quickly remove my left hand from the control wheel only long enough to snap the gear handle back to the "UP" position.

The whining of the motors and metallic thuds of the gear doors along with the increase in the drag asymmetry have confirmed that the process is completed yet again but the red "in transit" or "unlocked' light remains illuminated indicating that, once more, we have an unsuccessful operation in progress. But the asymmetry does not seem nearly as bad as before. I jerk the control wheel hard left to full stop the ailerons and again mash my left foot to the floor to stop the turn. My heading is about north for a crosswind leg and my right side window is a glowing white opaque mosaic. The lights of Kotzebue shine under the right against the frosted plexiglass, beckoning.

There has been a big amount of really heavy and rapid breathing for the last three minutes or so continually interspersed with grunts from both Dan and I. We struggle together to with our separate tasks. This has made for a real buildup of frost on all the cockpit windows.

Headed north still I have regained the seventy or so feet I lost in the right turn and am pleased to see that blue line is now giving me about a 110 FPM climb as I pass back upward through 500 feet AGL (or "above ICE level", in THIS case). I tell Dan I am turning onto a downwind as I begin the turn and at the same time announce clearly "PLEASE leave the wheels the way they ARE 'til I can get us some ALTITUDE!"

Dan says "Okay. No problem!" Looking up from the engine gauges to check the altimeter as his hands continue flashing from boost pump to mixture knob to throttle he notes the bright glow in the right side window and says "Hey!? Can you see town.?" When I respond in the negative Dan comes back with an obviously exasperated "Well ... SCRAPE DAMMIT! SCRAPE!" (Dan NEVER cusses....)

To appease what I consider at this point to be a LOW PRIORITY request, I let go of the yoke with my left hand as I jam it full left to begin rolling wings level again. I reach across to the right window and with three or four fingers quickly make four or five fast passes across the same piece of plexiglass with my fingernails resulting in a fairly clear hole in the frost no more than four inches in diameter just about eye level. Looking through it quickly, as I dare not lose my instrument focus NOW, I note two things which I report immediately to Dan.

"Hey DAN! The right wheel is about halfway UP now and I can see TOWN!" Instantly Dan shouts back. "GOOD! We're VFR!!" We're ... VFR! My God man. The whole world except us is VFR! I convulse into laughter so hard Dan stops flipping, pushing, pulling and whatnot on the controls. He looks up at me and says "WHAT!? WHAT is so FUNNY?!"

But just as I am about to reply, the right engine again BURSTS to life going from dead to balls out, as Dan had halted his "orchestra conducting" with both the mixture and the throttle in full forward positions. Immediately this is translated into an increase in airspeed which I promptly turn into more altitude by pulling the yoke aft until once again the airspeed registers blue line and we are climbing like a homesick angel in comparison to moments before. We are doing better than 700 FPM on the positive side and that's with one main gear STILL hanging half down!

Dan and I both turn to the engine gauges and stare in disbelief as now all the needles match up. Two manifold pressure gauges indicating 30 inches and are reading as one. We also have one set of matched RPM needles both at the 3400 mark on the tachometer. There are also two steady, unflinching fuel flow needles, one in either half of their shared, split-down-the-middle gauge, both pointing to the top of their arcs.

Dan speaks first, with a somewhat bewildered sounding "Huh! Well, whaddya' know! I'll try the gear again." I scream "NO!!' and his hand freezes in mid-air reaching for the handle. "Why not" he sez "they're running pretty good now." I replied "Let me get some more altitude before we tempt fate again, and besides we need to pull the left engine back in about sixty seconds or so as the thing has been running flat out for over four minutes and we're limited to five minutes at MAX power." He answers "Oh yeah. Okay. How you doin' OK?" To which I responded "Much better now, thank you."

Dan slumps back for a moment's rest. A break so unlike the previous few minute's pandemonium it seems almost surreal. JEEZ! That was close. Did that really happen? Ascending through two thousand feet a couple of minutes later I remark to Dan that we'd better pull the power back on the engines. And Dan agrees and says "Go Ahead."

I take the throttles in my hand and slowly slide them aftward watching both the manifold pressure(s) and fuel flow indicators slide slowly down. And as I begin sliding the propellor controls offa' their stops aftward, once again two surprised pilots hear a kinda' (very muffled) "whomphf" and warm air starts penetrating throughout the airplane. Now at about mid field on a right downwind leg and climbing through 2500 feet with the windows defrosting at a nice clip I again allow the airplane to roll into a fifteen degree right bank and Dan asks "Where're you going now?"

I said "Well Dan, I'm thinking I'll keep climbing 'til we get about four or five thousand feet under us so we got some room and time to work any MORE problems that might jump up and BITE US IN THE ASS. And I'd prefer to be directly overhead the airport in that case as well. So since we have the whole of the arctic airspace to ourselves tonight we may as well do it over the field and climb in a right hand circle as long as that damn wheel is dragging us that way anyway!" "Okay ... gee whiiiiiZ. Are you MAD or something??" he asks. I say (lying) "No. Not really. I'm just tired and hungry and that makes me grumpy."

Meanwhile Dan has been working the frequency selector knobs on the KX170 and as the digits click into position for 123.0 I hear Rod's voice coming over the speaker in mid-word saying "... uys doing up there? What's going on? Dan? Do you read base?"

Dan quickly explains to him that "the darn right engine must've ingested the last of the water I guess, but it was no big deal." (Speaking for himself obviously). It surely was a major deal for me! Then he explains our current remaining problem (the stuck right wheel) and says we're gonna' get four or five thousand feet under us and play with it for a little while. Now that the engines are doing "swell" and the heater continues to run, it has warmed the cabin to the point we can unzip the top of our snowsuits.

Rod cautions us to be careful and call him back as often as we have time to update him and asks how much gas we have adding "Man ... you guys sure scared us pretty bad down here when we watched you takeoff." And I ask Dan to please tell Rod the company owes me one pair of new size 34 waist (Boy. THAT was a long time and quite a few sizes ago) Fruit of the Loom Jockey shorts, at an attempt at humor, which he obliging relays. Since there are no less than oh, two dozen or so VHF scanners in use in OTZ at any given time; we all laugh realizing I have just announced to the entire town that I %^&$ my shorts with the same effectiveness as having it on a banner newspaper headline. I grab the mike on my side to add "just joking, of course." (Well ... I mean, I hadn't really. But only, I suppose for lack of food in the last few hours.)

Nonetheless we sign off temporarily as we pass through four thousand feet now well west of town out over the ice again, but within easy gliding distance of Kotzebue's gravel 17-35 if need be. And as our gently sweeping turn rolls us through an easterly heading again and town approaches on the right I am continuing to fly as Dan sits up straight in his seat and says "Well, this is pretty high now. Let's give this another try."

Lifting the inverse U-shaped pin lock guard to the other side Dan selects the gear lever to down as I now use the trim wheel to drop the aircraft's nose and maintain the 4300 feet that I have. When the wheels are all three showing down and locked in just a few seconds I can, for the first time in hours it seems take all input and pressure off the control wheel. Godfrey, I didn't realize how sore my left shoulder was getting from holding the control yoke almost continually for the last fifteen minutes, sometimes hard over sometimes less, but with steady resistance.

Now we cruise straight and level almost effortlessly, with no input at all on the controls from me.

As soon as the gear downlocks practically, Dan says "Here goes nuthin'" and attempts to again retract the gear. With the frost gone off the windows we both have a clear view (with Dan practically laying in my lap) of the right main gear bobbing up and down at least three times as it tries to retract. The doors for the other two landing gear have already thudded shut and I must now look away from the recalcitrant right leg of the aluminum beast in order to (sigh) again offset the resulting drag. This prevents me from seeing what I hear and feel, which is the right main landing gear making yet another "bounce" down motion in a six or seven inch arc of travel. Then, having "bottomed out" that bounce so to speak; the upward portion of the bounce take the wheel completely into the wheel well and THE DOORS SNAP SHUT! This is immediately confirmed on the lower instrument panel by a brightly glowing red light going out and a noted absence of any yaw at all! Well YAAAAAHOOOOO!

Now the question is ... will they come down? (All three hopefully.) The answer is apparent only seconds after the handle is again placed in the "down" position as both the left and right mains fall in sync and Dan, just as quickly as the green light illuminates, raises the handle once more and we both again watch the right gear which, this time with only two smaller bounces, restows itself in the wheel well.

On the next two cycles the gear operates smooth as new and after the red "in transit" light extinguishes for yet the fourth or fifth time successfully, Dan sits back, heaves a big sigh and says "Alright! Now I got my AIRPLANE back! Here. Let me fly 'er a while." I gratefully relinquish the controls, and mashing the fingertips of both hands inward together, pop ALL the knuckles and bring a great feeling of relief to my hands. This I follow with a large, loud and long exhalation and stretch of my tired arms to the fullest.

I take a few moments now to really relax and ponder the events of the last few minutes. I think about the inner forewarning that I didn't recognize and vow silently to NEVER ignore it again. And as I wonder how Dan could remain (mostly) so calm about it all, the radio breaks into my thoughts. "Hey. How you guys doing up there?" Rod is asking. Dan, who has started experimenting with flaps and slow flight and generally just exploring the "feeling" of the airplane he has been missing for these many month says "Go ahead. You talk to him."

I grab the slender tan colored Telex mike out of it's side window post mounted plastic holder and press the push to talk switch. "Yeah Rod. Everything's looking pretty good right now. The wheels are all up, and we ran 'em up and down a few times. The hamsters are all runnin' in harmony in their cages, singin' sweetly, and the heater could roast marshmallows!"

"Good. Good." he replies and then says, "Hey is Dan listening?" I answer "Yeah, go ahead. You're on the speaker." "Dan. What you think? Is she pretty good?" And now Dan, who was just returning to cruise from slow flight practice says "You fly some more", as he takes his microphone and says "Yeah Rod. I think she's GOOD again, uh?"

They spend a couple of moments discussing the past half hours events and potential causes and how the plane is performing now, which I mostly ignore. I am now really enjoying flying this "hot" twin. By far the hottest machine I've ever gotten my nineteen year old hands on and I am banking back and fourth in 20 to 25 degree banks flying figure eights. I concentrate on maintaining my speed at exactly 165 MPH and my altitude at precisely 5000 feet, with the ball centered directly and evenly between the two vertical lines on the slip/skid glass portion of the needle and ball instrument. So it take just a few seconds for the impact of Rod's two questions to Dan to hit me. "Hey Dan. So how much gas you got left and how many seats do you have with you???" Saaaaaay what? Now, Why would Rod ask that, I wonder.

Dan replies "Oh, I dunno'. I got good hour and a half's worth of go-juice and ... lemme' see ..." (this as he turns to look back in the cabin) ... "I think we got all seven seats here. Why. What you' got?"

"Well. Marie Armey called down from Noatak. I guess they got some people want to come down. But, you know, it's up to you. I mean since you're already up there 'n all. You know, if it runs good all the way to Noatak ..." and Rod leaves the statement hanging in mid-air as his transmission ends. Now they have my attention and I am looking at Dan intently, trying to discern his thought process. Surely, he wouldn't ... after ALL THIS?!

And then he looks at me, gets that goofy grin on his angelic chubby little face and, as he puts his right hand on his control wheel and wiggles it slightly to indicate he is taking control; he simultaneously starts a left turn out of the traffic pattern to the north and says to me "GOOD! Now let's make some money with this bird!"

Rod is again coming over the speaker saying, "But, you know. If you're not SURE ..." and again leaves it hanging in mid-air. To which Dan responds. "No sweat. I'm already northbound! We'll be there in 15 minutes! Got it covered!" Yes. Dan is sure as Dan can be. I too am sure. Sure that Dan, into whose hands I have repeatedly placed my life for temporary transport and safekeeping, only to just as often as not regret it, ... well ... I am SURE that Dan will teach me many, many valuable lessons in life.

With another heavy sigh and the slightest shake of my head I wonder to myself if I shall live long enough to make use of the new knowledge. I note that already, from this altitude, the twinkling twenty or so street lamps of Noatak are visible in the distance through the cold sparkling crystal clear air from a distance of over twenty miles. Ruefully, I look back over my left shoulder at the jumble of passenger seats that have fallen back into a pile in the center of the aft cabin due to the extreme airmanship and manhandling of the controls in the thirty minutes or so.

Seven seats. Five "stand alone" with their seat belts mounted to the side frames and two seats on the "bench" along the port side of the cabin wall. Seven legal passenger seats I think to myself. So at most, even by Gunderson standards, we can't POSSIBLY fit more than fourteen people back here ... (I HOPE.)

"Hi. I'm From the F.A.A.,
and I'm Here to Help."

1

Is That One STUFFS or Two?

I'm pretty sure it was late spring, maybe around the third week of May or even the end of the month. The sun was staying up pretty late but there were still snow patches scattered around town and the surrounding countryside.

The tinny jangling ring of the old 1950's over-sized black phone had jolted me from a pleasant afternoon daydream. Grabbing for the receiver occurred simultaneously with my black leather dingo boots falling off the edge of my boss's desk and "klunking" to the dirty brown and broken linoleum tile floor. The woman on the phone from Kivalina was asking for a price to move herself, husband and two small kids and another lady over to Noatak. As usual I quoted 1.6 hours of flying time. (A Kivalina round trip always being quoted at 1.3 hours with an extra 3/10's thrown in for a stop at Noatak). But the big question is always "How much stuffs you guys got".

Now, if you are unfamiliar with village travel, the word "STUFFS" is a general word that covers everything. From the dark green Hefty Plastic bags (generally used in the Lower 48 for lawn clippings and stuffing with dead leaves in early November) which are known throughout Alaska as "village Samsonite", it goes to anything up to and including steamer trunks and whatever may fall in between.

Ergo the response (this varies from "no stuffs" through "a FEW stuffs but not too many" right on up to "Lotta' stuffs too!") along with the conviction in the tone of the prospective passenger conveying the information is critical. Any personal experience with the passenger(s) if you already know them pretty good is also factored in then quickly analyzed by the pilot to determine which plane to take. Should you take the "big plane" (the 207) or whether you can get away with taking the 185 which is twenty dollars per hour cheaper for the customer, not to mention way more FUN for yours truly! The answer comes back in a fairly noncommittal sounding "A FEW stuffs …".

And, knowing that if I can get them to commit, then they can't get mad at me later if I see all their stuffs and say "No. Now you KNOW that is too much!"

"So maybe I should bring the big plane if you're not too sure about your stuff." To which she responds "How much more it will be". And upon hearing the new higher price she is now much firmer in her conviction. All their stuffs should fit, especially since the two kids are small she adds hopefully. With her assurance that they are waiting with cash (and stuffs) in hand, I tell them I'll be there in an hour or less and drop the receiver back into the phone cradle with a resounding "thunk". I jump up and grab my neon orange nylon windbreaker with the company's name and the picture of a Cessna 207 embroidered across the back pulling it on as I skip down the wooden stairs and trot across the gravel lot to where the 185 sits.

In five minutes the preflight is done. I grab the left windshield post and the top of the pilot's chair and, folding myself in half slide quickly into the left seat. As my right hand reaches down for the seat latching bar under the center of the seat my left reaches for the black tubular V-brace above the glareshield. In a matter of moments, a few fluid and flowing movements have locked the seat full forward, clipped the golden-brown soft cloth combination seat-belt/shoulder harness into place. I close the left door while at the same time both popping the plexiglass window open and locking the door from inside.

Mixture, prop, throttle in BOOOST throttle out and rotate the key to the right. GGGGRRRRRR! GGGGRRRR … GGGGRRRR … DAMN!

2

Remember the Alamo

For the last seventy-two hours we had been waiting for a new starter for this, my favorite bird, to come up from Wilbur's in Anchorage. The odds seemed to be fifty-fifty any time you reached for the key on whether or not the starter was going to kick in on the first, second or third try if at all. And it appeared I was on the losing side of the equation this time. Pulling the mixture knob and throttle fully aftward I reach under the seat, release the lock and let gravity drag me downhill.

As I lean forward and grab the parking brake handle to rotate it and pull it aft I give one last disgusted twist on the ignition key and release it almost immediately and ... DAMN! Wouldn't you KNOW it ... it engages and the prop spins a few rapid blades! So just as it's almost to a stop again after two or three revolutions of the propellor, I manage to twist the key in time to keep it turning and I mash the red mixture knob full forward. Presto! Lucky me she's goin'.

As the IO-540 barely ticks over at no more than 725 RPM, I quickly reposition my seat and resecure me to the airframe. With a quick slap from my open right hand the parking brake handle rotates 90 degrees clockwise. It unlocks and retracts forward under the panel with a solid thud. A slight goose of the throttle and this light bird is rolling across our gravel lot as I flip on the ARC radios and grab the mike out of the left windshield post holding bracket with my left hand

Rolling onto the asphalt parallel taxiway I mash down on the right rudder and the push-to-talk switch at the same time. The tail swings of the SkyWagon swings to port as I begin the familiar litany of the abbreviated flight plan ritual over the radio to the Kotzebue F.S.S. specialist on duty. "HELL-oh Kotzebue radio. This is Cessna 80124, flight plan when ready." Upon their response I continue, "124 will be round-robin. Kotzbue-Kivalina-Noatak and return. SOBs (souls-on-board) one, six and one. Two plus thirty enroute (I always give my planned time PLUS thirty minutes for contingencies) and four hours on the motion lotion. Advisories please."

And as the flight service fellow is rattling off the local traffic, winds and altimeter, I am rolling past the biggest structure on our little field. It's a faded blue and white corrugated tin siding combination hangar and terminal for Wien Air Alaska. Luscious Wien agent and part-time bartendress Sheila (see "Good! We're VFR!") I noted was escorting a good half dozen or more passengers out to the aft boarding door of 01Whiskey, Wien's Kotebue based Twin Otter. At the same time I see the crew emerging from the back ramp door to head for the business end of the machine. While I don't recognize the first officer I am glad to see the Captain walking out is my good friend Red Hotchkins. I see them both looking over at me sailing by and I flip off a jaunty right-handed salute that gives them a laugh and a reason to wave back. I detect Red giving the slightest bemused shake of his head.

Poor Red. I know my friendship with him can be a burden for him to bear sometimes. I have an alligator mouth which frequently overrides my 23 year old pea-sized brain at this point in my life. And Red's fellow Wien pilots and the other long-time Kotzebue aviators rib him pretty good when I'm not around to hear. Some fella' tells how "CloudDancer has gone and let his elephant ego overplay his limited flying skills yet again, only to have to turn tail and pull his balls outta' the vise at the last second". And Red'll come up with some minor comment in my defense. Oh, Red will laugh just as hard as the rest of the boys at the story but then something … maybe my youthful exuberance and niavete … or maybe just our common Texas heritage kicks in, and he'll make a weak stab at defending me or giving me the benefit of the doubt.

I mean, after all. I am STILL one of the youngest guys around and least experienced. At least now though, I am closing in on the bottom range of "average" for guys in these parts. That combined with the fact that the only other Texan to have come to Kotzebue to fly only lasted three days before wimping out (see "If You EVER Do That AGAIN"); usually prompts Red to mount some sort of verbal defense for me until shouted down by the assembled throng or my unannounced arrival occurs. Whereupon "the elders" then turn their good natured ribbing immediately my way until I (good naturedly, of course) suggest that they try something most likely anatomically impossible.

Red has given me every benefit of his hard won knowledge he picked up since being named Wien's Chief Bush pilot for Kotzebue. He has already been flying up here for a couple of years.

Of all the old timers and "elders" he has been the most forgiving and least judgmental and tries to see the humor in my "growing pains". Oh the other guys are all great mostly, and generous to a fault as well. But Red, I dunno, just something about his manner I admire. One of the coolest dudes I've ever met.

Taxiing by that day I reflect on all of that in merely a moment and look forward to finding him on 122.8 in the next few minutes as I suspect he will give me a holler. Just back from his days off in Anchorage he'll want to know if I've managed to stay out of trouble in his absence.

In another minute I am rolling out onto runway 08. Having already set the trim wheel below with my right hand (DON'T trust the little white plastic "indicator"; all the way forward and then three goods spins aft sets it just right for an empty takeoff each time) as the tail lines up with the centerline I'm already feeding in the throttle.

Full throttle slides easily and semi-slowly forward, and the tail is already rising as the throttle hits the stop with the airspeed passing 45 KIAS and increasing rapidly. My right hand drops to the flap lever sitting in the ten degree position. With a blood-curdling rebel yell I simultaneously depress the white button in the end of the flap handle, haul it up-and-backward to the 30 degree setting and smoothly pull the Cessna control yoke toward my belly. Up we go hanging on the prop at seventy knots indicated like a homesick angel. Below my left wing I see the number one prop on the Twatter just starting to rotate. LORDY I purely LOVE to FLY!

2

Blue Propellor Thingy

I was almost to Cape Krusenstern before I heard the voice of the Twatter first officer call "Kotzebue Radio, zero one Whiskey is airborne, time check please". As soon as he received his answer I grabbed my mike and said quietly ... "Hey Red. Come up on fingers." Fingers, of course a synonym (in our area anyway) for VHF frequency 123.45 which was used by many airborne pilots as a common "chatroom".

Seconds later Red is introducing me over the radio to his new first officer, a relative new hire at Wien who had just been promoted OFF the third (jump) seat of the Boeing 737 to the right seat of the "bush" machines, the Otters and Sky-vans. I congratulate him and tell him that he is lucky indeed to have such a fine Captain for his first ventures in the Arctic north and that Red had already taught me a great deal. This, I'm sure caused embarrassment much in the left seat and Red no doubt came back with some sharp witted retort.

Red and his partner were about fifteen miles behind me and headed up to Pt. Hope with a stop at Kivalina going outbound so in addition to having plenty of time to yak, I would get the added thrill of watching the big airplane land, and maybe even take off whilst on the ground loading up at Kivalina. So I passed the remaining twenty minutes or jawing about ... well, who knows. But as I approached Kivalina, angling downward from the southeastern skies in a cruise power high speed descent, I'm sure I switched over to 122 point eight or point nine to call out my arrival to any other traffic that might have been in the area. Now concentrating on my arrival procedures, the contents of the conversation were unimportant it seemed. Little did I know.

Back in those days, the most common arrival procedure on a pretty day was a "buzz job". Most all of us went roaring across the top of town anywhere from 50 to 500 feet above the tallest obstacle which was usually the HF antennae on the village clinic. Anything higher than 500 feet wouldn't really be considered adequate, as the whole idea was to alert the entire village to your presence and provide an airshow like thrilling entrance. Otherwise how would your passengers know to come to the airstrip?

Another common variation, which I chose today was to roar alongside the village no more than twenty feet or so off the beach. This allows the pilot the extra thrill of waving at the kids playing and adults working outside their beachfront houses whizzing past no more than twenty or thirty yards off your right or left wingtip. The village residents know the local planes and pilots and their "tactics" so well that quite often they recognize us in the brief flashing glimpse they have of our passing. In either case, with an empty plane inbound such as I have today, the arrival procedure will then transition to either a left chandelle out over the frigid waters of the Bering Sea to my left or a right chandelle at a point past the last houses if a landing on runway 12 is desired.

Today the clothing flapping on the clothes lines outside the houses clearly indicates landing back toward town. So as the last of the houses slide by on the right side of the aircraft I haul back on the wheel and crank her to the right launching myself upward as off a catapult and rolling to a heading of 210 degrees. As I do this, I look down to the right and see the first couple of what will be eventually be more than three dozen three wheelers and snow machines parked by the village's airstrip racing pel-mel to greet me.

In no more than a dozen seconds I have turned my hundred and forty-five knots of (literally) sea level airspeed and energy into almost a thousand feet of altitude heading briefly south over the lagoon to the immediate northeast of the village. I watch the airspeed needle as it sweeps slowly counter clockwise in the same space of time to stop a comfortable 15 knots under the top of the white flap arc. Rolling left to commence my downwind leg I quickly haul out the first three notches on the flap handle as I ease the throttle back slightly.

Allowing the nose to fall through the horizon I crank the prop control slowly right, turn after turn until, like the mixture knob, it too is flush with it's center panel stop. The still decreasing airspeed, now, thanks to the added drag of the flaps down to ninety knots results in a barely noticeable increase in RPM from my cruise setting of 2300 to now, maybe 2350.

Even in the (relative) much warmer temperatures of spring, say maybe forty-two degrees today, we always have "shock" cooling of our recip engines as a consideration. I ease the nose back up a little to get eighty knots and then add the final notch of flaps in. A couple more spins aftward on the trim wheel provides neutral pressure on the control wheel as the SkyWagon's trimmable stabilator does all the rest of the work for me. With those Fowler "barn doors" in their full forty degree extended position, lowering the nose to maintain eighty knots or so combined with two left hand banks for base and final should just about do the trick as I give up a good four hundred feet per minute.

Allowing the northwest end of the landing strip to pass behind my shoulder for a good fifteen seconds makes for an almost perfect base and final leg. I must only retard the throttle a little further for the last quarter mile of the final approach.

The left main hits once about a hundred feet from the end of the runway and then bounces me back into the air slightly before reconnecting with the World War Two pierced steel planking surface of Kivalina's runway to stay. And, having cut what remained of the engine's power on first contact with Mother Earth, the right main follows almost immediately thereafter. This allows me to pin the main wheels firmly to the runway with some forward stick pressure. My size twelve clodhoppers dance on first the right, then the lef … NO! The right rudder … some … more … hold it! The tail is falling … more forward pressu … and finally the tail quits flying and settles to the peirced steel planking with a rumbling and rattling. I seek to end that quickly with some good braking. Like many a tail-wheel machine; you ain't done FLYIN' this baby 'til she's about parked!

Speaking of which, I had decided that I was going to leave the engine running while on the ground at Kivalina to eliminate the potential for having to PROP the darn thing when it was time to leave, even though I really don't mind prop-ping the 185. It's much easier for instance than a three bladed 206 because of the angle or plane of the propellor arc. It'a another plane which I had often hand propped as well. [For one that will REALLY "keep you on your toes" try hand propping a dadgum Navajo with it's negative (sitting) angle-of-attack.]

Nonetheless, despite my "comfort" with the procedure, I would not intention-ally place myself in the situation any more often than necessary. I have already in my short life-time seen two people hacked to death by propellers when hand starting airplanes.

Therefore I now planned to pull off the steel planked surface early and park a couple of hundred yards down from the southeast end of the runway where we would usually park which would leave plenty of room for Red and his big air-sheen down there.

As I pass the cemetery conveniently located adjacent to the runway on the south side, (as it is in many small Alaskan villages statewide) I feed in left rudder and start a wide and fast swinging left 270 degree turn in the soft pea gravel that forms the peninsula on which both the town and the runway sit. With the need to work the control wheel as well during the turn because of the wind, I can only listen as 01 Whiskey reports herself "10 southeast inbound to Kivalina."

Finally bringing my bird to halt allows me to set the parking brake and insert the control lock into the little hole in the yoke housing. I slide the wheel back and forth 'till the pin falls through the hole all the way now immobilizing (pretty much) both ailerons and the horizontal stab. I grab at the mike, push the spring loaded push-to-talk switch and say "Hey guys! I'm down and clear just past mid-field on the south side. Your winds are all of about zero-niner-zero at fifteen and pretty steady." Thanking me the first officer adds a very formal sounding "Roger. The Wien Twin Otter 4901 Whiskey will enter a left downwind run runway 12". I think nothing of it though as I now have my own newly arising problems. This is evidenced by the half a horde of the fine village folks waiting for me at the END of the runway now leaping again onto their three wheelers to come "receive" me as it were.

Quickly I set the parking brake and rachet down the friction knob on the throttle as tight as possible before bailing out my left hand door. I run slowly from under the wing toward the oncoming machines waving them off with my outstretched arms, and they come to a halt halfway between the main group and my slowly idling 185. I holler over the rattling din of a half dozen two-stroke motors that they need to return to the main gathering area and I will tell them more. Immediately, used to obeying the pilot's wishes in and around the airstrips and airplanes, all but one spin around throwing pea gravel and race back to the pack. The Wien agent, already alerted by radio as to his incoming bird remains behind and motions me onto the back of his sled, saving me the 100 yard trot.

While holding onto the back of the sled I crane my face upward to watch as the DHC-6 in royal blue and gold colors passes high overhead on a left down-wind, not even descending for a low pass at all. Strange. Usually even the big-time airline pilots make a pass at 500 feet or so. I guess they (rightly) figured I'd given the place a good beating-up on my way in and they didn't need to attract any attention.

I quickly explained to my passengers that I would escort the two kids and one of the adults out to the awaiting airplane and that we should all carry as much baggage as we could. I selected the one grown man, lighter by a good thirty pounds at least than either his wife or (accompanying) sister-in-law to go out with the kids and me.

Between the four of us we were able to get all the suitcases and hefty bags ... you know ... stuffs ... out to the plane on the first trip. Surprisingly they really had only a moderate about of stuffs. As we get to the 185 I instruct everyone to drop their stuffs and tell the man to keep the boys motionless. I tell all three to stand together aft of the small baggage door behind the left wing until I got the bags loaded. As I ducked down to begin stuffing the aft cargo shelf full I noted the Twin Otter turning about a two mile final. Wow. Red was REALLY showing it to this guy "by the book" so to speak, it seemed.

In under a minute I had the cargo compartment loaded and the aft bulkhead re-secured and replaced the seatbacks on the two small stools that acted as or "Row Two" as I liked to call it in the 185. Quickly I opened the pilot's left door and, bracing it against the thrust airflow from the rotating prop I held it open with my back to it while hustling to get my passengers in and out of the wind. The man knew the boys role and bodily lifted them one at a time into the cabin urging them quickly onto the back bench seat. Then he clambered up and into the seat in row two on the right. Assuring him that the plane would be fine and it would not move so long as he never touched anything, I reminded him to get his boys buckled into their seat belts. We gotta' be SAFE around here ya' know!

He in turn assured me he had NO interest in the airplane moving without me in it, hence I could quite confidently expect his compliance with my "don't touch anything" edict! Oh-KAY! So far, so good. This is going well actually, and I slam the door secure and turn to race to the assembled group down by the end of the runway. About just passing the wingtip, the arriving Otter goes sailing by offa' my right shoulder taxiing down the center of the runway. I see Red clearly in the cockpit in what appears to be the standard awkward position of a Twatter Captain taxying his machine on the ground. It is a semi-uncomfortable position that I am still years away from knowing and becoming comfortable with.

The fingers on Red's left hand are split wide apart as he grasps both the control yoke with his thumb and pointer and then has the next two fingers spread wide apart and wedged over the goofily control yoke mounted nosewheel hydraulic steering "tiller". His right arm hangs ape-like from the two center overhead mounted throttles.

I throw off a juanty wave with what I am sure is a big grin plastered on my face and am puzzled as I get a brief glimpse of his face as he passes me by. He seems to be shaking his head in an almost disgusted fashion as he looks at me for the briefest of moments at our glances meet. Then he and the huge machine are outpacing me for the remaining 100 yards or so to the parking area.

Well, I can't make any sense of it I think as I continue the trot back to the assembled group and I arrive to grab the two ladies who have been patiently waiting. The Twatter props make that WHOOSHING noise that the Hartzells always make as they slip into their feathered position and in a couple of seconds as I am turning my back toward the airplane I hear the engines begin their whining slide down the musical pitch scale as, deprived of life giving Jet-A, they lapse into rest mode for a few short minutes at least.

I now, with a firm grip on each woman's forearm, propel them at their best forward speed toward our waiting steed. The old gals make good time of it considering the lighter of the two must weigh in about 200 or better and my front seat candidate is a solid two-fifty if there ever was one. Both gals are wearing traditional kuspuks or one-piece fabric dresses that are slipped on over the head and shoulders and go down to mid-calf and they start gaily flapping and snapping in the breeze of the propblast. While very comfortable and functional in almost all roles, they aren't necessarily conducive to ease of entry or exit in the 185, as they really aren't meant for climbing.

I station the larger of the two gals aft of the wing facing the tail with a "Stay here a minute" hollered in her ear and then turn to help the second gal into row two behind the Captain's chair. She actually accomplishes a fairly easy entry after I slide my seat all the way forward. This allows her first to get from the step to a kneeling position in the doorway from which she can relatively easily half-stand, spin and fall into her seat.

Cautioning both she and her brother-in-law seated beside her on the right to "watch your legs"

I then slide both forward seats to the most aftward locking limit. I retreat again fully outside into the prop-blast and while turning to get the remainder of my human cargo I take a quick glance through the rear window to check and see if the boys have been strapped in well by their father. Seeing that they are the subject of my attention even briefly, as all village kids do, they get BIG grins on their faces, wave and callout an unheard "Hi Pilot" quite loudly. I laugh, and having read their lips grin broadly and wave back.

Okay. Let's get this job done! And I grab the remaining gal and cautioning her to watch her head on the flap I back toward my door which I open by feel without looking and I am hollering in her ear. "Sadie! Be very ... I mean VERY careful! You are going to have to crawl across my seat to the other side OKAY?"

I had decided to have her "mount up" on my side and crawl across as opposed to using the right side door so that I would be near both the parking brake and the ignition key should she accidentally hit the throttle. I knew from her size no matter which side she entered she was going to need some form of assistance from me. Well. HELL!

Things just didn't go that well. With me and her both in the 185's doorway, the left door was straining at it's limits. She couldn't it seemed get upward beyond the boarding step onto either the floor with her knee or preferably my seat. Considering I'm standing on the ground yet, she is frequently falling against me with various parts of her anatomy. Now, up to this point I have tried to be respectful (she's my elder) and gentlemanly as well. But it has become quickly apparent to me that, short of a very small front end loader or forklift, I am going to have to take more … er … drastic and somewhat unpleasant measures here!

As Sadie dismounts the step for the third or maybe the fourth time I tell her. "Okay Sadie … when you get up on that step this time, I want you to reach inside and grab that black pole in the window and use it to help pull you up and I will … well girl … I'm gonna give you a little BOOST from BEHIND Okay!?" And laughing it off as nothing she says "Roger! Roger!' and prepares to mount the step again. I holler "Wait! Let me get ready first!" I press myself facing forward against the inside of the door with my right shoulder down low. I reach out and grab the throttle with my right hand and raise my left arm up over my head to get a firm grip on the parking brake handle.

Having assumed THIS comfortable position I holler at Sadie "Okay!! Get On!" and as before she struggles mightily to heft her bulk up offa' the step and onto my chair. When upward progress ceases, well … that's my cue to do my part. Wedging my right shoulder under her … posterior I begin a maneuver or exercise which, looking back, I wish someone could've taken a vidoetape of. There was no "America's Funniest Home Vidoes" back in those days, but if there was, I'm sure this would've rated highly. Much as I had muscled loads of hod and bricks in high school for a brick-layer friend of mine, I now tried to MUSCLE Miss Sadie into the airplane without hurting myself or the airplane.

She was grunting I was groaning. She was twisting I was turning. She was laughing … I was NOT. Her sister was pulling and I was pushing and there was small but NOTICEABLE progress until.…

A very strong tapping on my left (unoccupied) shoulder caused me to cease motion and quickly snap my head around to confront some stranger of an old white guy. I mean he had to be about like … FIFTY! And as he was wearing some green air force style parka and I instantly took him for a tourist or something. Whatever. He sure as hell didn't belong here.

As I opened my mouth he shouted at me … "Is this the way you ALWAYS load you airplane mister". Quite angrily I retorted "GEEE-ZUSS CHRIST!! Hey I don't know who the HELL you are but get AWAY from my airplane CARE-FULLY. I have NO time to chat right now"!! And I turned my head again as Sadie's struggle to overcome gravity was reaching a climax and … we were WIN-NING! Hooray! She's KNEELING ON MY SEAT! And I begin to coach her carefully across and into her seat when again comes the insistent POKING from behind me. I WHIRL ... eyes AFLAME ... prepared to unload on this ... this MOE-ron who had DARED to defy me.

I can't SEE his face. Because there, no more than four inches from my now rapidly cooling eyes are four fingers holding open a wallet sized leather display case. My eyes focus on one thing and one this only. The blue propellor like thingy under the words that span the top of the identification badge and read "Federal Aviation Administration". The badge is slowly lowered from in front of my eyes to reveal the same face, same guy in the green parka. "I'll try re-PHRAS-ING the question. Is your standard practice boy!?"

4

You In a HEAP'o Trouble Boy

As this obviously quite displeased federal official slowly allowed the hand holding the I.D wallet to sink lower it allowed me to see the fire in HIS eyes. Memories of my thus far short career flashed through my mind along with the thought "Well ... THIS probably screws the old airline pilot job all to hell". Now, I can bluff a crappy hand at poker. But I have never been able to look a person in the eye and keep a straight face whilst outright lying to them. I dunno'. Call it a personality flaw.

So I quickly avert my eyes to the ruff of his military issue parka, which is bending in the strong breeze from my idling propellor. And then, another tap from behind gives me a momentary reprieve as Sadie leans across my seat and taps me on the shoulder causing me to whirl to my right again. Sitting now peacefully in the right seat and struggling to wrap the seatbelt and shoulder harness around her ample girth she announces "CloudDancer! We ready now. We can go now."

I reply "Okay. Just give me a minute here I need to talk to this man for a minute" and then I turn back to ponder his parky ruff again momentarily before finally looking him in the eyes (which have not gotten any "friendlier"). Now, I did say I couldn't outright lie. I didn't say I couldn't B.S. with the BEST of 'em.

"Well sir," I respond with much less animosity in my tone. "You obviously know the gravity and risk of such an operation as well or better than I do given what I'm guessing your experience level is. (CAUTION ... moderate to HEAVY groveling ahead.) And if this actually were my standard practice as you called it, I don't know whether I'd be a bigger idiot for doing it or admitting it to you. So the answer is definitely not"! (pausing for breath) "As a matter of fact, I was KINDA' hesitant as (averting my eyes briefly) I've never really done this before."

Well my response only lowered the temperature in his eyes to the slightest degree. And as I listened to him speak ... behind my furrowed brow ... my brain was going into overdrive trying to figure which of a dozen or more ways to "explain" these actions stood the best chance of even minimizing slightly what I expected could be a severe career spanking.

"So what POSSIBLE reason do you have for doing something so downright stupid not to mention dangerous?" And before I can even start to answer that he adds "Isn't this one of Rod Gunderson's machines? Are you flying for Rod"

"Yes Sir it is and yes sir I am, and my guess is he probably won't be too happy about this either but you see ... really ... I thought I was doing O.K. here". At which point I saw the "temperature" starting to RISE again and continued quickly. "You see sir, it's just been the last couple of days ... and every now and then ... really hardly at all that the starter wouldn't kick in. So when I jumped in the plane to come up here and she took a buncha' tries to finally work, well I got to thinking on the way up here." Speaking a little faster by the sentence I continued. "I thought the way it behaved in Kotzebue it might just give up the ghost altogether and not work at all up here. So then I thought of all the options if that were to happen as far as me propping the airplane myself while the passengers sat inside alone or someone else here, trying to prop it for me. And well, by the time I got here ... I decided THIS was the best plan."

"This is a good PLAN!" he roared. "So you fully intended to do this when you left!"

"Oh ... No Sir" backpeddling furiously now...." When I left I intended to shut down ... load normal ... fire up and go like I ALWAYS would do. Normally! No sir! It wasn't the plan at all. As a matter of fact I almost brought the 207 because I didn't think this thing was gonna' start! It started on the last try I was gonna' give it up. Which, of course, gave him his next point on a silver platter to throw back into my face. "So why didn't you bring the 207 instead boy."

Treading water furiously in my head for just an instant ... I managed to come out with "Well sir ... you see ... these guys really couldn't afford the bigger plane and had to leave some stuff behind just so they could afford to take the trip at all. So I was just trying to help THEM out sir.

And HONEST (the sound of pleading now entering my voice) I SWEAR, once I decided on this as my SAFEST option (always use that word with the F.A.A ... it's their favorite) I did everything I could to ensure the operation came off SAFELY."

"You did, huh?" he grunted, obviously not buying it, although now that we had a "dialogue" going he was starting to seem a tad more willing to let me "explain".

"Oh yes SIR ... you BET! See, that's why I am parked wa-a-ay down here instead of where we normally park down by the Otter" glancing over his shoulder to the far end of the runway. "See ... this way I can control the access to the air-craft, and the passengers are loaded carefully and in such a manner so that no one gets near the airplane or the propellor."

"Right." He looks back over his shoulder to the Otter to see how far along they are in their loading and unloading process before looking back and riveting my eyeballs once again with a steely glare. His eyes are no longer "on fire" but his whole facial expression still makes it clear he is UNhappy and (in my mind) prob-ably hasn't bought a tenth of what I've told him.

"So ... were are you taking these people sonny?" "Well sir" I started to reply "I'm gonna' take 'em over to Noatak and...." "No. You're NOT." He inter-rupted. "I'm not?" now somewhat puzzled. "He continued "No. If they want to go to Noatak you will take them to Kotzebue in this airplane nonstop and then shut off this engine. You will load them in another airplane and have someone else take them to Noatak. And you sir, will keep YOUR ass on the ground until I get back from this trip whereupon you and I are going to have a little talk. Have I made myself perfectly CLEAR?"

Mind whirring with all sorts of jumbled ideas ... I looked up meekly into his very stern craggy face and mumbled "Well ... if that's how you want me to do it...." trailing off.

"No. That is what you will do because if I find out you did anything ELSE you'll be in even deeper trouble. You savvy me boy?!" (I swear ... every time he called me "boy" I'd get the impression of the stereotypical Deep South small-town sheriff who just pulled you over for doing sixty-five M.P.H. through HIS 200 yard long "city limits" stretch of four lane asphalt highway that's posted at 35.) "Yes sir. I understand." I respond now quite meekly. "Alright then. I'll see YOU in a few hours!" spoken with all the foreboding of a sudden rattling sound heard while on a desert walk. And with that final sword left dangling over my head he said "Now. Get outta' here and fly SAFE!" (See what I mean....) And he spun on his booted heels in the pea gravel and stomped away headed for the Twin Otter.

5

Pilot Police

As I watched the grumpy old goat go marching determinedly toward the east end of the runway I note that Red is closing the aft baggage compartment on 01 Whiskey as his co-pilot helps the passengers up the detachable aluminum steps into the back of the DeHavilland machine.

Mind still somewhat awhirl I turn and clamber up into my seat popping the window open and locking the door all at once. In two or three seconds I am harnessed in and ready to go (I think) and pop the brake goosing the throttle a little bit at the same time. It hits me the INSTANT the airplane responds to the increased propellor RPM as the wheels begin to turn. I lock the brakes having moved no more than an inch or three.

You never ... EVER pull onto a village runway without first having made at least some sort of "traffic call", assuming you have a VHF to use, which I do. Mentally I spank myself and, shaking my head slightly I reach for the microphone. I remind myself that I have people's LIVES in my hands and I must not ... repeat NOT allow my mental whirlwind to override my flying brain. "Kivalina traffic ... November 80124 Cessna 185 ... to back taxi from the cemetery to the west end for an east departure over."

When after ten seconds the only response has been silence; I again give the throttle a good shove and blast my way back onto the metal planking with a hard right rudder and the 185 begins to rumble her way down the center of the fifty foot wide runway. From my right I hear Sadie's voice break into my thoughts. "Hey CloudDancer??" and I turn her way as she continues "... whoWAS that strange nulakmi" (new-lock-me, Eskimo for white man)

"Oh...." I say absentmindedly as my thoughts are becoming more despaired by the minute it seems ..." he's just some guy from the F.A.A. in Anchorage, that's all." "Oh" she says back. Then ... "What's F.A.A?" I couldn't help the small laugh that escaped and I looked at her and said "Pilot Police" a term I was sure she could relate to. Now approaching the end of the runway I allowed the

71

airplane to drift almost all the way over to the beach side of the runway preparing for my U-Turn and departure and, as I brought her almost to a stop Sadie asked "Are you in trouble with pilot police CloudDancer ... he looked MAD."

I mash forward on the yoke release the left brake and add pressure to the right one all unconsciously and feed in a buncha' throttle while answering the old gal. "Well Sadie ... he AIN'T too happy ... but I'll figure out how to fix it." And as I finish saying that the nose has pivoted a hundred-eighty degrees around the right main wheel and we are now lined up in the center of the PSP runway again as I mash down on the left brake to stop. Quickly I do a last quick check and reset of the direction gyro (120 degrees) and the altimeter (eight feet). Mashing the black button on the mike again I announce to the world in general and anybody approaching Kivalina in particular.... "Cessna 124, a Cessna 185 departing Kivalina runway 12 straight out for Kotzebue."

Just at that moment Sadie leans over to me and says loudly "CloudDancer. You tell us if you need help. We'll tell that Mister F.A.A. man you GOOD pilot. You allus take good care of us and fly us good TOO!"

As I feed in full throttle and full forward elevator (I want the tailwheel off the steel planking to minimize the damn beating and vibrating the 185 takes on this runway) I laugh and say "THANKS Sadie ... I know you would and that means alot to me." And over the increasing roar of the engine and tinny intense rattling of the airframe she hollers back "We WOULD. And so will everybody!" Now with the tail lifting and all my concentration on tracking straight for another couple'a hundred feet 'til I get flying speed I just laugh loud and say "Thanks!". As I watch the Otter at the other end of the runway growing larger in my windscreen and see Red opening his door preparatory to mounting up I just sigh to myself and think "if ONLY it were that easy." Airborne before the halfway point I lift the Skywagon's nose a good twelve degrees and put in an immediate five degree right bank to swing me well clear of the Otter and out over the beach.

6

The Death Penalty

I'm passing 250 feet or so as the Twin Otter flashes beneath my still raised left wing and again see the left propellor just beginning to accelerate. Within the "hot section" of the Pratt & Whitney free turbine, the growing fire and expanding gases are converted to hundreds of propellor revolutions per minute from the tens of thousands of turbine revolutions per minute through the reduction gearing that actually turns the three-bladed Hartzell.

As the dark brown strip of beach slides out from beneath the body of my Skywagon I am passing 400 feet and abeam the first houses of the village. With the indicated airspeed now increasing to more than eighty-five knots, I grab the flap handle with my right hand as I roll from a right to left bank now to line up with the shoreline. I mash the spring-loaded white push button in the end of the johnson bar and quickly allow the flaps to be pushed to the ten degree detent by the airflow while the muscles in my right arm tense and flex to moderate the rate of retraction. It takes at most a second and a half and another push of the white button and the process is repeated again in two seconds this time as I retract the flaps to zero. With a clean airfoil the speed now increases to ninety knots as I straighten up in my seat again having had to crouch down and to the right somewhat, even with my long arms, to ensure that the flap handle locks into it's "zero" detent gently but firmly.

As I do my right hand move from the flap handle directly to the throttle where a gentle and steady pull drops the manifold pressure to twenty-two inches. A slight move to the right and three and a half full cranks counter-clockwise on the ridged propellor control reduces both the speed of the prop and the thundering roar noise level of takeoff power to the slightly quieter belligerent bellowing of a 25 squared climb power setting. Next a couple of equally quick spins of the red fuel flow knob on the far right brings the needle on it's vertical half circle scale down to the top of the green band.

In little more than another minute I have ascended through thirteen hundred feet and my right hand reaches down between the seats. Grasping the rear portion of the half of the heavy black large beaded-edged trim wheel, I start slowly rolling it upward and toward the front it's arc. Once and then again t-w-i-ice even slightly slower this time as my eyes focus on the altimeter.

The rate-of-climb needle falls ever more slowly from it's seven to eight hundred foot per minute range through it's left downward arc as the white hundred foot indicator needle on the face of the altimeter slows it clockwise race around the dial. The two needles reach their separate goals at virtually the same moment at the plane now settles comfortably at 1500 feet.

The airspeed needle remains on the upswing continuing to reflect the swift acceleration of our aluminum chariot, as the thrust which, no longer needed for lift is now converted to speed. As I watch the indicated knots increase through 125, now 130 and then135 I lean slightly to the right and holler over the noise "'SCUSE ME SADIE!" as my right forearm gentle shoves her matronly pantyhose clad left leg toward her right. I bang the corny-dog sized black hard plastic cowl flap handle out of it's detent with the inside of my right thumb as the rest of my hand closes around it and instantly starts it travel downward to the full closed position.

And in those few, maybe three or four seconds, our blurred propellor has increased our airspeed which is continuing to march upward, albeit at a much slower pace. Now passing one hundred forty-five knots it would, if left unchecked at this power setting continue to increase over the next minute or so to barely over 160 knots indicated with this load. Pretty impressive for a fixed gear straight tailed machine with struts. Left to right again across the three knobs in the "power panel" at the bottom center of the dash board sets up a twenty-three squared cruise power setting with an exhaust gas temperature 75 degrees centigrade on the rich side of peak showing a fuel flow of just about 15.1 gallons. Just right for this altitude.

A very gentle tug of about a quarter turn aftward on the trim wheel relieves the slight bit of back pressure I have had to exert on the control wheel since reducing the power by moving the trimable horizontal stabilator of the airplane. Unique for Cessna singles (I believe); the 185 unlike it's bigger family members the 206 and 207 Skywagons which I also fly daily, does NOT have a trim tab on the elevator. But rather like large jets, the front end of it's horizontal stabilizer is what moves up and down in response to movements of the cockpit trim wheel. Hence, since it function as both a stabilizer and trim came the term "trimable horizontal stabilator".

Airborne barely over four minutes now all this has occurred in somewhat of a fog in my mind. As I have spent so much time of the last few years of my short life in the three airplanes mentioned above it all happens almost completely unconsciously now. The same engine and horsepower ratings means the same power settings are set on identical engine instruments. The engine control knobs are the same shapes and sizes as are the cowl flap handles and positions on the right bottom of the center pedestal. The only significant differences in the 185 are the placement of the trim wheel between the seats, the flap handle and the relatively cramped quarters. Oh, and the 185 accelerates faster as well.

But after ... Lord KNOWS ... how many thousands of takeoffs behind these engines ... up until this moment, since becoming safely airborne and passing out of about three or four hundred feet when I lined up to parallel the beach ... the last couple of minutes and all the actions contained therein; including hollering at Sadie before pushing her leg have occurred in a veritable mindless vacuum. Seeing ... doing ... twirling ... shoving ... a routine. Now done mindlessly although with extreme accuracy. My mind has been meanwhile otherwise occupied with my newly created problem.

A very quiet voice is heard through my David Clarks. "Hey!" spoken in a hushed but quietly explosive kind of manner. It continues "CLOUDDancer! Are you on point nine?"

It's Red!

Grabbing my microphone out of it's holder I quickly respond "Yeah Red! TALK to me bud."

Immediately he comes back with "Go to eighty-five" in the same quiet but emphatic sounding tone. Uh-uh. THIS can't be good. Red wants me to switch frequencies to one where hopefully almost no one else will be listening. I reach for the frequency selector on the VHF and roll one click to the left and the nine-zero in the clear plastic window on the face of the radio is replaced with and eight and five. "Okay. I'm here Red. What's the scoop man?" I utter quietly.

As he starts talking I hear the sidetone in his transmission sliding down the musical scale and the roar of the propellors of the Twin Otter in the background also diminishing. And I realize the crew is setting climb power as he speaks. Man! I was so absorbed in my thinking that I must've missed their takeoff traffic calls from Kivalina I'm thinking to myself as I listen to Red's somewhat alarmed sounding but still quieter than normal voice.

"CloudDancer! What the HELL did you SAY to Bartelli?! (the FED) He's not just gonna' throw the BOOK at you. I think he wants the DEATH PENALTY!"

this last ending with a slight chuckle. "Oh ****" I mutter as my worst fears seem to be confirmed. "He's really pissed, huh?"

Still speaking quietly and now outright laughing, but TRYING to hold it in (I'll give him credit for that) Red continues. "Pissed!? Cloudy! I've known the guy for almost three years now and flown with him a half dozen times and I've never seen the man so MAD before. I mean he's a pain in the ass sometimes and a stickler for rules but man! The guy is SEETHING! He hasn't even put on his headset yet he's been back there writing notes and talking to himself ever since he got back on the airplane. Usually he won't even let us do our before START checklist without him getting on his headset first so he can listen to everything as well as watch it too. You have got the man LIVID son. I think you're in big trouble friend."

Obviously with Bartelli still off the headset I might have just a moment to say something to Red without the FED overhearing it. In desperation I plead "Red! Red! You Gotta' HELP me.!!"

Approaching now a few miles in front and to the left of me are the western end of the low hills that form a northwestern barrier for the Noatak Valley and lie between the villages of Noatak and Kivalina. And I hear Red saying into my earphones "HELP you. Like how am I supposed to help you?"

I've made the first and most pressing decision. I key the mike and the first thing I ask Red is "Hey. Confirm you are pointed west and proceeding toward Cape Thompson now, right?"

"Yeah we are westbound climbing to forty-five hundred feet. Why … oh … and HEY! If I quit talking in the middle of a sentence it means Bartelli is grabbing for his headset and I will not talk so don't call me back. Now what the heck are you doing?"

As I roll the airplane into a hard left turn I say to Red "Listen. I dunno'. Do whatever you can think of that might help me. I mean I know you don't owe me nuthin' or anything like that … but … JESUS man … I dunno' … see if you can calm the sumbitch DOWN somehow and tell him I'm usually really a good guy or whatever. Huh. Red. Whatcha' think?' And I snap the wings level now heading north and pointed at Noatak about thirty miles away. The silence on the frequency after I release the push to talk switch is loud. "Red … Red? Are you still there bud?"

Well. I guess I know what that means. I caress the trim wheel between the seats ever so slightly forward a few clicks … a half dozen … no more. 250 feet per minute down. Perfect. As I watch the altitude start slipping away with a corresponding increase in the airspeed, I mull my future bleakly as I catch sight of the Noatak River and make a slight course correction to the right.

I have decided that no matter what occurs later today my immediate problem is getting this load to Noatak. Quite conscious of the added cost involved in doing things the way the FED told me to do them (i.e. take these people to Kotzebue first, switch planes, etc.) I figure my loyalty to my paycheck and my boss says I take these people to Noatak as originally planned.

Noatak's runway is north/south and in spite of the fact that I am slipping down through 1000 feet and I cannot yet see any of the structures in town yet I know I am pointed the right way. The village will come into view soon enough now what ... HOW ... am I gonna' handle this guy when we meet in Kotzebue later? Lord! DAMN! A violation. Sum-ma-ma-bitch!! Man, I'll never get to be a Wien pilot now. Or any other kind of airline pilot either. I sure hope Rod don't have to fire me! (Altitude passing seven hundred MSL and I creep the throttle back a bit to retard the increasing manifold pressure.) CHRIST! Will I be able to get another flying job? Will I have to pay some big fine? Will I have to go get a CFI ... HELL ... CAN I get a CFI with a violation on my record. Holy crap! What if he suspends my license?! (Now passing five hundred MSL I caress the trim wheel halfway back to it's previous position. This slows my "descent rate" to more of a 110 foot per minute "sink" rate.) Good. There is the top of the clinic's antennae j-u-u-u-s-t peeking over the horizon dead center on the nose cowl. Maybe somehow Red or Rod can convince the guy to gimme' a break. I'll admit to flying "young and momentarily stoopid" and throw myself on the mercy of the court and maybe I won't get a firing squad. As the tops of the houses come into view in the far distance I am leveling off at 200 feet about ten miles south of town.

My plan is to sneak into town from the south as quiet as possible. No "rude awakening" one hundred fifty foot AGL high-speed loud noise event to alert everyone to come to the airstrip and greet the plane. Not today. I do not need a crowd. As I hit the ten mile south or so mark I hear (now back on 122.9) one of Leroy's boys in a Cessna 207 make a departure announcement that he is taking off to the south on runway one-eight. I reach for my microphone as well.

Well ... DOH! Talk about young and STOOPID!! I almost was gonna' mash the push-to-talk switch and make my OWN position report on 122.9. But I realized that I could well be inviting yet more trouble with the FED. See. The Twatter is most probably also listening to 122.9 as well, and I remember thinking to myself "HEY! DUMMY! This guy don't seem to need much more rope to hang me."

I am skimming the tundra at no more than a hundred feet above the surface and with just over a hundred and forty knots of indicated airspeed the occasional low scruffy bushes flash by as a dark green blur. I am approaching the village on a northeasterly heading of about forty degrees and suddenly, against the backdrop of the village buildings looming larger appears a dark black speck rising. It is one of Leroy's three dark blue and gold and white trimmed Cessna 207's staggering off the south end of the Noatak runway, no doubt every seat filled with villagers on their way to the "big city" Kotzebue for a couple of days of partying and shopping. It will take the loaded 207 almost one third of it's 43 NM journey to Kotzebue to climb slowly to the normal thirty-five hundred foot cruising altitude for it's 26 or so minute flight. I am always grateful to fly the 185 with it's far superior takeoff and climb performance.

As I close to within four to five miles south-southwest of the 3200 foot gravel strip it is time to concentrate now on carefully executing this "low profile" arrival. I drop down until I am no more than forty or fifty feet off the tundra and start V-E-E-R-R-RY gradually sliding the throttle back a couple of inches of manifold pressure each time, twice. After each power reduction, even though so small; three or four "clicks" of aft trim on the big black wheel between the seats is required to relieve the back pressure on the yoke as I maintain the altimeter's big hundred foot pointer motionless within it's glass face.

Finally acquiring a visual sighting of the south shore of the lake I seek just south of the Noatak runway I now bank gently right and exert the slightest back pressure while slowly cranking the propellor control two full revolutions to the right. The combination of the back pressure on the yoke, the very slight nose up attitude and the increased pitch on the variable pitch prop produce the anticipated effect and my airspeed has now dropped to just under the top of the white arc. A wee bit more back pressure and I'm at my goal of ten knots below max flap speed.

Very carefully, without looking … I lean forward and to the right stretching the fingers of my right hand to barely but firmly grasp the flap levers. I stretch my neck as well, as far as I can in the opposite direction, to keep as much of a clear view outside as I can. At this speed and this low altitude a moment or two of inattention and we could easily become just a wide area of scattered twisted aluminum and airplane parts on the tundra.

The added lift of the big fowler flaps as I haul 'em out into the airflow and lock them into their ten degree detent now helps boost the Skywagon all the way back up to 100 feet above the ground. This is well within the parameters I have set for my quiet arrival which I also don't even want to be seen. And now with the added thirty to forty feet of altitude the entire Noatak airstrip pops into view now no more than three miles away and I note with relief that I have the airport to myself, something that has become more of a rarity these days than even as recently as three years earlier. Back then ... it was EASY and often done that you would fly around all over the valley and not see another airplane until you came back to base (Kotzebue).

A short, quick left bank of twenty degree now brings me completely in line with the runway. And at the same time I crank the prop control forward steadily resulting in a further airspeed reduction. At a mile and a half south of the runway I am settled back down to about forty feet. But this close, my destination remains fully visible as I cross the south shore of the big lake that points the way to the airstrip. As I suspected, a final glance at the lagoon passing below me assures me that the surface winds are non-existent. A quick glance at the OAT mounted in the air vent mounted in the wing root show (no surprise) a temperature almost 15 degrees warmer than Kivalina.

As the next sixty seconds ticks off the clock I continue to gradually crank the prop control knob slowly clockwise, a crank or two at a time, toward full coarse pitch. Speed gradually continues to fall of and a half mile off the end of the runway as the airspeed needle drops through ninety knots I reach over easily now and grasp the flap handle in it's ten degree detent. A hard push of the round white plastic fifty-cent piece sized mechanical release button in the end of the lever occurs with a notable (as always) opposing pressure. It is intended to be, so that you can't easily or accidently unlock the flaps from their intended position.

It takes just a little more muscle to move the flaps to the next (twenty degree) detent. You CAN pull the flaps all the way to thirty of forty degrees if you so desire at this speed and going to thirty isn't too difficult at ninety knots either. But to lock the flaps in the forty degree position the Johnson bar is extended at about a seventy-five degree angle from the floor and requires that your right arm, actually your right hand, grasping the handle; well, it's purt near abeam your right rib cage. Since this takes a bit of leverage ... it is MUCH more convenient if you plan your approaches such that your speed is down to the 80 knot range or less when it is time to add that last notch.

Once again ... as did the procedural executions following our takeoff a mere twenty or so minutes ago ... most of what I've just told you occurred almost as if controlled my some internal automation. Although this wasn't necessarily a routine everyday approach, it was far from being an unusual or unfamiliar approach. There was any number of times I would execute the same type "low profile" entry approach to a village at the behest of a State Trooper or Judge seated beside me who often wanted to enter a village without attracting attention or any fanfare.

And sometimes, when alone usually, we'd wander the Arctic wonderlands at tree smacking heights just for entertainment or to practice. And there are quite a few times I can remember doing it just to stay awake! You'd be amazed at how ALERT you are when skimming the tundra at fifteen to twenty feet at speeds anywhere from 145 knots in your 185 or 206 up to 195 knots in your Navajo. Keeps ya' right on the edge of your seat with your eyes WIDE open. The airplane equivalent of screaming down the highway in my car with all four windows wide open and the car stereo rocking full blast as a kid!

So as I said … it all once again occurred in a very fluid and calm manner; and as the last quarter mile or so of tundra drifted ever more slowly forward to aft beneath our 8.50 x 6.00 Goodyears the speed continued to slip away until finally as the needle tickled the 75 knot mark I reached on last time and set the flaps to full. With the propellor control as well as the mixture knob all the way full forward I grasped the circular steel rotary friction lock on the throttle and wrenched it slightly left to a position allowing for more ease in throttle movement and with the heel of my right palm simultaneously nudged the throttle inward a half inch or so. Climbing the RPM back into the vicinity of 2200-2300 was perfect and it will remain the for the last few seconds of our flight now.

Five seconds more the tundra beneath our wheels is replaced with gravel as we cross the south edge of the strip indicating 75 knots. Back out comes the throttle slightly dropping the engine and prop revolutions to about 1900 to two thousand and the last ten feet between us an Mother Earth erodes along with the airspeed. At an indicated sped of about 70 knots the two main gear bounce lightly and skip back into the air no more then a foot and a half or so before settling down again. The second time they make contact I am ready an instantly apply gentle forward pressure to the yoke "pinning" the mains to the gravel while simultaneously reducing the RPM yet further to about seventeen hundred or so.

It takes very little dancing, almost none, on the rudder pedals to keep the tail and thereby the whole aircraft going in a straight line. I LOVE the challenge of a good gusty crosswind in the 185 … I just wasn't in the mood for it today.

For all the conflicting thought processes going on round and round in my brain that day, I had been unusually quiet and sullen throughout the short ride. It had not gone unnoticed by Sadie sitting beside me that I didn't (as I usually do) remove my David Clarks and hang them over the control yoke in cruise so I could chat and joke as I usually did with my passengers. It was my normal practice, and quite often I would not even remember to put them back on until I was calling inbound for advisories somewhere.

Now, as I looked forward and concentrated on where I was steering this still fast moving machine, I slide the headset backward off my head to around my neck and in a loud voice announce … "OKAY EVERYBODY! LISTEN! I will have to leave the engine running again So! We will unload exactly in the reverse from which we loaded … OKAY?! So Sadie I'll take you first and alone and then I will come back for you other guys okay?" Everybody assured me of their co-operation and I went on to say "I will stop just off the edge of the runway and then take you all a ways from the plane. You HAVE to stay away from the plane. Then I will bring all your stuffs (yeah … I say it that way too) to you at last, okay?" And again I get the confirmation I need.

7

Keep the Change

I slide the throttle fully closed and add full forward pressure on the yoke as we pass the halfway point of the runway and the tail begins to slowly settle downward. At the instant I hear the first contact of the hard little wheel spraying gravel I smartly pull full aft yoke while sliding my boots upward on the rudders to mash down on the brakes until the Skywagon's groundspeed has been sharply reduced to a comfortable taxi speed. A couple more jabs at the brakes and I am ready to take the 45 degree right hand turnoff that leads to the small parking area.

Mashing hard on the right rudder pedal momentarily sends me down the centerline of the angled turnoff with it's very slight downhill grade and rolling into the parking lots still ticking off about twenty knots or so. This is a perfect speed for I will need no further (attention-attracting) burst of power to swing my tail and roll a few feet forward afterward. With the throttle hard pulled against it's aft stop, I continue to decelerate as I grasp the sliver circular friction lock knob between my thumb and pointer finger. With the north end of the gravel ramp now nearing I now shove full left rudder whilst still applying some braking pressure to the right main to continue slowing.

I am twisting hard right on the throttle's friction lock and the (seemingly) sandpaper-like edged rotary lock is hurting my thumb and finger I note as the tailwheel instantly flops over into it's free swivel mode and the 185's tail assembly starts to swing fast to the right. Only a brief moment after the swivel starts I am mashing hard on the right rudder and brake to use the last of the aircraft's momentum to roll a few feet forward so as to allow me some distance behind the plane to take the passengers away.

I yank on the parking brake and as I pop my door open I turn to Sadie and say 'Sadie! Wait right here for me and don't move for a minute okay? We'll get you out your side a lot easier in just a minute okay?" This last is said as I reach across her ample bosom to grab the door handle on her side and rotate it up and aftward. Two thirds of the way through the rotation arc and the locking pin has retracted forward into the door frame from the fuselage and the door pops momentarily open and then back almost fully closed held there by the gentle prop blast.

As Sadie assures me of her compliance I reach down and unbuckle her seat-belt-shoulder harness assembly with my right hand as I am grabbing mine with my left. Hollering back over my left shoulder as I open my door I say "Watch your feet!" as I reach under my seat with my left hand to release the locking pins. I slide just far enough aftward to give me room to fold my legs under my ass and push myself outward to the ground in one smooth motion.

Immediately I reverse direction of the left front seat slamming it full forward against the metal "C-clamp" whatchamacallit type of stop that is pinned into the metal floor mounted seat track rails. And I again remind Sadie to "Stay Still" 'til I get back.

Grabbing the ankle of the lady seated behind me for the trip I shake it gently and say "Okay Darlin', you can get down now." And she grasps the door frame and leans forward to grab the top of my chair. I wince as I see the top of my seat starting to be pulled farther aft and bark out 'STOP!" (JEEEZ gal … Don't BUST my gahdam SEAT!! I think to myself) "Here!! Gimme your hand" I say while reaching for her right hand. Quickly we pull her forward off her seat onto her knees so she can spin around and dismount ass-in-my-face-first as I help her left mukluk shod foot find the small step welded to the airframe.

She's out in just a few seconds followed rapidly and quite spritely by Sadie's husband who is SO slight of stature in comparison to his wife I can't help but somehow, at this inopportune moment, get a vision in my head of these two engaged in … well … you know. The brief glimpse in my mind is again … more visual imagery that one needs to share. I shake my head to clear it.

I have the gal held by my right hand and as the man exits I grab his upper arm in my left and squeezing them both gently I holler into their ears … "just STAND here while I grab one of the boys." And, lucky for me, the man had already unbelted them and one was about to try and crawl over the removable seat back of the chair in front of him.

"Wait WAIT! A sec there big FELLA'!" and he freezes with a quizzical look on his face at me.

I said "Let's make it easy, okay?" as I snag my right palm under the open seat back and with a smooth upward stroke of my arm pop it free from it's bottom mounts and pitch it on the floor behind Sadie's seat. A HUGE grin returns to the kids face as he steps across the seat bottom with ease now and I grab him under the arms he grasps my forearms. As I am dragging him forward and lifting him I see his big brown eyes up close. They bore into mine ablaze with joy and enthusiasm for....

"CloudDancer! You COOL pilot! Flying is way FUN, UH!!" hollers the munchkin with an ear to ear toothy smile. "You LIKE it, Uh?" I respond in village English, me now with a broad grin on my face for the first time in a while. The kid's joy was infectious I noted as I dropped him to the ground and had a momentary flashback to every time an airline Captain had let me into the cockpit in flight.

I shoved the cherub forward and prodded the two adults in the back following them toward the tail as they held the boy by his hands between them. I announced loudly 'You guys go WAAAAAY over there by those drums and wait, indicating a stack of 55 Gal. Blue steel drums (the unofficial Alaska State flower) about twenty yards aft and slightly offset from the tail.

With them headed the right direction I turned and quickly bounded three large steps back to my door to find the other kid already standing in row two and starting to push at the door to get out.

Apparently far less enthused about flying his face remain straight and he said nothing as I set him on the ground and hustled him ahead of me toward the tail. And with a gentle push at his shoulders I only hesitated a moment to watch as he sprinted off in pursuit of his brother and the others before rounding the tail feathers to the right side of the plane. I noted in the distance, by the closest house a couple of hundred yards away, someone had stopped on their three-wheeler and was standing up on the pegs trying to get a better view of what was going on.

As I arrived at Sadie's door another glance back over my left shoulder now confirmed that he was headed (balls-out, of course) to the airstrip. Drat! I DON'T want or need any extra participants in this program and I swing open the door and reach behind Sadie's thighs and under the seat to the seat release which I pull sharply up on. Sadie is caught unawares as I mutter loudly 'Okay Sadie … your turn" and WHOOPS loudly in momentary fear as her seat takes off rearward and it seems to her the ground dropped out from underneath her.

Mass times gravity times the angle of … whatever. Sadie's seat slammed to a stop almost instantly. As I hollered "Sorry Doll! I shoulda' warned you first!" Now laughing she forgives me and her dismount is brief and uncomplicated. I head her off in a direction to join the others while now racing back to the business side of the airframe. A quick glance to reassure myself that everyone including the new arrival are remaining by the drum pile as I had told them to, and I dive head first into the small cargo door and rip the velcro mounted aft plastic wall/bulkhead out of it's flight position and throw it up into the second row. I will have time to deal with it when I get home.

Two quick trips over to the barrel pile laden with "stuffs" and I am ready to turn to sprint back to the plane and leave when Sadie hollers "CloudDancer!" And I turn back to see her twisting the small golden locking pins on the top of her black cloth palm sized coin purse which she has extracted from her large purse. Man, oh man am I lucky SHE remembered. I wait impatiently as she counts out one hundred and sixty-eight of the one hundred and sixty-nine dollars due me as the agreed upon price.

I am hearing those two cycle engines in the distance and look up to see … sure enough … three or four more three wheelers are headed this way and one of them carries two people with the guys riding in back carrying a large brown trash bag (suitcase) under his right arm as he holds on for dear life as the vehicles driver makes top speed attempting to get him to the strip in time.

Okay. This is what I DON'T need now. I tell Sadie, now actually fishing for coins to make up the other due dollar…. "Hey Sadie … no sweat this is good enough and I gotta' GO before those people get here, 'cause I can't take any passengers right now because of that F.A.A. man. So will you please tell those guys I'm really REALLY sorry but I couldn't take 'em??"

She's looking up at me trying to register all I blurted out so fast. I stuff the wad of cash bills in my right pocket and bend over to give her a little kiss on the cheek saying "Thanks!" and 'Bye, I'll see you guys. As I reach over to shake her husband's hand, a traditional one shake (up and down) deal and then tousle the wiry black hair of the one youngster still watching me with worship.

As I turn to sprint to the airplane Sadie hollers "CloudDancer!" And I whirl. Still blushing slightly from my unexpected peck on the cheek just a few seconds before she hollers "You be careful and don't worry to much about Mister F.A.A. pilot policeman. Rod will make him go away!" I laughed and waved as I sprinted the few short paces to my waiting steed. In under twelve seconds I was again airborne with the bellowing engine lifting me skyward. The forty-three nautical miles to Kotzebue, checking in with flight service for traffic advisories, the landing (full stall this time), all passed in seconds or minutes unnoticed. I flew unconsciously.

Only after I had landed and made the ninety degree turnoff taxiway and was taxying toward our lot where I could see Rod gassing up the Dornier did I return to the present. I had spent the entire 22 minute flight daydreaming about both the immediate future; the conversation with the FED when he got in, and my long term flying future. Or did I even have one after today?

8

Buy Ya Books 'n Send Ya' to School ...

Rod was balanced halfway up the folding six foot aluminum ladder with the black rubber fuel hose hanging draped over his right shoulder for comfort. Intending to top the Dornier's nacelle mounted tanks completely his mind drifted with the splashing sounds of the fuel serving as just background white noise.

CloudDancer had left a note on the schedule board and was due back anytime now accordingly.

Rod just wished he hadn't taken the 185 with the starter behaving on a 50/50 basis. To pick up a big load in Kivalina he would most likely have to shut down there at least as well as in Noatak to unload. Therefore he could expect the kid was going to have to hand start the plane at least once. And even though he, his brother Dan ... heck ... everybody took an occasional hand start as just part of the job; it still worried him. Well, at LEAST it wasn't the 207 with the starter out. Hand starting the bigger single, even with a TWO-bladed fan instea ...

Cutting through the soft noise of the green tinted fuel poring into the huge fiberglass tank came the slightly louder whistling sound the two-blade on the 185 makes at idle in the air. Rod took a quick glance offshore to the short final approach area of runway zero eight. Sure enough here was 124 (his REAL baby) in a mild slip with CloudDancer headed "for the numbers". Another fast glance at the tank (half-full) reassured Rod that he had time to spare and he could turn and critique the landing.

With the huge Fowler flaps fully extended and in a slight left wing down slip, Cloudy was giving up what remained of his altitude in a hurry, but still crossed the threshold a tad high. The numbers were out of the question as he kicked the tail back in line with left rudder while relaxing the downward pressure on the left side of the control wheel. Settled now well into ground effect the Skywagon "coasted" at three or four feet above the asphalt as the residual speed above stall bleed quickly away. Seventy-five feet or so past the numbers the remaining lift could no longer hold the empty Cessna off the ground and she settled to earth.

At the very last instant the nose of the 185 rose quickly skyward. She was done flying as all three wheels hit the pavement within a microsecond of each other. Rod noted with approval that the huge whites flaps retracted so fast that they were actually fully up and flush in the wing as the sound of the wheels hitting the pavement reached him now only two hundred yards away or so. The airplane immediately slowed to a calm, well controlled taxi speed. For the remaining minute or two it would take for the Skywagon to pull up alongside the fueling tanks Rod returned his attention somewhat to his chore.

With a sigh and a gentle shake of his head he found himself thinking back to over three years ago when his brother Dan had told him on the phone from his motel room somewhere in Texas that he had hired some "I dunno'. I think he's nineteen!...." year old ... KID with no time to speak of. What? He had about 250 hours or so, didn't he? Rod told Dan he was crazy. But Dan insisted he'd flown with the kid already and he could fly pretty good. So maybe we'll have better luck "raising" our own kid pilot from practically scratch like Uncle Ernie taught us when we were even younger ... remember?

With a chuckle Rod thought of CloudDancer and now, starting his fourth year, still ... this BURNING desire to be in the air. All the time! He just loved to fly and he was, for the most part, becoming a damn good driver. As long as he kept his EGO in check while at the controls! Twice Rod had to grab the skinny little bastard by the scruff of the neck; shake him fiercely and boot him in the ass hard; once even banishing the kid from the whole airport for a week. Each time the boy pushed himself along, with a load of passengers, WAY to far into a corner and only escaped by the grace of God.

One time Cloudy confessed his "sins" himself (the guy was honest to a fault) and one time his passengers complained. But each time it seemed, the lessons had the right effect and helped mold a better pilot. So much so, if fact Rod had relented after only three days of the supposed to be week-long airport "banishment" intended to give Cloudy a chance to reflect on how lucky he was to even be alive a pulling a stunt like he did.

A very humble and extremely remorseful kid pleaded to be off the hook and released back in the air having sworn quite sincerely that he had indeed learned his lesson. When Cloudy convinced Rod but Rod still wanted to hold fast; CloudDancer reminded Rod that, having already learned the required lesson QUITE clearly, Rod was the only guy still losing on the deal.

Over the dinner table with an infectious grin Cloudy cheerfully informed Rod that well ... he was off for another night of joyous carousing at the Pondu where he would most likely again for ... what ... the FOURTH night have to find some lovely lass to take home tonight and sleep IN with tomorrow morning, awakening sometime after he (Rod) was probably on his third trip. "And since the rent's paid" he continued, "and I'm not outta' money yet ... I guess ... jeez ... I hope you're not losing to LEROY since I'm not out there to...." Cloudy's boyish grin only doubled in size when Rod relented and lifted the chains. That grin. Good weather or bad. Drunk passengers or sober. Short trip long trip. Cloudy always had that happy face on coming or going in his airplanes. The boy had indeed been a good investment.

The 185 tail is swiveling around to slow gently to a complete stop simultaneously with the propellor on the other end of the airplane. Having parked with the tail no more than four feet in front of the DoorKnob, from his still elevated perch on the ladder Rod first see the bottom of the left door swing forward as two Levi and boot clad legs drop to the ground. Emerging from under the left wing and straightening upright Cloudy is heading over and Rod's cheerful banter over Cloudy's landing "performance" stops in mid-sentence. He's see the absence of a smile on the kid's face, instead replaced there by one real worried look ... "Jees kid. What's wrong? Did sumpthin' BAD happen? Are you okay?"

9

Bless Me Rod, for I Have Sinned

"Nope. Nope." CloudDancer responded as he raised his arms and shook his hands before stopping them palms outward like a traffic cop. Rod, who had released the trigger on the gas nozzle and started to take a step down the ladder now reversed his actions and continued pumping as CloudDancer continued. "No Boss. The plane is fine an ... except of course for the starter, you know ... and everybody's fine and the trip went ... um ... ooooohkay ... SORT of ..." and as he hesitated ... Rod prodded him. "Okay. Okay. Now what didn't go okay, SORT of?"

"Well ... ya' know when Sadie first called she wasn't too sure about the load, so I figured it would be a full 185 for sure. So I was thinking on the way up there tha ..." Here Rod interrupted. Although he really loved the kid like one of his own most of the time, Cloudy had a a way of getting to the point. It was the LONG way, as in never use two sentences when five will add more color. "Cloudy!' he snapped his name out mildy "GET to the POINT", what happened?"

"Uh ... well ... uh ... do you by chance know a Fed by the name of Bartelli?" having spoken this while staring at the ground where his right boot idly slides gravel back and forth sideways; Cloudy stops his movements and looks up at Rod on the ladder to gauge his reaction.

Rod groans audibly, rolls his eyes and again releases the trigger and the fuel stops flowing into the almost now full tank. This time he does descend the ladder so as to be more eyeball to eyeball with his young protégé before responding with "Oh no. Don't tell me you ran into Bartelli out there. Yeah I've know him since I was a ... since I was YOUR age! He can be a nice guy. He was pretty decent when he rode with me on the F-27 at Wiens. But, he can be the meanest S.O.B. on the planet when he wants to. What happened?" And this time he remained silent until he heard it all.

I was afraid Rod was really gonna' be pissed at me for NOT having brought the load to Kotzebue first and then having him fly it back north to Noatak. He did tell me he appreciated my concern for his "costs" of business but he still wished I had brought the load home first. And he did compliment me on my planning and execution under the circumstances, although he did say when he talked to Bartelli he was going to have to tell him he really chewed me out somethin' fierce. After he got back from taking my load up to Noatak (of course). And then he looked me square in the eye and said ... "Now. Do you understand what I just said to you?" I looked Rod in the eyes and answered that I did.

"Okay." Rod continued, "he'll probably come straight over here to talk to me after he gets done with you. You're done for the day anyway so hang out 'til you get done with him and the call me or come over to the house after nine tonight. And don't worry TOO much ... we still might have a chance with this guy." This last was spoken as Rod remounted the ladder and slung the gas hose over his right shoulder to finish the job.

"Now ... get outta' here and ... remember ... stay COOL. Stay VERY cool and humble when you talk to this guy. One thing I do know is the only time you can argue with him and stand a chance of breaking even with him is when you are a hundred per cent RIGHT ... an' you're just a liddle short of that here. Do not let your sometime alligator mouth get us in any more trouble today okay Cloudy?"

I looked up at Rod and told him I understood everything quite clearly and would make sure I did not put my foot in his mouth before this guy left town. I turned away and headed for the Wien hangar walking across the ramp. Sure didn't feel like Rod wanted me underfoot there and I just wanted to be alone. I definitely had some thinking to do before 01 Whiskey rolled in.

10

A Few Well Placed Words

And as it turned out I had plenty of time to ponder for the Twin Otter would take over three more hours to get back. They wound up having to divert to PIZ (Cape Lisburne) to sit on the ground for awhile shut down. Point Hope was socked in pretty tight with fog and Red decided since Lisburne was open and calm (a real RARITY for Cape Lisburne) he would go there first and sit on the ground for an hour or so. Get a good (fresh) coffee break in with the Air Force boys and have a chance to try and bend Bartelli's ear just a little bit if possible.

Meanwhile our young hero, unknowing of the delay, literally paced back and forth across the Wien ramp hundreds of times while awaiting the sound of a pair of PT-6's. There were only two airplanes in that corner of the world at the time wearing a pair of PT-6's. The other was a Beech 18 converted to a Westwind.

Deep in thought CloudDancer barely grunted an acknowledgment of a greeting to his friends who worked the ramp there. After the third one came by Cloudy gave him a very SKETCHY version of the story, apologized for being grumpy, and was left alone after that. Pacing. Sitting. Waiting as the sun moved from the west to the northwest starting it's evening and nighttime journey across the northern horizon. He stared into the large orange orb willing the DHC-6 to appear from it, burned kerosene exhaust fumes turning the fiery orb into a shimmering circular pool. He thought about a million different things at once.

It was ROD's fault because we never have any PARTS dammit! It was RED's fault for not warning me there was a FED on board dammit! (Although Red was positive that he had indeed warned me.) It was SADIE's fault for not being able to get her FAT BUTT into the damn plane any faster! Hell! It's Bartelli's fault. He's not even supposed to be concerned with ME! I'm a Part 135 pilot and he is a dadgum Part 121 Air Carrier inspector. He shouldn't even have any say or interest here ... RIGHT?! (Boy. Talk about your righteous indignation anyway, huh?)

Okay. I'm sure I can't go to jail. So that's good. License suspension. How long? I ponder what it takes to legally (or otherwise) change your name. But would the airline FIRE me if they ever found out? I could spend my life here I mean I DO like it and all. I don't have to go fly for and airline ... and on ... and on. For three hours every though of my past, present, and future raced around my brain like a carousel gone berserk. But most important ... there it IS! Turning final. I will face my accuser in just a few minutes.

As I watch the old man turn and kneel on the floor of the Otter in the doorway I am trying to decide how to play it. Bartelli's right hand grasps the rear door, still latched closed, for support as he slides his right leg out and down "fishing" for the aluminum stairs with his right foot. In moments he turns and sees me standing a dozen feet off the left wing as I try to stay out of the way of the rest of the passengers and the wooden wagon being wheeled under the wing toward the aft baggage compartment.

As he starts walking away from the Twin Otter I see Red appear in the vacated open doorway behind Bartelli and I catch his eye. Bartelli is looking at me and walking in my direction when he suddenly stops and glances off to his left at the Wien refueling stand. For whatever reason he has stopped and is now eyeballing it. My silent (but screaming in MY head) at Red is apparently heard. He gives me a VERY slight shrug of the shoulders a slight shake of his head with a wiry grin. Then comes two palms up quickly followed by a palm down shake of the right hand as if to say "cum see cum sa". Not much to go on but better than him dragging one finger slowly across his neck I guess.

All of this has gone unseen by Bartelli who now looks back at me. I try to read him. No dice.

Stern. Impassive. He visibly "snorts" and gives a slight shake of his head, almost in derision while looking at me as if to say "Boy! Don't even THINK about tryin' to mess with me."

He turns left and walks over to the fueling pit which is dominated by a stainless steel housing. The size of a good dining room table the top is perfectly flat and just over waist high. Clomping the few paces in his carharts and still wearing his grey USAF gov. issue parka he seems almost to waddle and I have to suppress a laugh.

I have yet to decide how to "play" this guy. Straight. Slightly cocky. Humble. Or obstinate. I mean if he's gonna' HAMMER me anyway I may as well fight. I just hope I can get through this without having to tell a lie. Then Bartelli decides for me. Throwing his briefcase down flat on the fueling pit top he reaches for the two locking snaps and rotates them. He raises the top of the briefcase and instantly slaps a big fat paw down on some papers the ever-present Kotzebue breeze tries to lift from his case. Turning right, the old man looks me square in the eye. He motions to me with his free hand and says loudly "Step over here into my ... OFFICE ... BOY!"

After all the tension and anxiety of the last three, no FIVE hours; after ALL the possible scenarios I had run through my brain and prepared a rebuttal to ... It hit me like a fist in the gut! It knocked the wind right OUT of my sails. I stared at the man for an instant ... and then I LOST IT! I LAUGHED! Now ... THAT's FUNNY!

I don't remember most of the whole conversation. I remember I didn't have to lie. I suspect only because the man didn't ask any direct questions that put me in that position. I also remember quite clearly him declaring to me his fondness for my boss Rod. Remarking how he'd known him since he was a kid and what a damn good if not the GREATEST pilot in the Arctic he might be. He then went on to say he was QUITE sure (and of course, I reassured him) that Rod would have never wanted or allowed me to do something that stupid! I replied in the affirmative "Yes SIR! I know Rod probably meant to take the key "off the board" indicating "down for MX." He concluded with "And I'm sure if I go talk to Rod he will tell me that he has already chewed you out I imagine."

And I very much remember the one thing that must have swung it in my favor as well, and that was that damn Red Hotchkins the Captain on the Wien Twin Otter. For Mr. Bartelli told me that while they sat on the ground lounging around with coffee that Red (bless his heart) REALLY went to bat for me. Said he'd been watching me for the last couple of years since he'd been the Wien Chief Bush Pilot here in OTZ. Said my flying was normally VERY safe and conservative. My weather reporting was accurate and reliable. And my judgement always seemed to be cautious. Why, he just couldn't understand how I could've just done what I did. Jeez. By the time Bartelli finished relating how great Red said I was; I almost believed it myself!

Well ... then of course, I laid it on as thick as I could in support of myself without (of course) appearing to be cocky. I apologized profusely for my sins and I'm certain, vowed that I had learned a great deal from the episode and that Rod in particular had been VERY adamant that I should "shape up" further. Out of breath, I finally shut up. Bartelli stared into my eyes and I didn't flinch. I knew my immediate if not long term future hung in the balance ... in this man's hands and ...

He ... let me OFF! Without so much as even a "Letter of Warning". Based far moreso on his trust in my boss, whom he'd know since childhood, and his two-year checkairman relationship with Red Hotchkins whose judgement he did respect ... I SKATED that day.

Bartelli was very clear and explicit in his verbal warning though. I remember it clearly. "But Mister CloudDancer ... if I ever hear ... much less SEE you do anything so foolish again I shall come after you for the whole kit n' kaboodle and ... TRUST ME ... you will wish your Mother had remained a VIRGIN! Do I make myself perfectly clear?"

PHEW! Bartelli, long since retired I'm sure, earned a ton of my respect that day. He was not closed minded. Among all the FEDs I knew in my many years in Alaska he was neither my favorite or least liked. But he ranked decently on the good side of the ledger.

Rod, my boss. I'll never be able to thank for ... everything. Red Hotchkins. What a piece of work that guy is.

After Wien was raped, plundered and pillaged at the hands of an earlier day version of "Lorenzo" and destroyed the pilots went mostly to Alaska Airlines or Southwest and Red wound up at Southwest from where he recently retired. His ties to Alaska and Kotzebue in particular are even stronger than mine have been as he managed to marry one of the ver best looking Eskimo girls in N.W. Alaska. (Not to mention one of the sweetest ... Hiya' Judy!) Their offspring, now college graduates have both earned flight ratings of some sort although they have wisely decided not to make a profession of it.

As for Red, he can still be found on rare occasions in a 737; now riding in back to and from his new helicopter job back in Alaska. Sometimes the ride in back is made far more tolerable by the fact the his life-long Eskimo love is the one pouring the coffee from the serving cart. All my professional life it seems, the former Twin Otter turned Boeing turned FLING-WING Captain has been unobtrusively standing somewhere nearby. At many turning points I sought him out. He was seldom, if ever in error, on issues of flight and our industry. I truly have always valued his counsel ... even when I didn't follow it.

And I know to this day ... on the very rare occasions that our paths still cross; now that I can no longer bump into him so often in the terminals our airlines commonly served; I know that Red takes some small matter of pride and satisfaction knowing that, since he had a role in my initial hiring in what became my current job, (Airbus Captain for a "legacy" airline) at least in some small measure ... his flying "lessons" live on to benefit passengers still.

For GODSAKES Red ... be careful out there in that airborne collection of noisy parts you fly around in these days. And THANK YOU ... for a lifetime of good advice and friendship.

The Jeremy Newton GCA

1

Meow, Meow, Meow

"Trans-Consoligamated 754, Seattle approach. SEATAC runway 16 right touchdown RVR now 700 feet, midpoint 800 and rollout 700. State your minimums." With a heavy sigh I momentarily restrained my first impulse, which was to key the mic and reply "A 12 year old Scotch, 38 D cups and 225 bucks an hour." Instead, peering through my "cheaters" at the small print on the Jeppeson CAT II/III approach plate I found the appropriate number and replied "Trans-YadaYada 754 … looks like 700 feet works for us today." The controller answers "Roger TC 754, this will be radar vectors for a Runway 16 Right ILS to Seattle descend now to one-zero thousand and turn right heading three five zero."

The first officer, who was still at this point flying the airplane, complied with the controller's instructions. Rotating the appropriate knobs on the upper center glareshield mounted flight control unit and pulling the altitude alerter knob, he initiated the descent. Meanwhile I focused my map light on the approach plate and increased the intensity of the bulb to it's full brilliance.

Within the next two minutes I had reviewed all the pertinent information on the plate aloud to the agreement of my partner. We both verified individually and together that all entries into the navigation computers were correct. Meanwhile our Airbus 320 had covered another eight or nine miles. Under the controller's directions were we now descending through seven thousand feet headed for five thousand.

My airline dictates that only the Captain may be the "Pilot Flying" during any Category Two or Three approach and landing. Therefore, as the first officer completes maneuvering the aircraft onto the base leg and rolls the airspeed select knob back to 190 knots in accordance with the controller's wishes, afterward I look over and say "my aircraft". And per procedure (gotta' get it right for the cockpit voice recorder you know, just in case) my friend sitting on the right replies "your aircraft". The sounds of our two IAE turbojets fade to a whisper. The autothrust system, having been notified by some series of electrons transmitted (somehow) from the 1st officers fingertips through the airspeed select knob to the FADEC (Fully Automated Digital Electronic Control)—think carburetor—now reduces our engine thrust to idle. Nevermind the "thrust levers" (Airbus terminology for throttles) remain motionless in a detent labeled "cruise" on the center control pedestal.

I watch the vertical airspeed "tape" on the left side of my Primary Flight Display tube as it slowly scrolls upward and the numbers get smaller and smaller until it passes 210 knots indicated. I slide my booted feet forward onto the rudder pedals and call out "Flaps One, please." In the right seat my flying partner glances up from studying the airport diagram to verify that the airspeed is allowable for my request. This is standard procedure ALL the time in normal and (almost) all NON-NORMAL operations. Seldom is anything done or moved without both pilots being "in the loop" so to speak. As he moves the flap handle to the first detent he replies "Flaps One" and we both glance at the upper of the two center mounted ECAM (Electronic Centralized Aircraft Monitoring) screens. We observe the pretty blue (in transit) pictures of the leading edge slats extending until they turn green when they lock into place.

In another couple of miles comes final instructions from this controller. "Trans-Consoligamated 754 turn left heading two zero zero degrees and slow to 180 knots. You are cleared for the ILS Runway 16 Right approach to the Seattle-Tacoma Airport maintain four thousand until established on the localizer. Maintain 180 knots until at least ANVIL or advise if unable. Contact tower at SODOE on one-one-niner point niner."

The "pilot monitoring" (the guy in the right seat now) replies and repeats verbatim every syllable the controller just uttered. By the time he has finished talking I have cranked the heading knob to the left initiating the turn even before I get the number 200 set in the window. I have also pushed two more buttons, one labeled "approach" and the other labeled "AP 2'", and follow that with a new airspeed setting. Both of us now look at our respective FMA (Flight Mode Annunciator) which spans the top of our respective PFDs and verify that (hopefully) all is well and our machine is "all systems GO" for lack of a better term. At the extreme right the approach capability reads in white "CAT III Dual". Indeed, we are "all systems GO."

I watch the bottom right of the PFD where at any moment I will see the chartreuse "diamond" that represents the localizer slide leftward (horizontally) across the bottom of the screen until it centers. When it centers that indicates we are on the localizer. As my lateral deviation milage readout now tells me I am down to less that 6/10's of a mile off the localizer centerline and closing it should "come alive" (appear) momentarily. I call for the next notch of flaps as the diamond makes it's appearance and the FMA announces we have "captured" the localizer.

Well HELL ... I think to myself. I guess this is what they pay us the "big bucks" for huh? I've trained for this in the simulator and done it a dozen times. We reviewed the two page CAT II/III "cheat sheet" in the QRH (Quick Reference Handbook) line by stinkin' line passing Yakima when it became fairly obvious that this might happen today. So far ... everything works just like the sim. The silence in the cockpit is eerie. It is the first CAT II/III approach for real for the first officer too. And I know that he, like I, is most likely mentally running through two dozen or so "things" that make a difference on this approach versus a normal Category One approach at 200 and a half.

The glide slope "diamond" falls from the top right of the screen prompting a 'Glide Slope alive" call from my slightly nervous friend on my right. I respond with "landing gear down, flaps three, landing checklist." The four item landing checklist is finished just as the glideslope is "captured" by the autopilots. And as the nose of the now captive plane drops slightly I call for full flaps. Yep. Works just like the sim.

Except this is REAL. One hundred fifty trusting adults passengers, along with three babes in arms and five very overworked and underpaid airline employees have just placed their hearts, souls, dreams and aspirations, not to mention their one and only ASS ... somewhat willingly in the hands of the humans who designed the 427 on board computers.

Now granted, only about a good two dozen or so of those 427 electronic marvels are really doing anything ... um ... important right now. And truth be told I could even LOSE a couple at this point and everything would still be hunky-dory according to the engineers. I on the other hand, along with my partner up here, can't help but remember that we (he and I) get to the CRASH SCENE just a split-second ahead of everybody else! And this ... this ... MACHINE ... of which I am supposedly in command of is rapidly closing the vertical distance between my seat (read ASS) and some very solid earth. As a matter of fact, given our current rate of descent and altitude remaining, something is gonna' happen here in the next minute and a half.

I've been flying this airplane for over eleven years now I remember, and seldom does a month go by (that's four four-day trips) where this airplane doesn't do something either weird or that I've never seen before. It is said truly, even by those who designed and built her, that you can not, and will not ever know all there is to know about an Airbus. Thirty-four years of professional flying. Over twenty-two thousand something hours. How many landings IS that I wonder briefly. And now, for the first time in my life, I am about to let an AIRPLANE land ME!

I am SO spring loaded as my left hand loosely grips my joystick … (no you sickos … the Airbus has a side panel mounted JOYSTICK instead of a yoke). My right hand rests curled around the thrust levers. I am READY to slam those babies full forward at the first sign of … hell … anything! I mean, at this point I'm so tense I don't think it would take even a Master Caution or Master Warning light and chime. A sudden unexpected loud fart or belch from the right seat would probably launch me into "go around" mode.

Now, with less than a thousand feet to go 'til … impact/landing? … I await the appropriate callouts from the first officer. I focus on my PFD and ND (Nav Display) exclusively. But for just the briefest second … I flash back to another place and time … when it was WAY easier. I can almost here Jeremy saying "CloudDancer. You west. Come EAST". I snicker loudly as I shake my head to free it of the now unwanted distracting thought which prompts the F/O to ask … "What's FUNNY"? As I reply "I'll tell you later" I watch the radar altimeter go down through six hundred feet.

2

East is ODD (+) 500, Right?

In the time passed since my flying debut in the arctic a few years earlier, the numbers on the bottoms of the logbook pages under the "total time", "airplane single engine land "and "X-country" columns had built into the thousands. One column however remained stubbornly below a hundred. It was the "actual instrument" column. This of course was due to a couple of very basic factors. There were no electronic nav aids on the ground anywhere other than Kotzebue, which now boasted a VOR in addition to the Hotham beacon. No nav aids means ... no fancy-schmancy radios in a lot of the airplanes either.

Hence ... all our flying ... was of course VFR. Oh, and occasionally ... SPECIAL VFR to enter and leave the control zone with less than three miles visibility. And CloudDancer, being the good Catholic lad that he is, raised to tell no lies ... must therefore NOT log any "illegal" instrument time in aircraft that were clearly not certified for it. Don't ask me how I justified in my mind writing all the time in the logbooks I spent sitting on the edge of my chair, hunched forward; peering into a mile or less of snow or fog whilst following a riverbank or shoreline at some altitude below five hundred feet.

Much less nerve wracking was the hundreds and hundreds of hours I had spent religiously maintaining the appropriate-for-direction VFR altitudes while sitting back relaxed in my chair solid on the gauges. A high overcast at night or even a moonless clear night in the far arctic can be blacker than ol' Hailey's AS ... er EIGHT ball! With sometimes up to a hundred miles between small settlements of as few as thirty to up to three hundred people and absolutely nothing else to be seen, you spend a lot of time not looking out the windshield. And the same holds true for many winters days when much of your VFR flying may be done with no more than vertical or just minimal slant range visibility. It doesn't have to snow too hard before a large amount of your airborne time, until the village comes into view, is spent also on the gauges. Oh ... uh ... vf R!, of course!!

With poor to marginally reliable to non-existent weather reporting from your village destination; quite often your go-NO go decision was based on the existing Kotzebue weather and the terminal and area forecasts. And the most valued weather resource was a less than an hour old pilot report from one of your fellow Kotzebue or Kobuk Valley based aviators. But only (mostly) from the professionals who did it for a living. I tended to somewhat discount what any of the local "leisure" pilots filed for PIREPS. Nothing personal of course as these guys were my friends as well. But, I don't know their capabilities and how accurately they can call the weather they see in comparison with the guys who are out flying in it and reporting all day every day.

So, quite often, after evaluating all the available weather intelligence, it becomes a choice to "Well … go give it a look and see what happens." So after working our way to within a few miles of the village (VFR, of course) how did we find our way to the ground you ask. I'll tell you about a few of my favorites.

3

The "State Flower" Approach

When dealing with what we euphemistically referred to as "kinda' poor visibility", generally taken to mean two miles or less; there were a couple of "standard procedures" generally employed by all. Essentially it boiled down to this. Go out visual and remain in visual contact with the ground continually if possible until reaching your destination. When you reached your VFR "limits"; which in my case varied from oh … 150 feet and three/eights of a mile or so … up to a high as five hundred feet and a couple of miles you had another decision to make. Big factors were always the village in question and the surrounding and enroute terrain. Whether the restriction was snow, fog or smoke made little difference. What is the icing level if any. How far to my destination yet? Can I set a reliable DG and pick a good heading? And most importantly what is the terrain in the immediate area around my target?

If all the answers came back positive and you were feeling frisky … you might just "punch up" … take a heading and watch your Timex. If you are REAL lucky you break out into an area of good visibility farther up the road, descend VFR and press on again visual. Or you reach your "time limit" and initiate a spiraling descent to your "pucker factor" limit. When exercising THIS option, my PF limit was determined by a combination of the destination's known terrain combined with how LONG I'd been "winging it". The longer (and farther) I had been unsure of my precise position the higher would be my minimum descent level.

For instance. To go anywhere up the Kobuk Valley in those days with two miles or less visibility in snow, Noorvik and the Kobuk River were the keys. Noorvik is 36 nautical miles from Kotzebue on the 076 degree radial or bearing in the case of the beacon. Depending on the strength of the east wind, even though I went on the gauges pretty much shortly after liftoff from Kotzebue, at some point between twelve and fifteen minutes from liftoff I will descend to as low as three hundred feet. I do this attempting to regain my two miles of visibility, even though I should be able to get by with a mile or a mile and a half.

I will call on 22.8 AND 22.9 giving my closest estimate of my position both to alert other "VFR" traffic and to hopefully raise any response from other aviators somewhere down the road for a fresh weather report.

I remember still. Within about a mile to a mile and a quarter on the south side of Noorvik there is a slough that enters the Kobuk at an extremely precise 90 degree angle. It is the ONLY such geographical feature of it's kind anywhere around for quite some distance. Hence even with a half mile to a mile visibility; meaning I would actually if on the south side of the slough, be unable to see the village, I can FIND it. If I happen (doubtful) to miss it to the north side I will stumble across the quite easily recognizable Kobuk River and ... off we go! If you can't find your way into Noorvik with a mile and a half visibility, you really have no business being OUT in this weather.

Many is the time I tried to make the upper Kobuk to get to Shungnak or Kobuk. It's an hour and twenty minutes no wind in my 207 as I cruise "VFR" on the gauges at 7500 feet in the inky blackness of a dark snowy night. I know from multiple past broad daylight VFR experiences that in this airplane my 075 degree VOR radial will begin to become unreliable and start wavering just past the Great Kobuk Sand Dunes about abeam Ambler.

I have kept very careful note of precisely what heading kept me on this radial at this altitude. I KNOW I lifted off at 17 minutes after the last hour. So. If I continue on this same exact heading until 30 or 31 after THIS hour (don't forget to adjust this number for estimated or known tail or headwinds) then ... in theory at least, I should be within a couple of miles of being on top of Shungnak.

But! Within about eight or nine miles straight north of Shungnak the foothills of the western Brooks range rise to a height of ... hmmm ... you know ... I can't remember the exact number.

But I DO know that 5,000 feet on my altimeter will keep me clear of anything within twenty miles of Shungnak by a thousand feet so, tonight's descent pucker factor limit is ... BINGO! ... five thousand feet. If I have not broken out of the base of the clouds, if I see no village lights, or a good three miles of identifiable ground (not likely tonight); I will point the nose west at the ADF needle and climb like a homesick angel to 8500 feet.

So how did we find some of those village runways in the dark and snow ... no runway lights ... ok ... maybe smudge pots if you're lucky. In later days some of the villages got light reflector "cones" for the runway edges. Just as the runways and runway lights were sometimes "improvised" ... so were the approaches.

Remember in "If You EVER Do THAT Again" (from the original "Chronicles" book) when Dan let me fly the empty 207 into Noatak and as we were on approach from the south landing north he pointed out the last electric telephone pole mounted streetlight on the north end of the village. As he spoke it was almost two miles north of us. Maybe a little less from our present position just a quarter mile south of the south end of the 2800 foot long runway. He told me to "Be SURE and remember it." Well, after that "learning experience" of a flight ended safely and we unloaded our three taxicabs worth of passengers out of our airplane, I asked Dan. "Hey. WHAT was the deal about the streetlight up there you were gonna' tell me?"

"Oh YEAH!. Come See." He says as he turns for our little office. Rummaging around the top of his desk he finds a clean sheet of paper and draws Noatak's runway and a crude representation of the river slightly off to the east. The village buildings are represented by dots and squiggles. Then he turns it upside down to face me. "Okay" he says "do you remember this is about what it looks like … right?" Upon my agreement he continues. Tapping an area just off the south end of the runway he asks "Do you remember what is right here?" And upon my admission that I had no idea he drew in a lake with a wide finger about a mile south of the runway. The wide finger pointed very close to north and slightly off the runway's "heading" of 360.

"Okay. You almost always land north at Noatak see … and you see this end of this kinda' fenger on the lake?" "Uh-huh" I mumbled in return. "Okay" he continued "when you get to exactly this place, the south end of the runway is directly … EXACTLY in line between you and that last street light I pointed out. So when you GET there, all you have to do is be at about three hundred feet and start "walking" your rudder a very little bit and within about 15 seconds you're gonna see the end of the runway!" And that's how you find the Noatak runway in a dark snowy night. 'Cause the LAKE you see is out lined by green trees and sticks out of even a dark night like a sore thumb. Admittedly, this IS one of the approaches that became much easier with the advent of the reflector cones.

Noorvik, just a few miles down from the mouth of the Kobuk Valley only had one runway in those days which was quite (in)conveniently close to ^%$#ing perpendicular to the prevailing winds usually blowing out of the valley. But. In addition to keeping you sharp on your crosswind landing techniques, the (usually) left crosswind always resulted in a left crab.

This was a quite fortunate turn of events as it just so happened that the road from town to the airstrip was on the left as you landed east. Going right across the top of one of the buildings in town (I honestly can't remember which, maybe the school) at a couple of hundred feet in a left crab did two things. One, it assured that you were lined up, at least at that precise moment, with the center-line of the 3600 foot dirt strip that lay somewhere in the inky darkness out the one to two o'clock position of your windscreen. And two, it assured that the beams from your left wing leading edge mounted landing and taxi lights would literally fall on the darkened dirt road that led to the airstrip.

So after passing over the last of the buildings, and dropping another fifty or sixty feet or so, you lights would now clearly illuminate the road as it reached the "parking pad" adjacent and even with the northwest end of the runway. As soon as the pad appeared it was a quick stab at the right rudder and drop the left wing to ... TADA ... and there's the runway ... (literally) right under your nose!

As faithful readers know by now, Kivalina is on the coast and subject to some serious fog days. However you could (if you WANTED to) fly from Kotzebue to Kivalina at a height of twenty-five feet and not hit anything by following the beach. Therefore the visibility required to successfully complete the outbound leg to Kivalina was pretty much determined by a pilot's individual pucker factor again. For me, that's usually one of those ... oh ... 150 feet and 3/8th's of a mile deals. Others have been known to do it a little tougher, but generally I like at least enough room and time to maybe change fuel tanks, hit the electric boost pumps, flare and holler "Oh ****!" prior to impact.

Well, in visibilities such as that circling to land upon arriving at the village is.... um ... DICEY at best and downright dangerous to be truthful. And fortu-nately since Kivalina in those days had something like 4000 feet of World War Two surplus pierced steel planking (PSP) metal to alight on, it was FAR safer to take a bit of a tailwind and land straight in. Well. Mostly straight in. See first.... at those um.... LOWER "approach" altitudes one had to be certain to MISS the village and a couple of tall antennae that were lying ahead in the fog between you and the runway. Approaching from the Kotzebue side, the last four or five miles or so (this in the days before the Cominco Copper Mine beach loading port was built) was pretty much unbroken even dark brown, almost black sand beach.

Of course, it was necessary to stay on the RIGHT side of the beach so as to not run into some guy going the other way, as well as retain as easy view of the beach. The problem was that ... WHAMMO! All of a sudden, there was the mouth of the slough between the lagoon and the sea, only a few yards wide. And when you crossed that ... you were essentially IN downtown Kivalina. Therefore, in the lowest visibilities, it was deemed there was a need for some "technical" assistance. Thus entereth the picture, Alaska's other "State Flower", the 55 gallon steel drum. An enterprising fellow working for one of the Gunderson competitors came up with the brilliant yet simple idea of using the drums as MILEAGE markers.

A group of three brightly green painted drums lashed together were planted in the beach three miles east of the slough. Add a set of TWO orange ones that were located a mile further west with a red drum placed just a mile east of the slough. It couldn't be any easier. Start slowing down. Slow down some more. Slow down to landing speed and configuration and move the hell over to the left some. Waggle your wings at the people outside their house watching you go by and then a slight sidestep to the right after the last house passes by. A quick glance at the windsock and you are down! It just doesn't get much easier than that. But my all-time favorite, the one you just WON'T believe, is the bad weather approach to Selawik. I am STILL amazed to this day how consistently it ... um HE.... worked!

4

With Apologies to Charles Shultz & Snoopy

It was a dark and stormy night. No. Really it was! I mean, think about it. It was the arctic. It was December. It was about 3 P.M. It happened alot! When you only have a mile to a mile and a half visibility in snow that is going sideways even faster than it's falling; with winds gusting between a steady state of twenty knots up to thirty-two rocking the airplanes in their tiedowns; you essentially have "a DARK and STORMY NIGHT!"

With Yours Truly at the controls, Comanche 7761 Papa lined up on the centerline (such as I could determine it) of Runway 08 in Kotzebue. The destination was Selawik to pick up a couple of school teachers to make the evening jet to Anchorage. Their destination was "points beyond", as in the Lower 48 where their distant immediate families awaited their arrivals to complete the Holiday tables. I would come to know it in years hence as quite an annual ritual throughout the entire region.

Not much has changed over the last few decades. Then as now, passengers often waited 'til the last possible day to leave, or left themselves only 48 hours to spare in their travel plans. Which, if you are going from Chicago to Detroit by air the week before Christmas can be risky enough. But if you're going from Selawik to Rochester, New York ... not leaving a MINIMUM of two days "slack time" each way is just DUMB! But people did it.

With the only phone in Selawik not working and very few pireps (none in the last two hours) and no one else known to be currently in the Noorvik, Kiana, Selawik triangle area this had become a go look 'n see 'n give it your best shot operation. I knew I would have passengers there, ready and chomping at the bit.

Now Selawik at about 62 or 63 NM on the oh.... zero eight-seven degree radial if memory serves, was just about one of the TOUGHEST places to find in a daytime whiteout before the dawn of a reliable and steady VOR signal, much less the help of DME, which appeared by the mid-seventies. And while both were of course limited to "line-of-sight" use they sure made it easy to refine a pretty good "guesstimate" of when you would be overhead the small village. Selawik village lay athwart two channels of the Selawik river in what you could I guess refer to as three "subdivisions". The river split in two just north of the village and rejoined just south. And of course, as you know from following the "Chronicles", following rivers to villages was always one of our favorite navigation methods.

Unfortunately in this case, the few miles between the river's mouth at the northeast corner of Selawik Lake, and the point just north of town were essentially useless. Unlike the Buckland and Kobuk rivers, the Selawik River offered little to no contrast with it's surroundings. Also it's (relative) extreme narrowness and more than 120 degree course twists, when combined with the real lack of differentiating terrain and an essentially flat-as-a-pancake ground run, made trying to follow it to difficult if not downright disorienting.

Hence, if you were lucky enough to find the mouth of the river at the northeast corner of the lake, a general heading flown for four to seven minutes, depending on the strength of the easterly wind you were flying into, would usually put you within a couple of miles of the village. But hey. This is one village where I know I was not the only guy to "lose" the village ("airport" and all) after having actually entered a downwind leg with the runway barely in sight.

But night COULD make it slightly easier to find the village, assuming the town generator was working. Once you found it though, night landings on the 40 to 50 foot wide 3200 foot unlighted dirt strip were generally made across the top of town. Usually there was no relaxing until the airspeed indicator was back down to zero on the ground. Fortunately for the pilots of the pre-DME days Selawik had something no other arctic village I ever knew of had. A one-man human "Ground Approach Controller" named Jeremy Newton. And it was nights just like this that earned Jeremy his reputation.

5

Can You Hear Me NOW?

Jeremy was a first cousin to Dan and Rod, my bosses. About the same age, they had grown up together as kids in Selawik. Like so many of the Gunderson brother's extended families of first, second, and third cousins, in-law's and out-laws, by blood or by marriage Jeremy basically adored his flying cousins with an occasional twinge of envy showing through. But overwhelmingly the Arctic communities feelings for the flying Gunderson brothers were awe bordering on worship and deep respect.

Over the years I would work with Jeremy in many capacities as he loved to be around "the aviation" as it was often called. Sometimes he would work for the Gundersons or other operators in town for periods of months as either a mechanic's helper or ramp lead man. But whenever he was in Selawik in these early (for me) days of the 70's he was the Gundersons main man for all purposes. I'll never forget the first time Dan told me about cousin Jeremy's special "talent".

On a fairly white early afternoon weeks earlier in October I had headed out for Selawik in marginal visual conditions. Dan told me if I thought I'd gotten real close, but I couldn't see it to "call Jeremy on the CB and let him steer you in if he can hear you." Well. This statement … spoken in the most off-hand manner you can imagine, stopped me dead in my tracks going out the door. I stood and listened as with a straight face, Dan explained to me that … somehow…. Jeremy had this … this special hearing ability. And Dan then told me that he'd used it in winds even up to almost FORTY KNOTS when the visibility was way down. Somehow, if you could manage to make it within a couple of miles downwind or three miles upwind of Jeremy's ears…. that…. by golly … he could guide you right to them. (His ears.)

Being as how he (and his ears) were most times at home, and home is on the "middle" or "island" portion of town and was directly in line with the runway on the east portion of the town; if this were true, then…. theoretically at least…. you ought to be able to nail down a pretty good "straight-in" approach to Selawik's

Runway 08. At least within 30 degrees or so of centerline which ... last I checked with the F o.f A.of A. qualified for "straight-in".

Sure enough only a few days later the opportunity came along to put Jeremy's hearing to the test.

The last few miles into Selawik from the northeast portion of the lake had been directional gyro and Timex only at 500 feet. I might as well have been swimming inside a milk bottle for all I could see. After eight minutes on a heading I resolved to go only a minute more to the east before turning back west again. Jeremy had already reported to me a half mile visibility. Maybe up to three-quarters of a mile visibility in snow with a steady twenty-five knot wind right down Selawik's runway. He could just barely make out the east end of the runway where it dropped off into the big (frozen over and snow covered) lagoon. Counting the distance between his house and the runway threshold across the river channel that was just short of about four thousand feet.

But wherever the hell I was at six hundred feet it seldom seemed that I could see any farther than three hundred feet whenever I ripped my eyes away from the gauges momentarily for a quick searching look. The second hand on my Timex hit "the mark" and as I reversed course to a 265 degree heading (turn right.... the hills are closer to the north) I fed in full power on my Cessna 172 and climbed another 200 feet to eight hundred.

"Hellll-Low.... SelawikSelawik! Jeremy are you there?" Shortly, Jeremy grabs the mike on his end and says "Hey CloudDancer! You can't find us so good today ... eh?" "Yeah Jeremy" I respond. "It's pretty crappy wherever the hell I'm at. But I went up a couple hundred feet so maybe you can hear me better I just turned west and I'll go three minutes and then turn east again.... Oh-kay? That way you'll have time to get dressed!" Jeremy replies that he has dressed in anticipation and is heading outside now, which I "roger"

Long, long before Verizon made it a part of pop culture lingo, I am sure I and many of my Alaska flying brethren repeatedly uttered the now catchphrase "Can you HEAR ME NOW?" Again I turn right to a heading of zero-eight-five waiting ... WAITING. And finally, Jeremy's wife is on the CB saying excitedly "CloudDancer ... CloudDancer ... make motor noise!" "CloudDancer! CloudDancer! ... Jeremy say ... come THIS way.... you too far NORTH. Jeremy say come ... liddle RIGHTliddleRIGHT!

I push the nose over hard diving to four hundred feet in a matter of a few seconds and ... BOOM! The world, or the "advertised" 3/4's of a mile (just barely enough of it for me to work with) comes into view and sure enough the north end of town lies a quarter mile offa' my nose in my two o'clock position. Well this ain't real good, but I can make it work I am fairly sure. I can't possibly bend this thing around and line up with the runway from here. But, if I transition to slow flight right now headed southeast and STAY at three to three-hundred fifty feet or so … nice 'n steady now. I should be able to go to the east end of the runway, make a right turn on the gauges to a "right downwind" and about the time I roll out from THAT turn…. With this wind I should be just at the west edge of town…. and then I can make one more semi-steep (30 degree bank) turn and I should be on a PUUURfect final!!

I quickly pull carb heat and throttle to slow down and snap in a short left turn to parallel the runway now directly below my right wing. I feed in some throttle after the second notch of flaps and quickly reset my directional gyro to the runway heading (hmmm…. not bad…. only off about nine degrees after all that crap). Another notch of flaps and more throttle and my empty 172 now barely covers any ground it seems moving eastward. More throttle and I pull up to four hundred feet before leveling off and now with close to seventy miles and hour showing on the airspeed indicator and again NOTHING to see out the window I smartly lay the machine into it's first 30 degree right bank.

Half way through the right turn to 260 degrees my peripheral vision in my right eye starts to pick up flashes of brown and I must resist the urge to take my eyes of the horizon and airspeed indicator until I roll the wings level. Again one more steep turn…. this one mostly visual with only occasional glances at the altimeter as I have all the houses and buildings to look at in this turn to give me some perspective. I a matter of less than four minutes from sighting the village I am on the deck trying to turn my Cessna 172 without getting it flipped over in the turn or the downwind taxi. Already I see Jeremy barreling down the riverbank on his side. An empty wooden is sled bouncing up and down and side to side behind his Ski-Doo as he heads for the smooth ice of the river.

And that's the way it's supposed to work. And in fact, it worked again that way a couple of times in November, even if it did take three or four east west passes the second time before Jeremy could "lock on" the sound of my engine and "bring me in". Absolutely dazzling to me. I'd never seen or heard of anything like it before. I mean not in a dadgum blizzard! So on this December night…. as the royal blue and cream colored Comanche 260 sliced effortlessly upward into the inky snow obscured skies; with at least four successful Jeremy Newton GCA's under my belt, I was quite confident Selawik was gonna' be a NOOOOOO sweater, as I was oft inclined to opine.

But I had failed to notice the ghostly presence of everyone's least favorite wingman, Ol' Murphy!

6

Every Which Way but ... UP!

Murph just started to play his hand out as I about figured I was over the east shore of Kobuk Lake outbound. After about twelve minutes of a smooth flight from liftoff, during which I shot up to all of fifty-five hundred feet and established a nice smooth cruise for the short thirty minute trip to Selawik, first came the bumps. Mild to begin with, over the space of the next five minutes I noticed a substantial increase to continuous moderate. Also I noted that during the same five minutes I had to add in over another five or six degrees to my southerly crab angle. Now holding an eleven to twelve degree angle to stay centered on OTZ's 087 degree radial. Hmmmmmmm. Now this is getting interesting.

At the 20 minute from liftoff mark I first reset my directional gyro. Then, still centered on my radial I nose the Piper over into a five hundred foot per minute cruise descent and pull back just an inch or two on the manifold pressure. After five minutes of descent I pass 2500 feet now almost fifty-five miles from the VOR behind me, and begin losing signal strength. But still, until the first slight wavering of the white course deviation needle, followed almost instantly by the first glimpse of the top of the red "OFF" flag as it rolls slightly fore and aft; a steady 98 to 100 degrees on the DG had held the course centerline. I commit to a descent to only eight hundred feet given this changing weather instead of my normal five hundred until I can get Jeremy on the radio and get an altimeter setting from him.

Up ... down.... WHAM!.... and the tail of the Comanche slews left as I reach across the right side control yoke for the CB radio on/off rotary switch. Trimming back for level cruise as we descend through a thousand feet starts the nose up and the airspeed reducing from the high of 165 knots it hit during the descent. It helps to soften some of the biggest bumps. Man! This is I think the WORST turbulence I've ever flown a plane in. Damn I hope those teachers got good stomachs.

I lean WAAAAAY over to the right and glance to make sure the barely dimly internally lit rotary channel selector in the citizen's band is reading number 11. Then I must lean even further as it seems to be off center requiring I turn it back and forth to ensure it is in the detent.

It's taken no more than five quick seconds and even though my descent rate was almost back to zero when I leaned over, that five seconds seems like an eternity without a look at my trusty gauges. So I straighten up quickly for a fast look out the forward windscreen and a comforting scan of my flight instruments. That was my intent anyway.... Murphy however ...

You know, I remember once. I was about fifteen or sixteen and my Civil Air Patrol event for the summer was a two-week flying encampment at Lackland AFB, a big pilot training center. Jillions of exciting things were available to an air-minded teenager to keep him or her inspired to fly, all of which were made available to us by the Air Force. And in preparation for rides in real jet trainers we all got a ride one day in the "Vertigo Chair". Now that is a SPECIAL chair that they use to demonstrate vertigo. The remainder of the group would gather around the chair in a circle as the "victim"-to-be was belted in.

The chair was built to be especially silent and practically sensory depriving. In addition the rider was given a box to wear comfortably over his or her eyes. The box was light, and fit quite comfortably on the face. And the inside was battery illuminated to resemble a dark (but notably) blue night sky with very dim "stars" emitting a soft light. The rider was instructed to sit up completely straight and relaxed in the chair as it began moving. Then the chair silently began to revolve slowly and gradually picked up speed over the next sixty or so seconds until it was stabilized at oh.... 12 to 15 revolutions per minute say.

The rider was asked a series of questions about the movement of the chair and consistently only got the first one right. It was 'Tell us when you start to move and in which direction". After that they we asked to announce when they had stopped, or the chair had reversed direction (if it did, which of course, it never did). Lastly the chair was truly braked to a halt, again noiselessly and gradually. Then the victim would try to announce when he or she had stopped, either often very early or very late. The instructor would position himself in front and to the right of the now motionless rider and say "Okay. Now quickly look over your left shoulder!" We laughed our ASSES off every time. For, sometimes gently and slowly, or sometimes violently and instantly, the rider would fall or almost catapult the upper portion of their body forward and to the right side. Kids ... meet VERTIGO! But I never had it happen in a real airplane 'til.... you guessed it.

As I straightened up, dragging the CB mike with me and looked into the blacked out windshield ALL CloudDancer inner gyros tumbled. Picture the WORST continuous tumbling crash you ever saw on a ski slope. You know ... where the guys falls halfway down the side of the Matterhorn ... skis go this way ... poles go that way.... ASS goes a third way altogether! WHOOOOAAA! I scream to nobody as my smacks into the left window and my body falls left until my snowsuit clad left shoulder come to rest against the same window.

Instantly I know what I've done to myself. Without moving a MUSCLE I rotate my eyeballs to see the horizon. It is telling me I am starting to roll left which is confirmed of course by the DG passing ninety degrees. I snap the wings level and find the altimeter. I sigh with relief to see it registering eight hundred and fifty feet. Having leveled the wings, I now attempt to simultaneously both erect myself in my seat and roll the aircraft right back to the proper heading.

I could rub one hand in right circles on my tummy and the other in left circles on the top of my head easier.

Half way to upright my internal gyros fail again and my body immediately returns to it's new favorite position, leaning on it's new best friend the left window apparently. It seems, at least for the moment anyway, that I should stay like this. I have no problem flying straight and level at least in this position and I am now holding my heading as well. I am also certain of two other things. We MUST be approaching Selawik now and this night would get a whole lot easier if I could PLEASE get some outside visual reference. Carefully raising the CB microphone to my lips I depress the button on top before saying "Hellooooo SelawikSelawik ... Jeremy boy. Are ya' DOWN there. Ol' CloudDancer's feelin' a bit lonely tonight...."

7

Oh Say Can You See

Nothing but silence interspersed with brief bursts of static come back from the overhead speaker. For over fifteen seconds, maybe twenty, I sat waiting to hear Jeremy's voice. After what seemed like a month to me I rekeyed the microphone pressed close to my lips again. "Hell-oooooh Jeremy ol' buddy.... CloudDancer's come to visit my friend."

The only sound in return is the continued roaring of the Lycoming under the cowl. Not even static back over the speaker this time. I know I've passed Selawik by now, and I must reverse course. I feel absolutely alone and very insignificant in the universe right now. I'm not really scared as such. But the combination of this turbulence, the vertigo, darkness and a lack of human communication is very unnerving. Apprehension. Yeah. There's a good word. I'm just apprehensive as HELL! Too young and stupid to realize just how far I am pushing my personal "envelope" this bleak arctic night. I MUST reverse course soon.

SIDEBAR *******

In later years ... after far too many "experiences" ... a more mature Cloud-Dancer would develop a few unbreakable rules designed to prevent ... um ... unpleasant flight terminations.

1. When your options for ending the flight in a positive manner are reduced to TWO.... select one of them and execute. Too often I've found waiting 'til your last option is left and then executing; (particularly if your last option is a 180) may well result in finding that circumstances have changed since you last reviewed your list.

2. There are two very key phrases that, when EITHER of them passes my lips or even silently runs through the bramble patch I call a brain; sets off ALL the internal sirens and warning lights. Any variety of the phrase "I think I can." ... like 'I'm PRETTY SURE it will work." If you ever find yourself wondering silently to yourself ... "Should I BE here doing this?" or "I wonder IF I should turn around?" Consider these to be RHETORICAL questions is my recommen-

dation! Thus endeth today's CloudDancer Flying Tips diatribe. Now back to our Lonely Eagle, eh?

****

I ve-e-e-ry cautiously and slowly this time erect my body in my seat taking a full three or four seconds to move the thirty degrees from resting on the left window to straight up and down in my seat. And although it is very difficult, I am able to override my intense desire to fall to the left again by sitting stock-still and only allowing my eyeballs to roam about the panel.

Dropping the CB mike between my thighs I reach for the throttle (still very slowly) and with the heel of my right hand push it in a 1/4 of an inch as I begin to roll the wings to the right. I focus solely on the faded white plastic lines of the horizon and wing indicators on the huge artificial horizon. I want to roll quickly into a thirty degree bank so as to stay as close to where I THINK Selawik is as is possible. But. Even as young and stupid as I am at this point I realize that I am walking a tightrope covered in strawberry jelly barefoot essentially. I therefore settle for slo-o-o-wly entering just a twenty degree bank.

For five or six seconds after the bank is stabilized at twenty degrees I remain rigidly focused on the horizon. Then I rotate my eyes down and to the right to the VSI which shows a descent of 100 FPM. I immediately ease the yoke back to center the needle on the zero at the left side of the face of the dial and VERY carefully and slowly give a half-crank of the silver rotary elevator trim handle. With the elevator pressure minimized, zero feet per minute on the VSI accomplishes the task of not giving up any altitude. No matter what your bank angle. Zero FPM on the VSI is easier to maintain an altitude with than trying to "chase" a moving target on the altimeter.

Back and forth between the horizon and vertical speed I go (with my eyeballs only). Every second pass at the horizon followed by a right and upward shift of the eyeballs to the "drum style" directional gyro face. I check the numbers rolling past the age-yellowed smokey dirty plastic rectangular window on the face of the instrument. The white numbers come into view on the right and march steadily to the left in sequence to disappear one after the other. 13 … 14 … 15 … and so on.

The rotation of my eyeballs continues as I sit rigid and motionless. And while I no longer have the intense feeling of falling (to the right) I am certainly far from over this attack of vertigo as my brain is still in serious disagreement with the artificial horizon. Only by continuous re-confirmation from the directional gyro am I able to believe that we are in fact in a right bank. My inner ear gyros are screaming "INVERTED" and "Full BACK All Engines" or something like that! I remember thinking I was damn thankful Dan Gunderson had insisted I show up with an instrument rating. Just as I again return my sight to the DG and the "S" indicating we are halfway through the turn passes dead center on the instrument a screeching parrot on my right shoulder blurts out "Gunderson Pilot! Are you THERE Gunderson pilot? Selawik here!"

The high-pitched female voice is scratchy sounding for two reasons. First, like most bush airplanes, this one is old and well used being a 1960 model. Hence the speaker quality in those days, like all the early sixties VHF communications arrived through any speaker in varying degrees of clarity. Add to it that the voice booming through the speaker was originating from an approximately eighty-some year old (why do people LIVE that long anyway?) woman. It is Jeremy's aged much beloved mother. A dear feisty ol' gal who insists on feeding me constantly, practically every other hour when I am staying over in Selawik: either stranded by the weather or waiting on my charter customers.

Selawik, like all the villages will be in a few years, is not yet home to it's brand new high school. Resulting from a recent settlement of the "Molly Hootch" case before the Alaska Supreme Court; the new high schools, complete with combination full scale basketball court, gymnasium, and cafeteria will become in later years the main layover refuge of young CloudDancer. Meanwhile charter pilots nowadays while away idle hours in the villages frequently as HONORED visiting dignitaries in the homes of the passengers or their respective company's village "agent".

Each Kotzebue-based charter company generally has such a person who, in return for scrounging up charter business for the company is allowed free travel back and forth to Kotzebue for him or her and their spouse and children whenever there is an open seat going to or from their town. They also store, safe from pilfering, very important stashes of extra aircraft gas in five gallons square tin Chevron cans in some villages. They help refuel and help us dig out after being stranded in blizzards. It's a goofy but effective system that pretty much puts a late thirties or early forties healthy strapping real ARCTIC world experienced grown adult man like Jeremy … at the beck and call of a snot-nosed twenty year old barely fresh up from the states charter pilot, looking to me for directions as to what to do to fulfill my needs. The Gundersons, being born and raised in Selawik as kids chose Jeremy, their closest first cousin since childhood as their agent making Jeremy's mom, Sarah, my bosses aunt.

The other critical criteria for determining which house I might have to spend my long hours in, especially when stranded for a day or two in winter blizzards, was the prospect for enlarging my growing circle of Kobuk Valley Eskimo …

um.... young female prospective.... um ... YOU know. And fortunately for me, young CloudDancer was pickled tink and driven to distraction by Jeremy's middle and oldest unmarried daughter, a scrumptious 18 year old named Selma. Selma would hold the distinction some day in the future of being the only Kobuk valley girl who actually makes mad passionate love to me, swears she's mine forever, and then tries to kill me within the HOUR! I mean usually that sequence of events takes weeks or (if I'm lucky) MONTHS to play out.

Frequently we would take Jeremy's boat, ostensibly down to the lake to "do a little fishing". But, as you've heard, the Alaskan mosquitoes, often mistaken for B-52's, can get pretty bad sometimes. "Fishing" while literally having had to BATHE your bodies and "fishing equipment" (mosquitoes being bloodsuckers of course) in Deep Woods Off does take a little away from the experience. Not to mention "fishing" in an open skiff does leave you open to not only the elements but the (unbelievably) rare prying eyes of one of your fellow airman who just happens to be in the right place to observe our "fishing techniques".

Yes. There were Selma and I in the front end of Jeremy's 16 foot skiff, "trolling" and "casting" and "reeling" in pursuit of "the big one" to the sounds of the Mama's and Papas blasting over the transistor radio (ambiance). When finally the drone of the engine of the plane as it circled lower and lower over our boat at reduced power finally was heard by us over the music and the noise of our ... um.... "fishing". Looking up mid-"cast" I recognized Leroy's 206 instantly. Selma however chose not to look up however. Rather, as before, she remained focused on "reeling in the BIG ONE!" which it appeared was beginning to um.... nibble on her LINE ... shall we say.

Now leveling off over a half mile away and configured for slow flight Leroy prepares for one last low pass a fifty feet for a final close up observation of my fishing prowess. As he flashed by Selma, now firmly "hooked" into a battle with the "BIG ONE", was INTENSELY focused on the thrashing about of her quarry. Doing everything I could to encourage Selma in battle with the monster and I had only one hand free which I DID wave at Leroy (sort of). For some reason the picture of some rodeo bronc buster, mid-buck, free hand and arm slashing through the air came to mind.

We often spent hours just walking around the "sidewalks" of Selawik. These were elevated wooden walkways built of 2 x 4's about four feet wide and mounted on pilings, as is EVERY thing in Selawik since the entire settlement is built in and on tundra and muskeg. Selma waved and shouted "Hi" to everyone she saw and of course was greeted similarly by everyone young and old, male and female. If I didn't know the person we would stop and introduce me. Almost every other person in this village of three hundred persons was either her cousin or second cousin or in-law … sometimes all rolled into one I think! By my reckoning having been introduced to the entire village by Selma over the first three months or so of my arctic life; fruit of the loins of Jeremy's mom was directly responsible for approximately a THIRD of the village's population in one way or another!

Nonetheless, still being the "new kid" in the valley, and Selma being well.… available … I spent most all my free time around Jeremy's large cabin in the winter. This always gave me the opportunity to watch Jeremy talk on the radio in person, as he would stride over to the wall by the front and only door leading out to the kunnichuk (an enclosed and roofed front porch with another door to the outside). The CB radio was mounted on a small 3/4 foot square ½ inch plywood shelf built especially for it and screwed directly into the log wall. The silver inch square holding bracket for the microphone was screwed into the log right alongside.

The radio was like a party line and with good atmospheric conditions the villages of Noorvik 27 miles to the west and Kiana just across the low Waring mountains to the north could all join voices on Channel 11 in a three village party-line gabfest that would put poor Sam Drucker's store and phone system in mythical Hooterville to shame. But the instant a PILOT broke into the often continuous steam of hunting reports, position inquiries about relatives from up or downriver boating by, and general gossip … the radio airwaves belonged to the agent and the calling pilot by common understanding until their conversation was done. This of course often gave all within radio range the added benefit of knowing who was coming or going where. There were very few secrets, about anything in the entire Kobuk Valley in those days. Given the altitude of the aircraft transmitting, quite often even the upriver villages got half the conversation anyway!

Now, as the "S" indicating south on the rotating drum in the face of the DG slides leftward, my right arm flinches momentarily. I desperately want to talk to someone.… even Sarah right now but … Based on the fact that my inner ears are still sending signals to my brain that we are riding a high speed merry-go-round I catch myself and resist the urge to move any part of my body until I roll wings level heading west again. So I stay frozen with the exception of blinking my eyes. Of course I needn't mention that "other" body orifice that has once again been twitching totally out of my control since the near panic of vertigo set in.

Finally I roll the wings level and the DG indicates "West". I exhale loudly and still motionless I ponder to realize that I hadn't even known I was holding my breath throughout the turn! I gently bank again to the right adding another five degrees until the tiny white mark at the top of the DG drum lies over the tinier on the drum between the big number 27 and the smaller number 28 to it's right. I had initiated the course reversal as a right turn from what I thought was the immediate area of the village so realizing that I would now be south of the village by some margin it seemed a course correction was called for. And after only a moment's thought I realized that five degrees wouldn't be enough.... so's I added in another five degrees. I guess that's literally the real life version of "winging it".

Carefully I reach between my thighs and extract the CB microphone just as Sarah's voice blasts through the speaker again "Is that Gunderson pilot? Are you THERE Gunderson's pilot?"

"Hi Sarah. Yeah it's me CloudDancer." It takes an effort to keep my voice sounding relaxed. "Hey. Where's Jeremy. I need to talk to him." (QUICK! PLEASE!)

One word comes back through the speaker. "Oooooooohhhh." Then silence. I ponder this as my eyes continue moving slowly right and left across the panel. The sweep second hand on the small Bendix chronograph mounted in the upper left portion of the instrument panel just below the glareshield is passing the 3 again. That's where it was when I rolled out of the turn initially. Unfortunately the reset and timer portion of the old clock has never worked since we got the darn airplane so you have to be your OWN timer.

Sarah! After four or five seconds my impatience gets the better of me and as I lift the mike toward my lips ... "Gunderson's pilot! You still THERE?" Barely containing my frustration at hearing Sarah's voice again instead of Jeremy's I respond as sweetly as I can "Uh ... Sarah darlin'. It's CloudDancer and I'm still HERE [Although I'm wishing I wasn't and wondering why that sweet but obviously feeble (with age obviously) minded kind ol' women thinks I might have gone in the last ten seconds!] and I sure need to talk to Jeremy pretty QUICK okay?!"

"Ooooooh. That's what I was gonna' tell you now CloudDancer. Jeremy go Anchorage this morning. You never see him, uuh?" Sarah responds. My brain.... which up 'til now, forty minutes deep into the flight had been running like say ... oh a kitchen blender mixing a fruit smoothie. Takeoff into the inky blackness of a snowy night (start blender motor). Transition almost instantly to routine IFR climbout (pour in apple juice). Turbulence starts (add in banana). Turbulence gets pretty bad (add in second banana before first one done getting "smoothied"). Now let's add in a container of frozen strawberries and blueberries (vertigo) and ohh and ahh as it makes pretty colors while the motor loads down in response to the thickening mixture.

Well the old blender's been running quite a while and all the ingredients are churning furiously although still relatively smoothly as the motor at the bottom of the mixer rotates the blades (gears, pulleys, and conveyor belts in my brain). You know the sound that the blender makes when you decide to add in three or four big ice cubes. You know. One or two at time they are sucked down into the vortex of ingredients until they crash individually into smoothly whirring blades at the bottom of the mixer. And there, upon colliding with the blade(s) ... there is this INSTANT ... out of nowhere NANOsecond long interruption of the mixing/blending function as the cube tries to stop the blade by wedging itself between the blade and the bottom or the side of the container.

And for just that tiniest moment you think the damn think has BROKE! It may happen half a dozen or more times before the whirling blades shred the ice slamming it loudly against all sides of the plastic container. "Jeremy go Anchorage." Three simple words that were the "ice cubes" that threw the "blender" that was my brain this night almost into overload. Synapses mis-fire. Jeremy go Anchorage! Gears seize for an instant. Jeremy.... go Anchorage?? Undershorts now halfway to my bellybutton ... from the inside. Jeremy go ANCHORAGE! My brain screams! Blender motor now faces definite possibility of overheating.

Finally the little gerbils in the wheel get their running rhythm back and coherent thought returns to the brain. Okay. No Jeremy. Maybe Selma's (very cute and tasty) ears are as sharp as her Dad's. I mean why not? It could be hereditary right? Maybe just no one's asked her to try doing this I think as again my eyes take in the sweep second hand on the clock now passing the numeral five.

CRAP! The clock! Um ... let's see.... that's two ... no THREE.... no WAIT! There's no way it's been three minutes, even though it seems like an hour. But I do have a definite tailwind. Most likely strong better than 25 knots and with a slight angle from the south. I mean that's usually how it works around here. Damn! I need to turn again NOW before I get to far from the village. Yeah, right. The village. I've got to be within a few miles of it but which way?

The needle on the ADF is holding rock steady and the tail lays 085 degree radial only 2 degrees off the Kotzebue-Selawik bearing of 087 And one thing good on this airplane is the ADF. It is rock solid and accurate I've observed in the months since we've owned her I roll into another right hand turn this time trying a twenty-five degree bank, and while I certainly don't feel normal the vertigo seems to be easing up somewhat. Maybe my brain is calming down my inner ears.

Cautiously I raise the microphone to my lips as I lock my head in place and start my rigid instrument scan again. "Sarah! Yeah I didn't know Jeremy went Anchorage alright. I didn't see him in town. Where's SELMA? Try lemme' talk to Selma?"

This time Sarah answers immediately. "Oooooooh. CloudDancer! Too Bad. Selma go to Noorvik this afternoon by sno-go to see her boyfriend too." Now almost completing my turn back into the wind I rea ... Noorvik??.... boyfriend!.... SHEESH. Well ... ain't tonight just turning out DUCKY! "So Sarah. Who's home but you?" I ask. I'm hoping for one of the younger kids.

"No. Only me. Are you coming? You need some-bo-dy to pick you at airport?"

"Well Sarah, I sure want to but I can't find town and I was hoping Jeremy could go out and listen for me to see if he could hear me." I answered, continuing unnecessarily "it's pretty stormy out tonight I think." The acorn of a last-gasp grasping at straws idea pops into my head and sprout as she answers back "oh YEAH CloudDancer. It real windy out tonight too!"

Rolling out of the turn on a heading of 105 I glance again at the ADF where the tail of the needle shows I have moved one degree north. Lesse'. I'm about sixty nautical miles from the transmitter (or so I think) ... each degree should be 1 mile ... I'm about three miles north of town ... still safe but edging closer to the Warings in the darkness and completely unconsciously I lean slightly right in my seat as I bank again. I roll the wings level and without looking, pat around on the right seat beside me until I find my flashlight.

Quickly I flash it on the compass and watch as the saucer shaped magnetized metal plate rocks gently in the alcohol inside it's case. The numbers and lines on it too are yellowed with age and I finally chose an average number between the swings and reset my directional gyro accordingly.

Glad I did. It was bordering on overdue after the last twenty minutes or so of this flight. Another seven degree right brings me to 110 degrees which I will hold until I'm centered on the 087 degree bearing off the Hotham beacon again. It could possibly actually bring me right across the top of town sometimes in the next two minutes. I ease the yoke forward and start a 100 foot per minute descent intending to level off at 600 feet and turn onto the bearing as soon as I reach it.

I'll give it one more shot. Remember. Jeremy's house is right in the center of the middle of town and no less than twelve hundred feet from the threshold. There are no runway light in these days But there is electricity all over town, and tall street lights on both ends of town. Hmmmm.

"Hey Sarah this is CloudDancer. You there still". "Go ahead Gunderson's pilot:" comes back.

"Yeah Sarah. Would you go and look out the door for me and see how far you could see from your house?" She replies "Okay! Gunderson's pilot. You wait. I go look now."

An eternity crawls by. Minutes pass. And I've leveled a six hundred feet and intercepted the bearing to track out bound on. This time I want to hold it for about three minutes as I'm positive I'm coming up on the village from the west. I glare into the inky blackness over the nose. The cowling is a dark blue and is invisible in the dark. I might as well be in a simulator. I WILL the snow to start "glowing" in front of the airplane but it never does. Finally after four and a half minutes I am fairly confident I have passed the village again . I called Sarah a minute ago with no answer back, but I do know she does move kinda' slow. I mean., don't forget. She's eighty-some odd. But I would like to hear back from her sometime soon!

As I suspected the wind was from the south of east requiring about an eight degree wind correction angle to the south to hold a steady bearing. Hence this turn will end on a heading of 258 degrees and ... "Gunderson pilot! You still THERE!". Oh good! Finally! Some news. Let's hope it's good "Hi Sarah ... still here ... did you go out? How far could you see? Could you see alla' town?

"Ohhhh Gunderson Pilot!. It RE-E-EAL stormy out! No good!" I'm slightly disheartened but press for more. "But Sarah. How far could you see?" And she came back with "Soooo bad. So bad I almost can't see house next DOOR". And I am discouraged until I hear her add "... but then again ... I don't see too good anyway". This evokes a good belly laugh practically doubling me over in my seat. I'm still laughing thirty seconds later when suddenly that damn parrot squawks again "You hear me Gunderson's pilot?" I assured her I did and told her I thought I was passing right now on the south side of town some where.

"Hey Sarah. Here's what I'm thinking" I said I should be back west of town and turned around for one last pass at you soon. Have you HEARD me yet tonight at all.?' Right away Sarah replies. "I never." Ooooooh-KAY then girlie. Here's what were going to do. I'm going to go couple of miles or so [ast the village toward the lake. Can you throw your parky on and go out side and see if you could HEAR me?" What the hell. Maybe it IS hereditary and Jeremy got it from HER!) "We-e-e-e-ll . I guess I could. Okay. I go listen for you outside." And then another interminable period passes. I shoved the prop control full in and out a couple of times when I think we are right on top of town. No breathless reply.

No response of any kind. I am getting nervous. Using an altitude this low for prolonged period in the dark gives me the CREEPS.

"CloudDancer! CloudDancer! Are you THERE??" "Yeah, yeah, Sarah", I reply "Did you hear me go by at all?" Much to my disappointment she replies "Gunderson pilot! Nooooo. I never hear you at all." There is silence only briefly before she adds an afterthought she almost forgot as I sit pondering my dwindling options. Sarah says "… but you know, I don't HEAR so good either!"

Another chuckle from me. I realize I've had it for tonight. I finally realize the water is getting JU-U-U-ST about up to my chin here. In reality, looking back from a present day vantage point…. I was actually breathing through a two foot snorkel without a face mask. I shove the throttle and prop control full forward and roll carefully into a twenty degree climbing right hand bank.

I key the mike one last time "Sarah. I sure wish I could come an' have some caribou tongue soup tonight. But the weather Gods are a little too tough for me dear. Thanks for trying to help though." "G'night Gunderson's pilot. Go home. Be safe." she answers. Smart ol' girl, wasn't she?

Epilogue

Six hundred feet. With calm winds my rate of descent is a steady seven hundred and twenty feet per minute. Just about fifty-some seconds 'til ... I flinch only slightly as a high-pitched tinny female voice grates in my ear like fingernails scraped across a blackboard "SEATAC TOWER!

Horizon 1512 is over SODOE inbound" Jeez. I think to myself. Are they getting them outta' junior high now?!

From my right seatmate comes the callout. "500 feet. Stable. Target. Sink seven." Meaning that the radar altimeter has just passed 500 feet and the aircraft parameters of sink rate and airspeed along with our proximity to both the electronic glide slope and centerline are within limits. Our airspeed is dead on the computer generated "target" speed for our weight and field conditions.

I grunt and mutter my standard "Rog ... that's airplane talk you know." It's as much to relieve some of the tension in my gut as for any other reason. And the tower controller responds "Roger Horizon 1512. Cleared to land Runway 16 Center at Seattle winds calm and runway 16 center RVR's are touchdown 700, midpoint 700, rollout 700 you are four miles in trail of a Trans Consoligamated A320. And all the way back from Shirley Temple's Good Ship Lollipop the sweet voice says "Cleared to land. Horizon 1512."

And now we're down to the nut-cuttin' in my cockpit and my muscles tense even further if that's possible. The thought passes through my brain quickly that I find it hard to believe these Alaska and Horizon pilots do this **** day in and day out like it's NOTHING! From this point on down a few things happen quickly in sequence. They must. They must happen. And they MUST come in sequence.

Somewhere "below 400 feet" radar altimeter altitude (as my pilot handbook reads) in the upper center of my Primary Flight Display [remember ... the one with the pretty "globe".... top half blue sky ... (sky is GOOD) and the bottom half brown (earth/runway.... solid.... VERY solid)] but NO LATER THAN three hundred FIFTY feet radar altimeter altitude (leesse'.... um.... FOUR hundred minus um ... THREE fifty is um ... FIFTY an' we're goin' down at.... um ... never mind!) somewheres in that stretch of time/speed/movement I am SUP-

POSED to get a boxed notice in capital letters that says either "LAND GREEN" (good)—or—"NO LAND GREEN" (obviously not so good). This momentous event is to be instantly and clearly relayed to me verbally by my fellow faithful flyer on the right.

The next significant issue as our remaining distance from the earth is reduced at what seems to me to be an entirely TOO rapid rate (that could ONLY be made scarier by a radar altimeter that had one foot readouts instead of ten foot increments) occurs as an R2D2—like automated voice issues from all speakers in the cockpit loudly stating "ONE HUNDRED". I now liken this to the hangman sliding the black cloth hood over my head, as we are still hurtling downward at seven hundred feet per minute … okay fine … seven hundred and TWENTY feet per minute. (I don't think the extra twenty is going to make THAT big a difference in how goddamn big a crater we make if this thing doesn't work.) My sweat dampened palm and right hand now grip the thrust levers like a vise.

Company procedures now require of me that…. at this INSANE moment, for absolutely NO logical reason, with NOTHING in sight, that I remain unmoving and clearly and calmly utter aloud but one word. It is said mostly to notify the co-pilot that I have not succumbed to the gut-churning apprehension inside me, had a heart attack and died at the controls and am still "in the loop". Failure by me to issue the word promptly would result in the First Officer having to pass through the elation phase of moving UP a notch in seniority instantly and TAKE COMMAND (something all copilots have dreamed of since John Wayne slapped what's-his-name in "The High and the Mighty").

I feel the coarse hairs of the rope noose on the outside of my hood as the hangman slides the rope slightly back and forth sideways. He is adjusting the large knots with the thirteen coils, setting it in just the right place to ensure a clean quick kill. With what I hope sounds like comfortable conviction and confidence, as proscribed by company procedures, as the Final Act approaches, I now utter my next line in this cockpit drama. One word…. "CONTINUING!"

Now…. WHY anyone in their right mind would WANT to continue downward from one hundred feet above terra firma at a rate of seven hundred or so feet per minute (a rate which eats up a hundred feet in…. oooohhhh … 8.57 seconds!) in what is at this point zero forward and most likely no downward visibility as well…. I don't really know. But I know this. It takes FAITH baby! It's one thing when you can see the runway rising to meet you, even if you don't catch even a glimpse of it until a hundred feet. Even THAT leaves enough time for your brain to assimilate the picture out the window and respond one way or the other.

In these last, brief seconds after passing one hundred feet; while essentially committed to the landing at this point.... it is STILL not a guarantee. There are still two things which could cause a mandatory go-around and missed approach.

One each side of the upper control panel, just under the glareshield is a (thankfully) now dark black one inch square pushbutton. Located specifically in an area just to the upper right of the flight display, it is so set to immediately and INSTANTLY attract our attention should it illuminate. If it does, it illuminates brilliant red and says but one word, AUTOLAND. I believe also some bells, whistles, and for all I can remember the sounds of rattling chains and an evil laugh come from four or five speakers around the cockpit simultaneously. This is NOT a light that I want to see any time between here and taxi speed.

Lastly we have the "Flare Mode" of the autoland system.

Now, when I can see where I'm going (a normal landing where I'm hand-flying) I normally break the aircraft's downward momentum at thirty feet. How do I know it's thirty feet? Because the radar altimeter annunciates every ten feet down to the ground staring with fifty feet. "Fifty ... Forty.... Thirty.... etc." Well. The autoland system "Flare Mode" engages automatically at forty feet and begins to pitch the nose of the airplane upward to arrest the descent rate. This too is displayed if front of both pilots eyes on the Flight Display by the "boxed" word "FLARE" in green replacing the "LAND GREEN" that showed up w-a-a-a-y back between 350 and 400 feet.

Now ever since I took control of the aircraft way back on base leg, the A-No.1 function of my right hand partner is not only to back up and cross-check my every word and motion, but to eagle eye everything on the panel and give me that instant alert and warning.

Should any of the last three items we discussed FAIL ("Land Green", the autoland light come on, or the "Flare Mode" fail to appear) this is known officially in Airbus lingo as ... get ready for this one...." DEGRADED LOGIC". Yes. I'll say that again. De ... GRADED.... LOGIC! Of course, as far as I'm concerned "degraded logic" FIRST occurred when some geek squad escapee came up with the idea to let some computers land airplanes!

Hopefully, by the time the R2D2 voice spits out the word forty, the word "FLARE" is annunciated and the nose pitches upward. Otherwise if it does NOT my partner is to, as fast as a rattlesnake's strike, say loudly and clearly "NO FLARE" which he or she will most likely YELL as this means we are now just three point four three ****ing SECONDS!! (3.43 ****ing) away from impact! Never fear oh trusting passengers. For, like all other critical (heh-heh) NON-normals, I have practiced this many times in the simulator. And so far, everything works just like in the simulator.

When I heard R2D2 say "Fifty" my eyes automatically flashed from wherever they were to my radar altimeter readout to watch for the number 40 to appear 0.86 seconds later and then again instantly flashed upward. If it ("Flare Mode") were not there INSTANTLY ... it would go something like this.

The second syllable of R2D2's measured "Forty" callout would be unheard as my companion's NOT so measured and utterly dis-believing voice would state the words "NO FLARE" in a tone that would most likely stir a cadaver. And simultaneously the cockpit voice recorder would be recording yours truly ... a highly trained, regimented and disciplined Captain begin my well rehearsed abort and go-around procedures.

In a microsecond I SLAM the thrust levers forward with all the intent of shoving them clear out the nose of the airplane at this point whilst simultaneously making my practiced, by-the-book callouts clearly. "SHIIIT! TOGA POWER! GO around flaps!" Okay ... sorry. So S**T! Isn't an official call. I figured ... as long as I was DOING it anyway ... And "TOGA" means take-off, go-around power (i.e. balls to the wall baby). And we raise the flaps up one setting to lessen the drag for the initial go around.

Now (hopefully) I did this as trained and with my usual lightning quick reaction speed for if I failed or was a little too slow.... well ... the Airbus might get confused. It'll go right through "DEGRADED LOGIC" right into it's "I don't have a ****ing CLUE where we are" LACK of logic. If I was lightning quick at forty feet in initiating the go-around, then the thrust levers hit the stops well before the wheels had a chance to hit Mother Earth.

Yes. In almost all cases, a promptly and well executed abort/go around maneuver will result in the A320's or A319's main wheels ju-u-u-ust missing the runway by three to eight or nine feet as the nose continues to pitch up and the engines(finally) kick in hauling you, your crew, your 150 passengers, and your soiled undies back skyward into the murk for another try. (Oh Boy!)

In the event that your disbelief and even SHOCK overcame your senses for more than a half to a full second, slowing your reaction time to initiating the go around; the main gear may hit the ground and bounce you back in the air. Or even (heaven forbid) if you were real slow you might wind up with the mains AND the nose wheels on the ground which then presents you with an almost overwhelming conundrum! For, you see, once having initiated the go-around, you are committed to the go-around. It is STRICTLY VERBOTEN to try to abort the go-around.

So there you are, if only for the briefest of moments with possibly all three sets of wheels on the ground. You can see you are in the center of the runway (oh good! At least THAT part worked). Voices in your head are screaming GROUND! SAFETY! LET'S STAY HERE! Yet with your brain and sphincter both in overdrive at this point you must remain motionless as the nose wheels bounce or lift off the runway again to take you back into the gloom!

Oh. And if by some chance you were SO slow that getting the thrust levers all the way to the TOGA detent occurs AFTER the main wheels touch the runway well.... now.... now you've REALLY screwed yourself be-e-eCAUSE; unfortunately for you, even though you have successfully albeit somewhat slowly relaunched your behind and all those with you BACK into the gloom; navigationally speaking, your flight terminated when the main wheels hit the concrete.

If you had gotten the thrust levers all the way into the "Go Around" detent BEFORE the main wheels hit the ground then this.... this supersmart airplane knows you haven't "arrived" yet and you need to go around the pattern again. Therefore, as might be logically expected, it continues to display where you are and ALL that is around you as well as everything you need to continue navigating.

But if you let the wheels hit the ground first, before the thrust levers hit the microswitch at the TOGA position.... well. We must be there FiFi assumes, right? (Wherever "there" happens to be.... your "destination".) Ergo ... it has done it's job (it thinks) and promptly resets to duh! (Startup mode) awaiting input for it's next flight. So there you are now back up in the air with ... a freakin' heading and nothing else to go on! Quick! Contact departure control. 'Fess up! And get vectors while you "set up" the magic again! Sheesh!

Fortunately for the 150 trusting souls who paid their hard earned dollars to TransConsligamated Airlines for transport to Seattle-Tacoma tonight (and thereby my paycheck as well, Thank You); everything goes according to hoyle. And just like in the simulator (when on the rare occasions the instructor actually lets everything go right for a change) my eyes flash up at the forty foot mark, see the word "Flare" in the green box and note with approval that the nose is rising and the sink rate is decreasing rapidly. Instantly a few hundred feet of runway appears over the nose as the R2D2 voice continues "Thirty ... Twenty...." and then hollers the word "retard!" repeatedly at me until I close the thrust levers to idle, as though I am even too STOOPID to figure that part out without it's help.

The main wheels VERY gently kiss the earth (ooooh.... I AM impressed ...) And the nose lowers to the surface slowly whilst my partner in the right says loudly "'Spoilers Green" indicating our spoilers have deployed on both wings to destroy the remaining lift. My eyes flash quickly to the landing gear panel where a green "decel" light confirms for me what I can already feel in the seat of my pants. The autobrakes have come on line and are now slowing us smoothly as evidenced both by my airspeed vertical tape reading and more importantly by the fact that the white centerline stipes are going under the nose at a progressively slower rate also aided by me having placed both engines into full reverse. I want this OVER with!

As my first officer calls out sixty knots I step on the brake pedals (just like a Cessna ... the tops of the rudder pedals). This knocks the "auto" function offline and now puts the braking under my command again. Gee. I'm finally in charge of something here now. I continue to decelerate until my groundspeed readout is indicating thirty knots and watch carefully for the gentle left arcing line of green lights that will lead me off the runway centerline onto one of only two allowable taxiways under these restricted visibility conditions.

Slower.... slowly.... careful.... I know there is a plane landing shortly and I must get clear of the runwa.... Oh! There they are. The lights are coming into view.... and just as they start sliding under the nose I begin cranking the nose wheel tiller to the left gently to fo ... what the!.... dammit.... the tiller (steering wheel) seems to be fighting me and.... god-DAMMIT! The ****ing autopilot is still engaged! It keeps trying to steer me back to the center of the runway! I forgot! I am supposed to dis-engage the damn thing myself before I try to turn off the runway.

The F/O laughs as I curse all things automated and mash on the brakes harder as I hit the disconnect button on my joystick and quickly return my hand to the tiller, now having to crank hard over left to get back to my green guide lights and clear of the runway.

We very. and I mean VERY carefully listen to every syllable of the controller's taxi instructions. Repeating them slowly word for word, following the proper taxiway marking very slowly we eventually reach our gate. But automation and computers are not done with me yet. Our company has installed a new computer sensor guided automated parking system replacing the HUMAN (with eyes and a brain). You know. The guy you always see down on the ramp with the orange "wands" waving his arms to signal the airplane up the yellow line into the gate.

Now under the yellow line, embedded in the concrete, are sensors. If I can manage.... somehow.... to possibly find my way ... ALL BY MYSELF.... and get my nosewheel anywhere near the beginning of the "lead-in" line the sensors kick on and now I watch a "light show" mounted on the terminal wall instead of the real man on the ground. Arrows point straight up (green) as long as I stay on the center of the yellow line and quickly go to horizontal (red) left or right if I drift. I have green yellow and red (just like a traffic light) for the last thirty feet which counts down 30—20—10—5,4,3,2,1.

Three … Two … one … RED! And I ease the plane to it's full smooth stop. Quickly snapping the parking brake handle to "On" and pointing at the brake pressure gauge with my right index finger I verify it as well. For it too is controlled by computers. The gauges show pressure, and I pull my feet from the brakes hesitantly…. ready to instantly mash them full on again if I detect the slightest motion. After two full seconds I slump in my seat, let out a huge sigh of pent up stress and reach for the engine cutoff switches on the center fuel console. It is OVER.

I hear the sigh come from the right seat too, and I sense and feel the relief spread from that side as well. Silently we shuffle through our post flight ritual of folding charts, filling out logbooks flipping switches off. We are exhausted. The airplane spends the night so I go through the "Securing" as well as the "Shut-Down" checklist. As I struggle to get my bags assembled for the trek to the hotel van area, the first officer heads out the jetway do to do a quick postflight inspection to see if we need to leave maintenance control any heads up on any discrepancies. I remain in the cockpit doorway bidding the passengers. Many of them complimented me on the landing. What else could I do. I just said "Thanks" and let it go at that.

My First Officer returns from below as I wait now in the jetway. The airplane goes dark as he kills the power before emerging into the bight neon lit glare and as we trudge still silently up the incline walkway to the terminal he speaks his first words since we hit the gate. "Oh … hey! What wazzit made you laugh at six hundred feet of all things."

I now give a small but very REAL laugh and shake my head as a picture of Jeremy's face fully fills the picture in my mind. It is winter. It is a howling blizzard. His face is surrounded by a parka ruff whipping in the gale. "Well … see…. you probably won't believe this but…. there was this old Eskimo who … ya' know what. It'll take too long to tell ya' now. How about I tell ya' over dinner?"

PostScript—One Pilot and a Dog

I was watching a CNBC live report from either the Paris or Farnborough Air Show (I can't remember which) oh ... almost a year ago whilst sitting in my hotel room in ANC early one morning. One of the anchors was interviewing the CEO of Seimans Corp., which is the company that provides the unmanned drones for the government.

In closing the interview he stated that it was his unwavering opinion that within ten years (by 2017) that either Federal Express or United Parcel Service will be operating the first unmanned full-sized cargo jets. He further stated that within ten years after that he anticipated the commencement of pilotless passenger flights.

Now before you pooh-pooh that notion ponder this. Seventy years ago who would think of getting in an elevator without an elevator operator? And even forty years ago who (besides Walt Disney and a few others) would have considered riding on a train without an engineer?

My "Breakfast at Gwennie's" transport arrived shortly after I had seen the piece on T.V, and the driver happed to be one of my former bush pilot friends now driving for FredEx. I told him about the story and jokingly offered that he might consider an upcoming career change.

He was far too serious as he told me that it was only a foregone conclusion. FedEx indeed had already operated a real Boeing 727 around the pattern at Roswell, New Mexico more than once with absolutely no intervention from the three human pilots sitting in the cockpit. They just sat there and watched it all happen from startup to shutdown.

Given all airline CEO's antagonism towards employees (cost units) in general and PILOTS in particular; as we are generally the "leaders" of the employee groups followed closely by the mechanics (currently you could keep moving passengers and some airplanes for three or four days without mechanics 'til they were all broke ... but no pilots ... no zoom-zoom); and whatever we by our bargaining strength (or lack thereof) gain or lose in OUR contracts sets the bar for every other employee group at the corporation; the "Bonus Buddy" CEO's would love nothing more than to get rid of us at the earliest opportunity.

For centuries man navigated by the stars. One the earliest wooden boats there were navigators. The sextant came along and made it official. On storm tossed seas awaiting a break in the clouds overhead; or calm and placid sea under a clear sky blanketed with millions of stars.... navigators would raise there sextants to their eye and search our Orion, Ursa Major or one of the Dippers.

The days of airplanes with "navigators stations"; little areas with a cramped fold down table for charts and an overhead mounted window or even dome for star sights is long gone. Navigators replaced with all sorts of acronyms like ADF and VOR at first to which we now add INS and GPS. So the four man crew became a three man crew.

Microchips, RAM, megabytes and FADECs (Fully Automated Digital Engine Controls). If you can find any of the few hundred men and women left who can honestly this day that they make their living as a Flight Engineer ... try finding one that uses an engine analyzer inflight to ascertain WHICH spark plug is the SICK spark plug out of the hundreds out there on both wings firing by looking at a small green screen with flashing squiggly white lines on it. And so the three PILOT cockpit became the two pilot cockpit.

Many times I've read stories of the old mariners. Often there was a 'ship's mascot". A mongrel dog. Often a stray picked up by the crew along the way. Helped retain some semblence of sanity and normalcy on a long voyage. A dog any crewmember could talk to when lonely. And often the dog, while adopted by the whole crew belonged to the Captain.

By merely automating two or three more functions on my flight deck, my A320 or A319 could be operated entirely by remote control from a keyboard on an earthbound desk. As it is already my maintenance people can talk to my airplane (not me) as we sit at the gate in Anchorage from their desk thousands of miles away. Airborne or in-flight.

Oh. Aqua-Jet does the same thing too. Yeah. Remember that Aqua-Jet Airbus A320 flight that landed live and in living color on television at a major west coast airport a few years back. It had the nose gear cocked ninety degrees off. Essentially sideways. Well, seems the Aqau-Jet maintenance controllers works ALL the way across the freakin' CONTINENT at some console in some dark room in operations control in New York.

Well ... by golly he TALKED to the damn airplane. And he and the AIRPLANE., independently of and with NO input from the pilot, came to the conclusion that is was a faulty indication!

This, even though it had already happened a half a dozen times to other A320s (including TWICE at my airline). The maintenance controller told the pilot that

HE (sitting safely in his chair over 1800 NM away) after having had a good discussion with the airplane felt there was no real problem and that he should just go ahead and do a normal landing back at the airport where the flight had originated.

The pilot, being a kindred spirit of mine obviously, decided he was not in a hurry to trust the computer and bet his whole wad on the first approach. So he, using his poor limited gigawatt, low RAM human BRAIN decided to first do a FLY-BY of the control tower. The fellows in the tower with their binoculars then assured him (the human pilot with the human brain) that indeed … the nose gear was NOT normal but instead cocked off to the side ninety degrees. Maintenance Control can KISS my HUMAN ASS!

I heard the tapes for myself! Thank God those people had not just a human pilot, but one with a WORKING BRAIN that just doesn't follow "orders" mindlessly. The joke around the industry is that there will never be pilotless passenger airplanes. The two pilot plane will become....

One Pilot and a Dog. The pilot's "job" is to feed the dog. The dog's "job" …

The dog's job is to BITE the damn PILOT if he tries to touch anything ELSE!

May I never live to see the day.

"Weren't Nobody SHOOTIN' at Me?!"

1

Gotta' Know When to Hold 'em

By the autumn of 1978 I was back working for Leroy and Velma for the second time. It was job number five in a career that was barely five years old now. But that was not all too uncommon for a pilot in those days.

Headstrong pilots would clash with headstrong owner-operators, their wives or family members who ran the office and did the scheduling. This resulted quite frequently in a verbal "quick draw" to say "&%$# YOU! I QUIT" before one of them says to you "&%$# YOU! YOU'RE FIRED!!"

Knowing there was nowadays more business and flying than you could shake a stick at, Bounce and I never worried about getting another job. Bounce, myself and one other fella' newly arrived from the states the previous year made up the flying force of Leroy's operation. We gave no indication of ever wanting or planning to leave Kotzebue. We each had by now at least a few years experience under our belts and some four to six thousand hours apiece "in country". Leroy was sittin' pretty with us in his stable.

This was of greatest importance to an owner operator for business was building in the arctic. The effects of the Airline Deregulation act of 1978 were creating a great demand for new pilots stateside. Hence there developed sort of, two kinds of pilots in most bush communities. There were the core "regulars" with experience like me, Bounce, and our buddy and co-worker Dirk Freeburg. Dirk had started working for Leroy about a year and a half ago after arriving with a buddy on a flying vacation two summers earlier in their own plane.

But nowadays, MOST of the full-time pilots hired by bush operations were young Certified Flight Instructors with 800 to 1000 hours total. If you were lucky you could occasionally land a newly minted 1500 hour Air Transport Pilot.

They were here simply because the Alaskan bush was gaining a reputation among America's West Coast aviation community as a place to go. You log alot of flying hours (experience) at a good rate of pay. And then hopefully Horizon or Cascade or Metro Airlines or Rio or some other "commuter" airline would hire you. Then you were on the road to airline riches and retiring as a multi-million-aire after a life of relative leisure and privilege. (Damn! Didn't ol' CloudDancer miss that train!)

All four or five of Kotzebue's "on-demand" air-taxi and charter companies were booming and had anywhere from two to maybe even six or seven hired pilots. In addition, as part of the fallout from the Wien Air Alaska ALPA pilot strike of 1977 to 1979, a Nome based company in a precursor to what is now common practice in the industry, subcontracted a fleet of BN2A Islanders, Grand Commanders, and a Dornier SkyServant. They had replaced the long time Wien Twin Otters and Skyvans that had devoted their all to serving Alaska's smallest villages for decades. So with the five pilots for that company along with up to fifteen "local" full time pilots and four or five F.A.A. Flight Service/part time pilots, hell, there were planes and pilots everywhere you looked mosta' the time. Quite a change from three or four years earlier when you could fly around the valley all day and never run into another soul in the skies.

If you were only flying 125 hours a month as a full-timer you were generally considered to be a slacker. A normal month was now considered to be 130 to 145 hours and anything over 145 hours was considered to be a good month.

I had spent the previous week in Waikiki in a little joint called "The Hide-away". It was Leroy's "home bar" during his annual island retreat which now, given the rich flow of money and flying business throughout the Arctic, was turning into a solid three winter month per year refuge from the Arctic winter for Leroy and Velma. They even purchased a condo in a nice building just down the street.

Sidebar—At the intersection of Ala Moana Blvd and Kalia Road in Waikiki is the Wailana Coffe House, a super good place to get breakfast. Come out of the coffee shop and turn left on the sidewalk. Proceed down the street until a 7-11 convenience store appears around the bend across the street. Stop momentarily and look to your left. That's where Leroy and Velma's condo was. Cross the street and hang and when you get to the 7-11 hang a right and go down the alley just the other side of the store. About 50 yards down on the right you'll find the Hideaway. Tell 'em CloudDancer sent ya'. I been drinking there off and on for thirty years ever since Leroy introduced me to the place. Although no one there knows me by the name CloudDancer, if they know me at all. I only get there two or three times a year for a couple a days at a time anymore.

Don't worry about showing up right after breakfast either. Even if breakfast is at 6:30 A.M. The joint, like all good local gin mills opens at 7A.M. one of only a handful of local bars that does.

Good thing too. 'Cause alotta' the time Leroy was well past thirsty by 7A.M. in those days. And I generally tried to crawl in for a little hair of the dog by nine A.M. myself so as not to miss the opportunity to possibly score a freebie from one of Wakiki's gorgeous young hookers. They generally wandered in after their (shift end) morning breakfast at the Wailana or the Denny's down on Kuhio street.

I mean, hey. I try not to judge anybody. Hookers are people too. They get thirsty too ya' know. They put their quarters in the juke box and play music just like you 'n me. Hookers need love too! HaaaarummmmpH! Why I consider it an honor to help reinforce the girl's sense of warmth, dignity and well-being after a long evening spent dealing with some of the bums they must run into. You know, sometimes in life it's nice to just lie there nekkid, cuddle up to somebody and talk.

As I said, I'd spent the previous week in Waikiki dividing my time between the pool and pool bar at my hotel where I tried to spot one of the many unattached females who may be seeking a vacation fling romance. The (former) Outrigger (now called) Ohana West on Kuhio street has been my favorite for decades. And no, I did not pick that as my hotel because Kuhio was the "red light" street in Waikiki. HONEST! I didn't even know when I picked it. And I still stay there today as the Outrigger/Ohana chain has always been very generous in their travel industry rates. They allow airline employees to cancel on the day of arrival without penalty if they are unable to get on their "space available" flight.

Daily I would meet with the Boss over at the Hideaway for post breakfast libations, dice lessons, hangar flying and an update from the home front. It was over the pay phone from the Hideaway that Leroy would run the family business with daily, multiple if necessary, phone calls from the bar to the office in our new hangar at home. Always answering the phone in the office would be Leroy's eldest daughter DanniKay.

She was known to immediate family and closest of friends (including us pilots since we lived downstairs with the kids in earlier years) by her nickname Pepper. It was short for peppermint, which apparently was her absolute favorite candy as a kid and which she still devoured at a rate of one per hour as a college girl. This girl was the old man's soft spot for sure and she adored and loved him fiercely as well.

But Pepper had learned the business at Velma's knee. And having taking a couple of semesters off from school after her freshman year, this was Pepper's very first time to be entrusted with the family business at the tender age of twenty.

Really, I think Velma was too tough on Pepper. The girl could seldom completely satisfy her mom but it sure wasn't for lack of effort.

Pepper was very, very pretty and one of the nicest human beings I ever met. She had an inner beauty and innocence that radiated joy and tranquility on everyone (but Velma) that she ever came in contact with. I think, I'm pretty sure I kissed her once when I was working for her parents and living downstairs in one of the six small "guest rooms" that used to house polar bear hunting clients in the days before I arrived. Leroy's kids lived in three of the rooms and we pilots lived in the others.

I remember having long serious talks with Pepper late into the wee hours of the morning about life, love, and our futures when she was a high school girl. That was the first time I had worked for her parents. Now she's my boss at work. And much to Velma's credit and training, young miss DanniKay don't take no crap offa' nobody. Drunks, customer or passenger or not. And she takes no guff from the pilot employees either. Leroy made it clear when he left for the islands. Pepper is in charge.

Probably one of the only good looking girls in Kotzebue I never even gave a serious thought to trying to "score" could now go from being my buddy and sharing a laugh and a joke to verbally kicking my ASS in a heartbeat! But Damn. I admire her to this day.

So I had wobbled up the astroturf covered steps into the Hideaway one day last week to find the boss on the phone giving instructions to Pepper as usual. But when he sees me coming in the door he tells her to hold on. Dropping his phone hand he turns and says to me "WHAT day are you gonna' be back in the saddle?" This being Thursday I tell him I will be at the office at "oh-eight-hundred Monday morning".

He puts the mouthpiece back to his face and says "Okay Pepper. Cloud-Dancer just came in and confirmed he'll be there Monday morning. So I'm gonna' have the new guy show up on the morning Weinie Bird so's Cloudy (acting as asst. Chief Pilot) can get all his paperwork and training done before the FEDs show up Wednesday." He pauses then continues. "Yep. Already talked to those bastiges this morning. We're on their calender for Wednesday afternoon for two rides. Okay baby.... bye-bye." With a dull crunchy clicking sound, he deposits the grey plastic earpiece, scarred and melted in two or three spots I note with brown stains into it's metal two pronged receptacle/cradle. Drunks with cigarettes no doubt.

Meanwhile I've continued toward a couple of empty barstools. In front of one is two packs of Salems and one half-full and two full vodka screwdrivers.

Hmmm. The Boss has been on the phone for a while apparently or else just won a dice "side bet". These items clearly indicate temporary ownership of said stool by Leroy. So I pull up the empty stool next to it and exchange morning greetings with the regulars. The bartender hollers "Hey CloudDancer the usual?" as he reaches for the rum bottle from the top shelf behind the bar against the dirty mirror, smudged with countless hand prints. Although it borders the entire back of the serving area only half the bar can be seen in the reflection. The rest of the mirror is covered by assorted worn, dirty and autographed dollar bills and dozens of Polaroid pictures. They are black and white and color snapshots, some faded and yellowed from times of yore. There are also a half dozen or so pairs of panties taped to the mirror as well. Colors vary. Also autographed.

As the Boss slides onto his barstool he nods at me and give out with a "'Mornin' kid. Get out yer' cash 'n I'll shake ya' for the 'bank'." "I lean sideways on the cracked faded red cheap plastic padded stool to reach in the pocket of my shorts for my wallet. I respond to his greeting with "Well. I gather from what I overheard that we got a new driver coming on Monday. Did you mange to get one with some experience??"

The Boss cocks his head sideways and gives me that shit-eatin' grin he likes to give me when he's puttin' one over on me. The same grin I see when I'm down to my last of three dice shakes without having even matched an initial pair yet while he holds four of a kind. "Oh. This guy is no low timer. And he's got plenty of 206 time too. Should be easy to get ready for a ride on Wednesday. Talked to him a couple of times yesterday after you left." The tone in his voice is mischievous, leaving me to wonder.

I suspect there is more that he is not telling me about this guy. And my inquiries into his age and hometown are rebuffed with the Boss growling and snapping at me that he can't remember all those little details after talking to so many pilots all the time. Why don't I just shut up, thrown the bones and deal with this guy when I get home!

My right hand twists side to side and the five small spotted cubes rattle around the inside of the brown leather dice cup, The open top of the cup sweeps rightleftrightleftright in three seconds.

Stopping the sideways motion with the cup at a 45 degree angle, I tap the lower side of the cup's bottom rim three times quickly in succession on the bar in front of me before loosening the grip of my right thumb just enough to allow the left side of the cup to slide level. With a practiced smoothness of repeated efforts I now lightly pinch the rim of the leather cup between my right thumb and middle finger. Extending my arm quickly just six inches to an abrupt and instant stop allows the weight and "mass in motion" laws of physics to start the bottom of the dice cup swinging out and away from me.

Snapping my hand downward with force instantly does the rest and the upper rim of the cup, now completely upside down SMACKS into the hard wooden bar with good thud! The dice are quiet. They have landed and I lift the cup to find ... DAMMIT.... not one pair!

Snatching the dice off the bar I throw them into the cup, now resting in my left hand before being tossed to the right hand to start the performance over again. From the snatch of the worthless first hand, through the identical shaking ritual, to the thud of the dice cup again delivering news of my immediate financial success or demise takes no more than five seconds total before I again raise the cup to find ... no pairs again! DAMMIT!! This is a thirty dollar per person pot!

I snatch the five traitorous black and white spotted cubes off the bar to throw them into the cup for my final shake. I decide possibly a sip of a good drink might influence the cubes to roll in my favor. Illogical? Maybe. Irregardless.it can't hurt. As I raise the glass to my lips I glance at Leroy. The old bastige has that damn grin on his face as he watches me drain the glass. I hate that look.

2

Mercenary Pilot ... or Novelist??

In accordance with Leroy's wishes Monday morning at 8 AM found me atop one of the three "Captain's Chair" barstools lined up along and behind the counter in our new office hangar. The stools were for the Boss or his pilots only, although occasionally visiting pilots from our competitors were allowed to sit in one if we were out flying.

The passengers and visitors were afforded the more modest comfort of hard plastic multi-colored school cafeteria type seats. These lined the longer wall of the 18 by 12 office addition to the hangar's west wall. The opposite wall behind the counter was covered with a floor to ceiling and wall to wall map of Alaska. Bounce and I had put together from sectionals. Of course, it had the ubiquitous eyehole screw into the map at Kotzebue through which threaded the red yarn that, on the map, headed out across the Kotzebue Sound. Just nicking the corner of Cape Krusenstern, the red string of yarn then proceeded across the Bering Sea to someplace in northeastern Russia where in passed through another eyehole screw. From there it dropped straight down to the two pound free weights it was tied to that kept it taut when not in use.

The effects of twelve hours of uninterrupted sleep and a good greasy breakfast along with the second gallon of coffee were starting to clear the final cobwebs from my brain. My hand again barely now steady enough to be able to light a match to the tip of my cigarette without my head having to bob and weave like a punchdrunk prizefighter just to keep the flame near the cigarette.

Lord. Would I ever learn moderation in life? (Apparently.... no time in the 20th Century it seems!) Oncet agin' I had done rested and recreated myself for six straight days and nights to the point of almost being comatoast! Just yesterday morning I had taken the bus down to the Wialana Coffee House with my suitcase in tow for breakfast followed of course by schlepping down to the Hideaway where Leroy was just helping open the joint a little after seven AM.

An hour later the regulars had bought me three or maybe four Bon Voyage morning "eye-openers" and I'd played (not well) another half dozens rounds of Four, Five, Six with the Boss and his cronies. It was time to call a cab and head for the airport where a nonstop five hour flight to Anchorage on the Hawaiian DC-8 awaited as the first of two legs home.

Handshakes all around, a few pecks on the cheek and lingering hugs from some of the "girls" (Ooohhhh BABY! Parts of you feel so GOOD next to parts of me!) Having taken the last of my vacation cash after yet again another losing streak with the dice cup; I get a 100 dollar "draw" from Leroy outta' my next paycheck for cab fare and "incidentals" on the way home. Soon I'm waving good-bye to the Hideaway gang as the cab heads down the alley.

Well naturally.... it being the last day of my vacation.... the cab ride was probably the longest I went without an "incidental" from the time I left the Wialana yesterday morning 'til I fell face down on my bed twelve hours later. At last I could now return to being a productive member of the aviation community and society in general. By the time the morning Wien 737 from Anchorage plops down on the snow covered numbers of runway 08 around ten-twenty in the morning, I'm feeling pretty good.

Now a lot of our business, like all the operators on the field, was booked in advance. Sometimes folks scheduled weeks in advance from places as far-flung as New York or Houston. We even had one regular customer who had come from Germany for three years in a row. Most local business, even governmental local businesses such as the school district, the State Troopers, and the Borough, often booked no further out than 48 hours ahead. The surrounding Kobuk Valley village traffic.... well ... that was about like a New Yorker stepping to the curb to flag a taxi. The phone would ring and off you go. But, each and every passenger jet that landed offered the prospect of walk-in traffic about twenty minutes after the engines were shut down.

So as the late autumn sunlight attempted to filter increasing amounts of daylight through the overcast, I was not surprised when the ramp side door to the office was flung open to admit an unfamiliar face.

Pepper, having been instructed by her Dad to use me as a last resort if need be had sent Bounce and Dirk out already. So together we had sat talking and awaiting the arrival of our new pilot who was supposed to be in on this airplane. Often believe me, quite often, these guys get to Anchorage and chicken out or stand in the aft doorway atop the first step of the telescoping folding airstairs staring in disbelief. Some have been known to never make it any farther than the ticket counter at the terminal in places like St. Mary's, Bethel, Aniak and Kotzebue.

Without ever stepping foot beyond the terminal they purchase their return ticket to wherever the hell the came from.

Heck. I'm just happy they do that before me, Bounce, Dirk and the Boss have to waste any of our time on these losers! So, I'm never too surprised if one don't show up. But since this guy has obviously just come from the terminal, OTZ baggage tag visibly dangling from the shoulder strap of his G.I. issue duffel bag, our new pilot should be hot on his heels as we are just 100 yards or so down from the terminal. Oh well. I'll worry about him when he shows up. Pepper and I simultaneously rise from our seats (Pepper at her Mom's desk) and say at the same instant "Hi! What can we do for you?" cheerily and then turn to each other and burst out laughing.

The old man's creased and weatherworn face and brow wrinkles further as he stops mid-motion in trying to shuck his obviously heavily laden duffel. He joins us in a hearty laugh before saying one word. "Stereo!" And as he finishes shedding his load, he stretches his right hand up and pulls off the fur-lined cap atop his head to ... JEEEZUZZZ MAN!!

Standing under the florescent light the glare from the toppa' this fella's HEAD! Jeez! Does he polish that thing? The two atlas road maps serving as my eyeballs this morning squint only slightly as I try not to let my facial expression give away my sentiments to the old duffer. I mean the guy's gotta' be fifty-sum. I mean. He's older than Leroy even. But I note to myself he's also in much better shape. Heck, I think he's even leaner than me! First to find my tongue again I ask hospitably "Were you lookin' to FLY somewhere today Mister?"

Father Time is now kneeling beside his upright duffel and is working the rotary combination knob on the MasterLock holding the bags contents secure. He stops and looks at me with a twinkle in his eye, and a very familiar facial expression. It's just like the one Leroy wears from time to time. "Why yes young fella'. I think a little flying together sounds like a good IDEA." He responds with a grin.

The old codger kneels down, now thankfully no longer under the direct glare of the overhead florescent light. I watch him unhook the strap end holding his duffel shut as I ask "Well sir, whereabouts would you like to go today?" He gives a quick upward glance at me with a blank look on his faces as he replies "Oh ... I dunno' ... I figured I'd let YOU decide that." And he again turns his attention to the now opened bag and starts digging in it.

Pepper and I exchange somewhat bewildered glances at each other and I have a brief thought that this is maybe one of those "kook tourists" who appear out of nowhere with no real agenda other than to "experience the wilderness". Over a couple of decades I would run across a dozen or more of the type. Some were crazier than others and some completely rational. LIFE magazine profiled one of these idiots based on a diary recovered alongside his frozen carcass in '81 or '82. The former Silicon Valley software designer turned "Grizzly Adams" (or whatever) ran out of food and starved and froze to death in the Yukon winter.

Meanwhile the fella' is pulling out some nice big Eddie Bauer mittens followed by a Colt .45 chrome plated hogleg! Ohhhh.Kaaaay. The guy is either prepared or DANGEROUS. The Alaskan bush has always, and still is I suspect, been seen as a good hiding place by various nefarious ne'er-do-wells on the run from the law in the Lower 48. However, this doesn't always work out too well. The smaller the town to try to hide in.... well.... let's just say it didn't always work out the way the bad guys wanted. And that was way before the internet days or "America's Most Wanted".

A few more seconds of silence and the guys pulls out a large book Pepper and I both recognize instantly. He tosses it on one of the plastic chairs where the embossed gold leaf print on the worn black hard cover is easily legible. It reads "Senior Pilot Master Log". Pepper and I both glance at it. We read it. Then like some pair of dim-witted bookends, reminiscent of the very earliest "animatronic" DisneyLand moving characters; we stand rooted to the floor. With our hands on our hips, mouths agape, we stand looking first at each other, then back down at this ... this OLD man! Back to the logbook.... and finally back to each other again.

Spritely scrambling back upright, the old guy takes in our "show". He laughs at scoring first, takes a couple of steps to plant himself square in front of me and sticks out a beefy right paw.

Glaring up at my eyes from a two or three inch height disadvantage he enjoys my obvious discomfiture and with a big grin says ... "I'm Dave, your new pilot! I'm guessin' you would be CloudDancer?"

Now, Momma CloudDancer had taught me young that a person's eyes are "the door to the soul". They almost always tell the truth about a person. This had steered me fairly true through life thus far. Dave, having scored the first point was now looking into my eyes, and I into his. Caught momentarily off guard in the last few seconds, as I grabbed his hand firmly within mine and shook, I fumbled for something to regain my mental balance with. What came out was "Damn. You're a lot ... BALDER than I expected!" Which busted both Dave and Pepper into a good guffaw! As I let drop his hand I felt I had to take a shot back and I asked "Do ya' polish that thing?!"

Dave's laughter ended as abruptly as it had erupted. Again looked me in both eyes as he responded in a slow and measured tone "Simonize. You like it?" The tone was neutral. But the eyes had JUST a new ... wariness, with a hint of menace in them. Hey, wait a minute bub. This is my place I remember thinking. With a bravado supported by good ol' youthful ignorance once again I responded "We-e-ell.... it don't really do nuthin' for me you understand. But I 'spect summa' the girls in the villages around here might mistake you for Telly Savales (T.V.'s Kojak) and that could be helpful ta' staying a little warmer some nights if ya' know what I mean!"

Dave responded with a laugh that was reflected in his eyes and said "Well. I'm here and I came to fly. What say we get started doing something. Leroy said I gotta' ride with the feds Wednesday afternoon at three. By the way. How was Hawaii?" And I, having moved to the coffee pot by the end of the counter responded by rasing an empty white porcelain mug. As I waved it toward our newest addition I asked "Fresh mud Dave?" "Lord yes! The coffee on that Anchorage bomber was the worst I've ever tasted and I've had some bad crap substituting for coffee in my day." he replied.

With a full cup in each hand, as he repacked the mittens and the shiny .45, I motioned him to assume one of the Captains swivel chairs behind the counter and set the cup in front of it. This indicates his (at least tentative) acceptance as a pilot here.

I resumed the conversation where it had been interrupted, by commenting that my week in Hawaii while being a nice break from flying every day had taken it's toll on my liver to which Dave merely smiled and nodded knowingly. Then I just had to ask. "Speaking of your day Dave.... uh.... um ... when.... exactly WAS your day? I mean I don't mean to be disrespectful but it's pretty obvious this ain't your first hoedown."

He said "You mean how old am I?" to which I mumbled an soft and somewhat embarrassed "Uh ... yeah. I guess." He answers "I'm a few weeks away from fifty-one yet. But I can still manage to drag these poor ol' bones into an airplane every now an' agin' and get some work done without hurting anything. Not to mention this girls Dad here" and he turns to look at Pepper and says "I assume you are DanniKay?"

At this Pepper bounds out of the seat and says "Yes! And I am so happy to meet you! And CloudDancer IS right about one thing." "Oh? What's that" he said. To which Pepper responds 'The girls are going to just love that head of yours. I think it's sexy!" Dave laughs, takes Pepper's hand in his and bows slightly from the waist and kisses her hand while saying "Tis indeed an honor and a privilege to meet a woman so young beautiful AND wise." He continued "You may well be the most enjoyable boss I've ever had."

Pepper answered. "We'll see what you say in a couple of months. You've talked to Dad and CloudDancer here is a real softie at heart." (sticking her tongue out at me mockingly while saying this). "Mom runs the organization and handles all the scheduling including dealing with the pilots. Dad may have hired you, and Cloudy will make sure you're fit to fly and keep an operational eye on you 'til Mom and Dad get back from Hawaii; but MOM is the one who will fire you in a heartbeat if you mess up too bad around here. And she trained me!"

Still holding Pepper's hand in his, the old guy turns to me with a quizzical look and arches one eyebrow in question. In response I nod solemnly and say "Dave, I have yet to ever say no to either of them. I value my gonads too much!" Suspecting that there may still be more to the story Dave drops DanniKay's hand and says gallantly 'Then it shall be as you WISH mistress.!!"

"Good. That's the company spirit I want to hear," Pepper says as she drops a pile of blank forms in front of the newest aviator in Kotzebue. "Here. Fill all this out to start with."

"Oh Lordy" sighs Dave as he drains the cups and slides it along the yellow Formica counter top toward me. "At my last job they weren't real big on pilots filling out a whole lotta' paperwork. Well, I guess it's back to the real world and the federal government. Wouldja' mind putting a fresh head on that one for me please??" he asks sliding his now empty coffee cup back down the long formica counter top. As I pour Dave a refill I ask "So what was the last flying you were doing Dave and how long since you've flown?"

"Oh, I took a couple a years off. Thought maybe I'd try writin'a a book. Doubt you ever heard of my last job it was on the other side of the world from here. Little outfit called Air America."

He said it all without looking up from the paper he was writing on. I came up beside him slowly and placed the full cup alongside the form he was filling out. Setting the pen down he picked up the cup and as he raised it to his lips he asked "Do you know anything about 'em?" He was staring me in the eye. His eyes were as emotionless and cold as a shark's eye.

I responded "Yeah. Yeah Dave. Believe I mighta' read a little bit about 'em' somewheres."

In actuality I had only heard whispers and rumors about America's "secret air force" in Southeast Asia. But if that's where he came from, it was a start toward answering a few questions that had been forming in my brain. "Hmmm" as he again picked up the pen and looked intently at the application form he was executing in the most precise penmanship I had every seen from a man's hand. "I'd be surprised actually." The sentence was spoken without ever looking up from the paper. "Don't think there was too much written down about our outfit. But, I could be wrong I suppose." Although he knew damn well he wasn't.

3

Groundschool, On the Rocks Please ...

Forty-five minutes later, feet propped up on the counter top, I was slouched down in the Captain's chair going over Dave's application and record of flight times. No wonder Leroy jumped all over this guy. He had better than 22,000 hours! Four times more than my pitiful 5,100 hours. Hell. Dave had almost THAT much time just in the turbine column for chrissake! And the score sheet also listed a good three thousand plus hours in 206's and 207's. I wonder where he did that time?

Every few seconds I would glance out the window to observe (hopefully unnoticed by Dave) as to how thoroughly he conducted his preflight of one of the company's three Cessna 207's.

Nowadays, as Captain for a large airline, I fly with literally hundreds of total strangers sitting to my right. Of course, for almost eleven years prior I flew with literally hundreds of strangers sitting to my left. But no matter which seat I was in for the last seventeen years; how the other guy or gal attended to the mundane everyday duties of cockpit preparation was always a good clue. Not just the paperwork preparation and checklists, but the often unbelievable variety of problems presented to you for your divine intervention by the gate agent, loadmaster, or senior flight attendant. How a pilot handles these mundane but essential chores is quite a tip off. Grace and good humor? Anally fixated? Strictly "by the book" or does he or she take a couple of extra minutes perusing "the book" for a possibly unique or creative way to (safely) resolve an issue.

Generally, before I cross the "hold line" and enter the runway ... 99.2% of the time, I'll have an accurate idea of what kind of pilot this person is.

Thirty years ago I made that judgement (mostly accurately) based on the way a man would preflight his air machine. Mainly because at one point mid-way through MY second full year of Arctic flying I got pretty, no, very lackadasical about my preflight inspections. Until twice in one week I had serious incidents, one of which resulted in an unplanned landing. They could've both been prevented by conducting a good preflight. Not an anal preflight. Just a decently good preflight! So now, I watch Dave and not surprisingly I am pleased by what I see. Very thorough in a timely fashion with a smooth flow of action. I can tell I am going to enjoy flying with him.

Twenty minutes later I am sitting in the right seat watching as his hands flow across switches knobs, clocks, and dials smoothly adjusting the panel for flight. Stopping in mid-motion he says "Hey. Jeez. I'm sorry. I was just doing this the way I've always done it. I suppose you want me to use a checklist huh?"

Now I give him the look and say "Well Dave. If you use the checklist each and every time you fly one of these things then ... yeah ... I guess you'd better use the checklist. However in the remote chance that it might get lost some day en route, it might be good to see how it is you'd get by without one."

To which Dave's knowing grin of a response let's me know we both understand how the real world works. And the coal black blades of the propellor merge into an indistinct blur of a disc with a yellow edging created by the yellow painted blade tips. And after instructing Dave in the finer points of the local F.A.A. F.S.S. radio system and the "local" flight planning procedures, I sit back in my seat and wait to be entertained.

It was somewhat of a let down. Although Dave complained multiple times about himself and his performance to me, I could find very little fault with his portion of the flying. So much so that after only thirty minutes I called for a little time out and allowed Dave to taxi back. Rather than waste anymore time or 100 octane I figured in light of Dave's obviously (but for a little rust) very accomplished performance, we may as well get to the meat of the matter.

So after topping off both the aircraft's two wing tanks as well as our two coffee cups during a half-hour break I thought I'd put a little more pressure on. I gave Dave a few minutes to peruse our most current copy of the NOS flip charts showing the NDB 17 and VOR 26 approaches. I gave him all of five minutes than took the book away.

We then put our jackets back on and proceeded into the hangar where I told Dave as I hoisted another to grab a case of engine oil and follow me. Out to the airplane we went. Back and forth a half dozen more times, until finally in addition to the full tanks of gas, the airplane would also carry four cases of engine oil in the nose baggage compartment and another ten cases. With me 'n Dave both weighing in at about 170 apiece (Yes, I was skinny once long ago.) This brought us to somewhere within a couple hundred pounds of legal gross weight and was just slightly under the "average" 207 load. The "average" usually being full or slightly over full. Which of course means that many flights were more than "just slightly over" full to get the average.

But my point is and was and has been throughout my career this one. It's oh-KAY to teach people how to fly in empty or far underweight airplanes. But one way or another, ensure that before you turn them loose with a precious cargo of human lives, assure yourself that they can fly a full airplane too! Most times I would just add 20 per cent of the useful load using some sort of ballast each or every other training session. However in Dave's case it was blatantly apparent that only one more or at most two training sessions would be involved. I grabbed the instrument training plastic "hood". It's a device that restricts a person's vision down and forward Picture a baseball cap except with a foot long bill that is curved downward three or four inches on both sides. It limits the wearer's sight to only the instrument panel when worn in the plane and they cannot see anything out the windows. After one last check with Pepper to verify there weren't any "pop-up" trips I needed to do, Dave and I mounted up again.

Once more we worked through regular, turning and accelerated stalls and steep turns. If anything Dave was even smoother than two hours earlier. Damn man! This guy IS good. Time to see how smooth the old boy is with his vision restricted to the gauges. On with the "hood".

Damn. This guy still nails 'em all. Well. I guess we'll go try a couple of approaches. Finally,.... FINALLY the guy screws up! But first he absolutely nails the non-directional beacon approach with a strong westerly crosswind from procedure turn inbound. All the way down! (Much to my disgust) Then he messes up the VOR approach to runway 26 offa' the 10 DME arc! 'Course it's ONLY 'cause he mis-set the OBS by ten degrees on the final approach course and then discovered it about two miles outside the VORhouse. He reset it quickly but got all buggered up trying to recapture the radial that close in. So he wisely declares a missed approach and we go around and (no surprise again) nail it cold on the second try!

I've seen all I need to see from this guy. The hood comes off in the middle of the go around from the second VOR approach as we are passing six hundred feet or so in a left turn. We are about the one third point of the runway in a climbing left turn as I direct Dave's visual attention to the VORhouse off to the left discussing it's relationship to the threshold. You ALL know what's next. Don't ya'. Having properly distracted him my right foot slides back from my rudder, under my left leg and with the toe of my boot I hook the end of the black plastic fuel tank selector arrow at the bottom of the pedestal ad push it to "off".

As the engine dies abruptly just touching 800 feet Dave's head whips around to look first at me for just a split second and seeing the grin on my face looks down to confirm his suspicions. He then looks back at me with THE most patronizing look of indifference I have ever seen as he begins to drop the nose and tighten the bank. He punches the flaps down to ten then turns his attention back out the window. He nails it one more time.

Bounce and Dirk are back when we taxi in. Having both been CloudDancer "victims" in their new hire days, they had been eyeballing us from the ground as Dave showed his stuff around the pattern. They are both loading to go out again and take a couple of moments as we shut down to come over and meet the new guy and hear my assessment. As Dave heads off to get the fuel hose I briefly relay the happy news that we've got a winner it appears and not someone we will have to watch out for or babysit for a long while. They are also happy to hear that, in my humble opinion anyway, even though he is by a long shot the oldest of us, he's not some grumpy old man, but seems to enjoy life and a good laugh.

By now it is pushing three in the afternoon and Dave and I are both hungry. I convince Pepper that with nothing else on the books, having planned on keeping me free for the whole day if possible, that I should take the rest of the day off after our late lunch and get Dave squared away at our "bunkhouse" of sorts. I remind her that Dave and I still have much book work to go over. And I watch as which Dave turns away, but NOT before I see the slight roll of his eyes.

After dropping Dave's gear at the house and enjoying a decent lunch I remind Dave that groundschool is part of every job, and the Boss expects me to have him up to speed in less than forty-eight hours. Reluctantly Dave climbs back into the company pickup truck. As I turn north in the center of the village Dave asks "Where are we going? Aren't we going to the office?" I reply to Dave that I often prefer to conduct groundschool in a setting more conducive to learning. It's easier without the distractions of noisy airplanes and phones ringing and customers wandering in and out. He appears to be mulling this over, as if trying to figure out if I am serious or jerking his chain.

Dave's been in the Arctic for all of about six hours now. He hasn't a clue where the hell he is.

I pull up in front of a building shut off the car and leaping out of the truck I holler at Dave "Let's go. School's about to start". And I bound up the three wooden steps to the broad porch and the single wooden door. As Dave gets to the top step I fling open the door and the sound of the Bee Gee's "Jive Talkin'" comes wafting out along with the smell of smoke. Dave gives me a slightly puzzled look as I bow slightly motioning him in ahead of me and I ask as he passes.

"So how do you like your groundschool? Straight up or on the rocks?". With a big grin in return he says to me "Oh, on the rocks, of COURSE! Always on the rocks!"

4

"Maintain Visual Separation"

Three or four weeks had gone by and Dave had shown himself to be one hell of a hard workin' old man!! He kept up with us kids in the air and on the ground. He'd bought a brand new Yamaha kick butt racing snow machine to get around on. He'd paid cash I discovered. He was never seen to be cruising at anything other than the fastest possible speed, unless slowing to stop.

But he babied his airplanes and the engines and handled those throttles with a great degree of smoothness and finesse. The contrast was remarkable really, until I thought of how Bounce, Dirk and I behaved on our ground bound machines. It was just, I dunno'.... WEIRD to see some old guy act like us!

Further he had no problem keeping up with anybody when it came time to relax and "unwind" from a hard days work at the Ponderosa or the Whale.

I had noted during our "new-hire groundschool" conducted at the end of the Ponderosa bar, Dave could beat up on a fifth of Canadian Mist every bit as good as I could a fifth of Bacardi. After covering the basics of the Cessna 206 and 207's fuel and electrical systems including what slim emergency or alternative procedures there were, I found not surprisingly, no gaps in his knowledge. I declared he had scored 100 % on his oral examinations and was now ready to begin his "ride-alongs". I had then tried to turn the conversation to talk about him.

Might as well have tried to learn more about the origin of the ciderblock wall against which my shoulder comfortably leaned. Every question was either coyly deflected, answered with another question to me or just plain ignored. And when I mentioned Air America, and that some of the things about some of their operations I'd heard were a bit, uh, shall we say questionably legal? Ol' Dave just turned to me and pinned my head back against that cinderblock wall with the absolute ICIEST stare I'd ever seen. Quietly he said "Now, I wouldn't know anything about that." He then climbed offa' his stool and headed for the jukebox. Discussion closed.

His "ride-alongs" (what today we call Initial Operating Experience) were pretty much none eventful as well for the next day and a half. On the legs with passengers Dave would sit in the right seat furiously scribbling notes in a green covered loose-leaf spiral notebook. Headings, milages, frequencies, and making lots of circles and notes on his sectionals. I was impressed.

On the empty legs I would get in the right seat letting him fly and get comfortable some more in preparation for the checkride with the FEDs. Neither of us was interested in continuing this any longer than necessary as only I was getting paid. He was supposed to be "learning". And after a leg or two I get tired (at least at that point in my life) of having to "share" my flying time.

And, as you would imagine, Ol' Dave wowed the F.A.A. inspector. They were used to quite often getting the beJEEZUS scared out of them by all the newly hired young kids fresh up from the States.

So now here we are a little over a month since Dave hit town and as Snoopy (in his frustrated author mode) liked to start out…. "it was a dark and stormy night …". Except really, it was kind of a gloomy and dimly lit stormy winter's day.

The %$#^ing on again-off again generator for the OTZ VOR had crapped out a couple of days earlier and this was about our third day in a row of doing things the old (pre-VOR days) way. And to add a little spice to the days events the weather was jeeeeest barely good enough to keep flying. The control zone would go from marginal VFR to IFR to marginal VFR. Back and forth, hour after hour. So we'd fly circles over Nimuik Point, the mouth of the Noatak River, Lockhart Point just north of town a couple of miles, and down southeast at Reilly Wreck. With one radio on 123.6 we'd listen to and communicate with flight service, and with the other VHF we'd gab amongst ourselves on one twenty-two point eight.

Some of the gabbing was just gabbing and some was important!! There might be three guys holding at the mouth of the Noatak, two over Sheshalik, and maybe four over Numuik Point.

All of us are (supposedly) VFR, even though maybe half of us can't see anything past our wingtips and are circling and blabbing whilst focused intently on the attitude indicator, directional gyro and the altimeter.

Visibility may be anything from vertical only to as much as four miles. That's the best it's been all morning. It depends on which band of snowshowers is covering the neck of woods you're holding over right at the moment. Hence it is extremely important that each and every airplane know the whereabouts and accurate altitude of the others holding in it's immediate vicinity at the same place. So we talk to each other.

The ATC specialist on duty at Kotzebue Flight Service has added our tail numbers one at a time to his list along with our "holding" locations. He will again begin to issue Special VFR clearances into the control zone to one aircraft at a time in order, as soon as the National Weather Service observer reports a mile visibility. But will that be in five minutes or thirty-five minutes? Who's got enough gas? Not enough? Does anybody have a medical emergency on board?

In some infrequent cases we will let one of our competitors even cut in line if they really need to. Hey. What goes around comes around, you know? For now at least, we are past the days of stealing each others loads and not enough work to go around. So us poor ol' rank and file line drivers do what we can to help each other out.

The FSS people will try to help out by combining more than one airplane into one SPECIAL VFR clearance. (I actually think our record was twenty-two airplanes on one Special VFR clearance. But that was for a group takeoff clearance in summertime fog.)

But if you have planes at the mouth of the Noatak River, Lockhart Point and Sheshalik they could (in theory) be within sight of one another. Hence, upon noting that the next three airplanes in line for a clearance into the zone are located at those three points the Flight Service Specialist will transmit the following "Cessna 47 X-ray (over Sheshalik) and Cessna 33 Quebec (over the mouth of the Noatak) and Aztec 63 Charlie (over Lockhart Point) are you able to MAINTAIN VISUAL SEPERATION?"

Quick as a wink you hear "47X-Ray roger ... 33 Quebec roger! ... Aztec 63Charlie ... you bet!"

Now these guys.... they don't even know where the others are most likely. I mean hell. There may be a dozen planes out there. The FSS guy, he's the one with the pad and a piece of paper. But that don't matter. Here comes the clearance. "ATC clears Cessna 9247 X-Ray, Cessna 7633 Quebec and Aztec 3563 Charlie to Enter the Kotzebue Control Zone. Maintain one mile visibility and remain clear of the clouds. Maintain visual seperation and report arrival this frequency.

Before the FSS specialist is even halfway through issuing the clearance all three aircraft have left the "holding fixes" and pointed themselves at the airport. Therefore, as soon as the FSS guy gets offa' his transmit switch three (in sequence) acknowledgments are rapidly transmitted back to him so that all three pilots can hurriedly switch over to 122.8. They are all within a few short miles of the airport and pointed at the same place. To avoid a collision there must be collusion.

Each pilot states his position and altitude first to insure we are at three separate altitudes. (Hey! Three hundred feet is a great place to be as long as no one else is there!) Then in a matter of moments who ever is second closest says something like, Okay … I'll stay at five hundred feet until I hit Arctic Lighterage and then I'll widen way out over the ice onto a left base and stay at five 'til you call short final. To which the third guy says Okay. I'll fly across the top of town at eight hundred and enter a right downwind to runway eight. I'll turn my right base when you call short final.

In a matter of three minutes all three planes have landed safely and canceled their clearances to make way for the next arrival or group of arrivals. And I never even caught a glimpse of either of the other two airplanes in the air. I mean, isn't that what they mean by "maintain visual separation"? I mean … ifn' I can't see the guy, I must be visually SEPARATED. RIGHT??!!

5

The Faith of our ForeFathers

So Ol' Dave had been pretty much on his own right outta' the gate, as it was quite apparent he didn't need anybody holding his hand. He was also damn smart. He continually, for the first few weeks after his arrival "pumped" Bounce, Dirk and I for tidbits of local flying knowledge. Of course this generally occurred while sharing adult libations after the day's flying was ended. Given the depth and variety of his experience, this continuous probing quest on his part to amass all the local flying info was further impressing to me. I reported confidently and by now quite infrequently to Leroy that our "newbie" was already comfortably shouldering his share of the load.

As this rather challenging (weather-wise) day reached it's peak of daylight at shortly past noon, I blasted off for Buckland in my favorite Cessna 206 focused on the difficulties of completing my assigned trip under these conditions. This was about the worst weather Dave has had to contend with since his arrival. I was fairly sure based on what I'd observed personally and through others that he would take good care of himself and by obvious extension, our passengers as well.

Calling "Clear of the zone" to Flight Service passing Reilly Wreck southeast bound released me from monitoring the radio. At 1500 feet with two miles flight visibility in light steady snow I eased my Midnite Blue, gold and white Cessna 206 into a gentle left bank. Changing from my base course of 127 degrees a few degrees more to the east will allow me to keep the western shore of the Baldwin peninsula comfortably in view. This, as opposed to flying a straight line course with the same visibility if the VOR been in service and providing course guidance for the first 30 miles at least. With the VOR down we now reverted to the "old" way of doing things.

This basically boiled down to the following semi OH-ficial proCEEdure. You go out VFR and REMAIN VFR until unable to do so. Clearly contact flying of the most basic kind accomplished by pilots in the 1920's and 30's all over the globe.

You know how ... sometimes it is rainy, overcast and a steady rain. Steady in intensity and visibility for miles and miles. And then sometimes you're under a semi-ragged overcast with ragged uneven cloud bottoms. You fly into clear areas with five or six miles visibility and you can see up ahead there is a shower "cell" (for lack of a better term) and it is pouring out precipitation in a noticeable gray shaft. Maybe it's a half mile across or around or maybe a couple of miles around. But you can see it and have the (airspace) ability (not really a problem in the Arctic) to fly around it without so much as a drop for moisture hitting a wingtip.

Well, for those of you who haven't flown in snow, it is quite often the same type of thing.

And this is what I was confronted with for the first two-thirds of my trip until reaching the north shore of Escholtz Bay. Sometimes I had five or six miles visibility and sometimes only one or two. I drifted slowly in and out from a base course line as required to keep the shoreline in sight or underneath me as the case may be. But upon crossing the base of the peninsula and looking out across the bay I was confronted with a different challenge. On a line as far as I could see from west-northwest to east southeast lay a solid line of heavier snow obscuring all that lay behind it. Now we were in for some serious contact flying!

This was due in part to the reduced visibility. The other big factor was the remaining geography between my destination, Buckland, and the soft cushioned seat in the artificially warmed cocoon of aluminum which was hurtling through the atmosphere at a cruising speed of 135 KIAS.

A straight course to Buckland would require crossing the south shore of the bay and then flying over terrain which rose and fell awkwardly and gradually from two to three hundred fifty feet above sea level. This would mean an altitude of at no less than five hundred would be required just to keep from smacking into anything. And I'd prefer to have six hundred feet at least to cruise comfortably. Also the terrain immediately prior to reaching Buckland on the base course has no really good distinguishing features and will be for all workable purposes useless. It would be a complete whiteout situation. Additionally to the immediate east side of Buckland across the very narrow river on which it sits, no more than two miles or so from the runway the ground slopes upward quickly into a low hill of about eight or nine hundred feet or so. And in the other direction a few miles further away (maybe about eight or so) but still uncomfortably close for "blind" flying lies a row of higher hills between Buckland and Candle. As I remember, one of them stuck up pretty good like close to 2000 feet or so.

Ergo, planning for the worst determined a rather large deviation. I took one last deep drag on my smoke as I rolled the airplane steeply left and let the nose fall. Exhaling, I stub out my smoke against the sidewall mounted ashtray and snap it shut. The brief metal sliding against metal scrapping sound lasts but a half a second. The click of the cheap metal ashtray cover colliding with the tin edging trim bordering the wall mounted receptacle indicates without my looking that it is shut securely and no further hazard. I snap the wings level again with the sound of the ashtray closing and revel in the speed building. The ground, or rather the frozen snow covered surface of Escholtz Bay coming closer and closer flashes by outside.

On a heading of eighty-five degrees now I am aimed at a point on the east side of the bay four or five miles ahead. The snow covered ice now streaks by me five hundred feet below at almost 160 KIAS as the excess speed from my "cruise" descent slowly drifts back to a more normal cruising speed of 135 knots.

For the third time since leaving Kotzebue I call out on both 122.8 and 122.9 one after the other.

"Heeeellllloooo down BUCKland way! This is Cessna 756LS over Escholtz Bay headed for Buckland. Anybody down Buckland way today???"

Receiving only silence for an answer or both frequencies.... I follow those transmission with the following, again on both frequencies. "Hey alla' you aviator type dudes (no girls back then) Six Lickety-Split is over Escholtz Bay at 500 feet headed for the east shore to try to follow the river up to Buckland. There is a BIG, I mean HO-rizon to HO-rizon walla' %^$# down this away. It looks like it goes from maybe all the way somewheres over by Shishmaffy (Sishmaref) to as far as a guy can see over toward Huslia. Hard to tell yet if'n it's moving northward or not. Seems almost stationary. I don't see anymore of the east shore disappearing as I'm getting closer but it's kinda' hard to tell.... I'll let ya' know!"

Now that transmission gets responses on both frequencies. A couple of "fly careful"s and the expected "Tell us whatcha' got if ya' get the chance after you get into it!"

"Roger that cat! Lickety-Split'll give ya' the news when I can get a hand free. Uh-oh, yeah boys. This &^%$ is definitely movin' north, headed our (Kobuk Valley) way. The east shore of the bay is disappearing moving northward. I think it should start covering south side Selawik Lake in another ten minutes or so. Startin' to look pretty thick. I gotta' hang up now. Talk to ya'll in a while!" Three or four more "thanks" and "be carefuls" in response and then I am again alone with my airplane.

Less than a mile to the east shore as I start screwing in the propellor control and ease the manifold pressure back to 20 inches. The airspeed needle drops to just under the top of the white (flap extension) arc at 130 KIAS. I wait until I see

120 and then drop the first notch of flaps which slows me further. I have let my altitude drop by another 100 feet and now inside a half mile to go to the beach I start a gradual right bank which will put the east shore line with the beach just under my left window and wing. I give the prop control another slow gentle full crank rotation.

At 105 knots indicated as the wings roll level again at four hundred feet I barge my way into the oncoming snowstorm. OOOHHHH Yeah Baby! This is gonna' take some work!

Visibility is now somewhere between three-quarters and a half mile. Yep. Looks like I'm gonna' hafta' earn my pay today. Oh well. Just so long as it don't get much worse I remember thinkin' to myself. (Sigh) I GOTS to quit thinkin' to myself.

6

"Weren't Nobody SHOOTin' At Me!!"

As I had time and again over the past years I "butt-crawled" slightly forward on my seat giving up the comfort of reclining back against the upright portion of my chair. I don't know that it helps. We've all done it. It just seems to be an almost universal natural reaction to the lower visibility. We feel as if somehow, it is good to have your eyeballs that extra three to five inches closer to whatever is coming your way. As though it might afford you that mere extra NANOsecond of reaction time that will allow you to avert making a gooey sizzling mess of your innards all over the suddenly no longer in flight cylinders and engine block. Dumb, but we do it.

With little more than two miles or so to the mouth of the Buckland river I barrel along confidently still. Even though in the Kobuk Valley region this is one of the more difficult contact flying areas. Like the area immediately west of Selawik when coming from Kotzebue, the eastern shore of Escholtz Bay and the Buckland river yet to come are very, very sparsely vegetated. Flying the Kobuk river is so much easier for instance. There are such large and lengthy areas of tall green trees bordering both sides of the river as well as a significantly much higher riverbank on one or both sides.

The Buckland riverbanks are comparatively much lower in height and have many gradual slopes to the water. Also there are no trees whatsoever from the mouth of the river to the village. And although the distance is only about fifteen miles or so (no counting the twists and turns of the river) it can seem much longer if the visibility really starts getting tough. With just the sparsest amount of green scrubby small bushes and what appears to be some occasional batches of straw sticking up through the deep snows.... well ... there ain't much to look at.

It's a very tight marriage of both instrument referenced quick glances to "what's out the window" quick glances. That's why since the beginning "the elders", the Gunderson Brothers, Leroy and the other old timers had pounded into our heads an oft repeated lesson. Spend lots and lots of time down low learning what the world looks like from five hundred feet or less. And we did it over and over on good days until we did learn it. I new which way the next turn in the river was going to be before I got there. I had to. I couldn't afford to miss it if I wanted to find the village.

So now, as the mouth of the river passes three hundred feet below the belly of my 206, I remain alert and a little keyed up, but quite comfortable. I've given up more altitude and now with the visibility a consistent and solid half mile, I shove the flap lever to the twenty degree setting and crank the propellor control in two more turns. The increased pitch of the Hartzell and drag of the flaps now take my speed down to a more comfortable eighty-five knots and I note with great relief that there is absolutely no change in the temperature and no ice accumulation at all. That would put a kibosh on this deal immediately.

My airplane is empty. It is quite light and responsive to the controls as I bank first one way then the other then back again. The reduced speed also means less steep banks to make the turns. That too is a relief under these conditions.

About a third of the way upriver to the village I commit to an "approach pattern" mentally in my head based on the existing conditions remaining the same. As soon as I see the village I will line up and fly down the center of the three thousand foot gravel strip. After all this twisting and turning I must have an accurate directional gyro setting in the pattern to make this work. Flying the runway at ten feet or so will allow me to accurately reset my altimeter to field elevation. I'll also reset the DG to 120 degrees with the airplane centered on the runway and get a good look at the windsock. Then I can cogitate a wind correction angle for the upcoming turn. I anticipate the winds will most probably be out of the east-northeast. They usually are when these storms come blowing through.

Reaching the end of the runway a climbing right turn to 200 degrees and four hundred feet Then hold that and wait 15 seconds going straight ahead. Next a steep (25 to 30 degree bank) left one-hundred-eighty degree course reversal turn will be done totally on the gauges to a reciprocal 020 degrees. I'll hold that heading wings level for twenty seconds before making another left turn onto "final" and descending to 300 feet on the altimeter. Make the "final approach" heading about 310 to 312 degrees for the wind and, within no more than a dozen seconds or so, Buckland should appear out of the murk ahead. Even with the low visibility, I should still have just enough time and room for a final alignment with the runway if I am off a little bit. A n-o-o-o "sweater" all right. As long as it doesn't get no worse.

But, of course it does. As another couple of miles pass beneath my serpentine-like, "slithering" up the river 206, I am forced to drop my final notch of flaps and crank the prop control all the way forward dropping my speed to "just barely". Hanging (literally) on the churning propellor and the lift of the flaps, I butt-crawl forward 'til my forehead is almost pressed against the left side of the black metal floatplane brace in the windshield. %#^&! %#^&! %#^&! I-I-I-I. HATE it when it gets like this!

Now down to seventy knots indicated and with only 150 feet showing on the altimeter visibility is decreasing. I know I have only five miles or less to go! Damn, damn. Double dog DAMMIT! I fear now that this may become one of those times where you get to see the village. Maybe just one quick glimpse and then it's flashes by and is gone. And having not been able to carefully set yourself up completely as I described for a decent approach; you must now just punch out and point for home!

Higher ground is just east of the east bank of the river and I hug the west bank tightly in what is now three-eighths of a mile visibility at best. If I can just hang on for another....

Looking up from my every-other-two-seconds check of the altimeter I crane my head left and have it practically wedged between the metal V-brace and the left windshield post. I see.... Mother Mary! No more than a few hundred feet away I am about to enter something that is dark grey and very scary looking. That's it! I am outta 'here! I snap the wings level, slam the throttle home and pull the nose up ten degrees. My Cessna chariot responds as if launched from a cata-pult. As I lock hard onto the gauges the world grows a little darker .

In a few seconds the altimeter is shooting up through three hundred feet and the flaps have completed a partial retraction to twenty degrees. My vertical speed keeps increasing upward to a 1000 foot per minute climb. As soon as the big hand on the altimeter passes the four I start rolling into a thirty degree right bank and bring the flaps up to ten.

The Automatic Direction Find is tuned to 720 for KOTZ radio. The needle on the face of the instrument is swinging it's way counterclockwise. I start rolling out of the bank and retract the last ten degrees of flaps as it passes the ten degrees off the nose to the right position. It settles in the twelve o'clock position as I look out the windshield just in time to see a slight yet definitely perceptible lightening of the darkness around me. There is the very finest slight coat of rime icing on the plane and the forward portion of the underwing area. No doubt. Getting out was the only thing to do.

A glance at my DG shows a heading of 330 which I know can't be anywhere near correct. With the compass is still swimming around, I reset it to 305 and leave it at that for a while. If the ADF says OTZ is straight ahead and I was within 5 miles of Buckland when I U-turned, then 305 is close enough 'til I get straight and level and the compass settles down for a good reading. Back in very cold air again I am solid on instruments but there is no ice accumulating. I decide to take her up to 6500 ft since I am light and reach for the microphone.

"Hellooooo … any traffic for Buckland this is 756LS climbing out of Buckland area to 6500 feet direct Kotzebue … anybody headed this way?" Immediately Dave's voice comes back at me from the transmitter in one of the company 207's and he reports he's on his way to Buckland from Kotzebue and has just leveled off at 5500 feet. Saaaaay what?! I quickly pass onto him all I know and I've just been through and there's a pregnant pause. I assume this has given him sufficient reason to turn around. And WHAT the heck is he doing at 5500 feet ANY-way??

Dave asks again how close I got to the village and reconfirms the perceived direction of movement of the weather in general. He then tells me "Waaaa'll %&$#!! I'm up here already anyway. May as well go one down and take a look-see. My Timex is workin' pretty good and the ADF is too. I know he is on listening on the overhead speaker and his passengers can probably hear me. As diplomatically as possible I point put that I don't see it getting any better and he's still pretty close to home." He replies that the passengers said they will pay just to "take a look" in hopes of getting home so he may as well give it a shot.

I urge Dave to exercise the utmost caution and have a safe trip. I switch radios and wait another five minutes to ensure I have passed safely over and beyond his airplane and then crank in some forward trim. Once again Lickety-Split goes tearing downward in a high-speed cruise descent.

I break out at three thousand feet about fifteen miles from Kotzebue with Reilly Wreck off the nose. With four miles visibility and 1200 overcast skies, for now the control zone is VFR. After getting traffic advisories I give a long and detailed pilot report to Flight Service concluding with "… in my opinion, based on the darkness of the areas I believe there may be large areas well below marginal VFR." The Flight Service specialist receiving the report knows only too clearly the exact implications of my phraseology. This ensures that if and when he passes that report along to any other airplane headed that way, they will get the appropriate emphasis in the right places.

Three hours later the storm is approaching Kotzebue, but I care not. I am already happily ensconced in an alcohol induced haze on the last barstool swilling my seventh or is it my eighth drink of the evening so far. And by golly, here comes good ol' Dave. With a cheery "Howdy Cloudy!" the old geezer plops his lean frame on the barstool next to mine and hollers at the bartender for his Canadian Mist on the rocks as he begins shedding the upper portion of his snowmobile suit! As the large rocks glass hit the bar in front of him he grabs it, turns to me with his ever-present wicked smile, raises the glass a few inches and says 'To another fine day of Arctic aviating!"

With a sigh and a smack of the lips another small sip is partaken of before he turns to me and continues "Yeah.... just barely got in from that last Noorvik before the %$^# hit! And I sure didn't ..." "Hey Dave" I interrupt without thinking. "What happened on that Buckland deal? Didja' go all the way down there?" "Oh yeah." sez he. "Made it in just fine." "Oh" I say. "So the weather lifted for a while?"

"Oh no. No. S'Matter a' fact, you called it purty good Cloudy. I started gettin' a little vertical about four hundred or so ... 'n then about three hundred I got that half to three-eighths a mile you wuz talkin' about. Liked ta' miss the damn place altogether!"

"O.K., O.K." I say, shaking my head a little to try and clear the enveloping rum fog that is slowly numbing my brain. "Lemme' get this straight ... you were going down there at fifty-five hundred feet right?" and he answers in the affirmative to which I continue. "So ... so ... you let down on ... you let down on what? The ADF and your TIMEX fer' crissake!?" Now, with a look on his face, at me,.... something like ... what is wrong with you boy Dave responds "Yeeaah. Izzat a problem for ya' sonny?"

"Well ... GEE Dave! I don't know! Don'tcha' think that was drivin' just a little too tough!?"

His response was immediate and spoken with the absolute most bland face and inflection of voice. Just a statement. One statement. "Weren't nobody SHOOTin' at me!!" he said.

Stunned. That is the only word that could describe my response. My mouth flopped open fully twice and closed. Finally on the third try my vocal chords kicked in and I responded, "Weren't nobody SHOOTING at you! Weeeell hell Dave. I guess that just flat takes alla' the challenge right out of the day don't it!" With an exaggerated sigh he turned slowly halfway toward me on his stool and spoke quietly. "No CloudDancer it don't. But it does make it a damn sight easier to concentrate on your flyin' problems."

I paused and thought for a moment of all the newsreel footage and gun camera films from three wars I had watched in my life. I've never had to dodge surface-to-air missiles, small arms fire from the groundlings or .50 cal or 20mm cannon fire from other pilots intent on knocking my ass outta' the sky while at the same time trying to manage the normal problems of a complicated flight. I realized that as tough as I thought I could fly…. I was nothing compared to those that had.

So. I shut up and bought Dave his next drink. I think that was the night I first heard him talk about Comanche Jones. Another real airman branded under fire.

7

Two Kinds of Legends

I'd been hearing about Comanche Jones for three or four years before I finally made his acquaintance.

We've all heard the term "a legend in their own time". This of course is very different from the similar sounding "a legend in his own mind". The latter is a self-affliction I now embarrassingly admit to being guilty of more than once or twice in my younger and less intelligent days.

I was quite fortunate that "the Elders" as I liked to call them would wait until ju-u-u-ust the right time. When I had sufficiently bragadociously verbally hung my ass out on a limb and they were tired of hearing about it; they would challenge me to prove it! And, of course, I would promptly go out the next day.... jump in my 207, 185 or whatever; and make a complete fool of myself trying to do what they knew I wasn't good enough to do anyway.

(Next time any of you 180 or 185 drivers think you're pretty good. Try and see exactly how far you can roll the tailwheel down the runway without breaking contact with the ground. With the mains OFF the ground. I dropped some major cabbage on that bet and then watched Leroy, completely hung over and operating from the right seat take our '67 model 180 down the centerline of the runway. The main wheels remained airborne with the tailwheel splitting the white centerline stripes in half. It was a good three thousand feet or more before Leroy lowered the mains gently back to the asphalt having more than proven the point.)

But there really are a few living legends. Jack Jefford was one. Bob Hoover and Chuck Yeager and Scott Crossfield come to mind. And maybe ... just maybe Comanche Jones if we're talkin' Twin Otter drivers specifically.

Now before everbody gets their gonads all in an uproar and hollers at me ... there were many many dozens of superlative DHC-6 captains throughout the various "unimproved" hinterlands of the globe. And maybe we all knew the greatest Twin Otter pilot ever. I personally served as first officer to two or three really great ones. But Comanche Jones stood out from the crowd and I had heard much about him before I flew with him. Much of it was pretty intimidating to be honest. He was a big, gruff, grouchy fearsome character who didn't speak much. Boy. Was that an understatement.... part of the time!

I think it was flying job number eight ... or nine.... maybe ten for all I knew. I'd been hired by this outfit outta' Barrow that was expanding into other areas of the state. I would be driving their singles and piston twins and also serve as a co-pilot on their Twin Otter based in Kotzebue. And I'd heard that one of their Captains was the notorious Comanche Jones. So, you know who I got for my first Captain don't ya'!

8

A Man of Few Words

I showed up at oh-seven hundred for an 8:30 A.M. takeoff for my first trip with Comanche Jones. I wanted to make a good impression on my new company, not to mention my new Captain. I knew he probably wouldn't show much before an hour or forty-five minutes early. So I figured he'd be impressed that I had already "unwrapped" the airplane from her winter night clothes and along with our two-man ground crew had the plane half-loaded with cargo before his arrival.

The Twatter's passenger seats, doubles on the right side of the cabin and singles on the left side of the aisle were of two varieties. One style hinged to the wall and collapsed and folded up when not in use. Otherwise, the far more work and less desirable variety were not hinged to the wall. They had to be mounted and locked in to both the wall and the floor.

In either case the seats took a continual hell of a beating. And every DHC-6 pilot (working in the bush at least) has spent hours cursing the designers and manufacturers as we struggled to put seats back up that we had just taken down at the last stop maybe as little as 15 minutes ago! Cargo on, some seats up. Next stop … cargo off … lotsa' peeps … seats come back down! Until we get to the next village where people get off. But there are three electricians and 1700 lbs of toolboxes to load so … put the same damn seats BACK up so we can get the tool boxes amidships. And so on and so forth. Three or four trips a day of as many as four legs each. Basically we just flew back and forth to work all day.

Sure enough, about five 'til eight I see the headlights pull into the parking lot and a huge hulking figure of a man in a green snowsuit with the hood pulled up emerges from the company pick-'em-up truck and waddles slowly toward the hangar door. He stops and I see him reach for the door with one mittened hand. But before opening it he half turns and launches a dying cigarette butt into the air toward the ramp. I follow the glowing ember arcing through the dark morning sky 'til it disappears into the snowbank with an unheard sizzle as the terminal door slams shut.

For the next fifteen minutes I keep watching the hangar door which opens to the ramp side of the security fence. Surely the Captain will come forth to, if nothing else, give final supervision to the securing of our fully loaded airsheen. But it does not happen. Finally at 8:15 with the loading and preflight completed one of the ramp hands says "Hey CloudDancer. You better go see what Jonesy wants for gas if you guys are gonna' get out of here on time. "Uh ... yeah right" I reply and head for the building. Pulling off my face mask and mittens as I enter, I am hoping for a quick cuppa' hot mud before we blast. But apparently I've not got the playbook quite memorized just yet.

There, behind the counter sits Jonesy. A Winston hangs between his lips. The other end of the cigarette gives off a curlicue of smoke which merges with the curlicue of steam rising from his freshly poured coffee. I stride over and introduce myself and get a one word reply. "Howdy." This was followed by complete silence and a blank stare. "Hey Jonesy. Uh, how much gas you want.?" I ask. "Whatcha' think?" Jonesy responds. "Well.... we're goin' to Noorvik, Kiana, and Selawik ... so I'd guess about 1700 oughtta' do 'er...."

"Aaawwww-right" from Jonesy. That's it. Nothing more. He remains firmly seated and takes another long pull on his Winston and then leans back against the wall. Well, even I can take that hint. I guess it means I'll do the gassin' up for this trip as well. Trying not to let my slight irritation show on my face I turn and proceed outside at the same rate I came in!

I'm reeling up the fuel hose when Jonesy emerges from the hangar via the ramp door and walks to the nose of the aircraft. He carries a large metal thermos in one hand. He looks upward at both engine intakes in the still dark late autumn sky. Satisfied apparently that someone (our rampers) had pulled the foam engine air intake plugs and stowed them in the nose baggage compartment, I watch Jonesy hoist his green clad bulk up into the captain's cockpit door as the last few feet of heavy black hose winds itself around the spinning takeup reel.

Heading for the aircraft I hear the metallic "THUNK!" of the batteries being brought on line. At the same instant the hydraulic pump kicks on to bring the accumulator up to pressure and the sudden glow of the nav light bathes the snow packed area through which I am walking in a soft red. Passing in front of the pointed nose I am reaching upward to grasp the handle to my cockpit access door as I hear a loud "CLICK!" It is followed immediately by the SNAPSNAPSNAP of the dual igniters and the whine of the PT6-20's turbine shaft as the internal rotation begins.

"Apparently" I think to myself as the feathered propellor slowly starts it's rotation a mere four feet from my left shoulder "it must be time to go flying now that all the work is done!" I wrench my cockpit door open to see Jonesy staring down at me impassively over his right arm which is raised to engage the spring loaded three position starter switch on the overhead. As my buttcheeks hit the canvas covered seat cushion the Pratt & Whitney free turbine lights off. Just as I am closing the door the first waft of burnt kerosene sneaks into the cockpit. God! I love the smell of burnt kerosene in the morning!!

9

The Golden Triangle

I hurriedly attach myself securely to the aircraft using the five-point seat belt-shoulder harness-crotch strap restraints. Jonesy fires off the other engine and watches it stabilize in a smooth and slow idle. And since turbines are ready to go to work as soon as they light off he wastes little time in getting us underway.

His bare huge paw of a right hand.... (That's it. This guy reminds me of a big ol' grizzle bear just awakening from hibernation) ... moves methodically around the cockpit adjusting lighting rheostats and flipping on com and nav radio switches with fingers the size of small hot dogs. He jams the hand back into a huge padded black mitten that extends a good six inches past the wrist and over-laps the snowsuit sleeve by just as much.

Then like Pooh swatting at a honey bee the now mittened paw raises up to take a swipe at the overhead center ceiling mounted engine control knobs. By turning his hand sideways he manages to just nail the two small box-like silver "knobs" that control the propellor pitch without touching either the throttles on the left or the fuel flow red knobs to the right. They slide forward an inch or two before "falling" over the feather lock position. Jonesy's right paw then curls around the throttles and eases the controls aftward to the Beta position. I hear a loud metallic "THUNK" from down below in the darkened recess of the Capt's rudder pedal well that indicated the spring loaded parking brake release has been actuated.

The right prop, with just barely slightly warmer internal oil (having run a whole thirty seconds longer than the left engine already) slips into full coarse pitch just a second or two earlier than the left. But Jonesy is already pulling both props into the Beta range through the use of the throttles. The airplane, as he had planned, barely starts rolling forward as I reach back over my head to snag my David Clark headset off the hook on the back cockpit bulkhead.

As Jonesy starts a right turn out toward the taxiway I, without thinking at all, drop the David Clarks over the top of my head! EEEEEE-YOUCH! Even before the headset is fully released from my hands and their built in tension clasps the black rubbers seals around my entire ear; I can feel the icy cold of the earpieces spreading throughout the sides of my head. As I rip them back off my head I see Jonesy, curious as to what might've provoked my outburst, looking at me as one would examine a specimen under a microscope. Sheepishly I admit out loud "I guess I forgot how cold these can get". Jonesy responds with nothing more than a grunt before looking back out the window.

I drag the rubber earphones rapidly back and forth, up and down my right Levi covered thigh to warm them via the laws of physics (friction) while Jonesy taxies to the west end of the ramp. This place is quite often the runup area for eastbound takeoffs and Jonesy again wheels the Otter into the wind. Silently and with no prompting or input from me, he runs through the various propellor tests one after the other. Overspeed. Auto feather. Beta backup. Having well over ten thousand hours in the Otter alone, the scrolling glareshield mounted checklist remains uncalled for and unused.

Wanting to at least play some limited roll in the proceedings I have correctly assumed it must be my job about now to file a flight plan and get airport advisory services. This takes me all of about thirty seconds … the same amount of time it takes him to do the prop checks.

The "THUNK" of the brake release and once more we are moving out onto the runway when Jonesy finally cuts loose with one whole word to me. "Flaps!" I quickly reach up and grasping the overhead mounted flap handle with my thumb I release the handle safety lock and set ten degrees which I know from my training to be the company standard takeoff setting.

Now lined up on the centerline, Jonesy waits until the center windshield mounted flap indicator white needle ends it downward slide at exactly ten degrees (thank GOD). Satisfied that I can at least do that much correctly he shoves the two throttles forward and the DHC-6 accelerates briskly down the runway.

With 65 knots on the airspeed indicator Jonesy eases the y-shapes floor mounted yoke aft. The Twatter slips the surly bonds of Runway 08 with the nearby spinning propellor tips creating a noisy din that even through the David Clarks eats into your eardrums. At five hundred feet I see Jonesy's right paw beginning to slide the throttles back. I grab the propellor control levers and slowly slide them aftward as well. I take great care to ensure that the RPM on both engines remains in synchronization throughout. The WHA-GAH WHA-GAH WHA-GAH sound of unsynchronized propellors may not irritate the boxes in the cabin as it would passengers, but it is a matter of pride and professionalism to do it well all the time.

We climb into the dark moonless morning sky under a blanket of brilliant stars. The bleed air cabin heat, with the engines now really making some fire and heat at climb power, begin to produce the excess pressurized heat our air cycle machine needs to begin warming the cockpit and cabin . This is the biggest airplane I have ever flown so far in my life and as part of a two man crew, I really feel like Mr. Big Time Heavy Iron Driver now! At 3500 feet Jonesy levels the bird off and already I can see the first twinkling lights of Noorvik come into view now just thirty miles away across Kobuk Lake.

Not a word one has been spoken since becoming airborne five minutes earlier. Gazing ahead at the lights of Noorvik slowly approaching, Mr Big Time Heavy Iron Driver must face the grim realization that this might just be a "one man show". I do know my other job for sure and reach for the aircraft logbook while unzipping the top of my snowsuit to find my pen.

Less than 15 minutes later we slide sideways to the north a little before a gentle right bank lines us up on final for Noorvik's sole dirt runway a mile and a half ahead of us and now just beyond the lights of the village. As we cross the Kobuk River and sail across the top of town at no more than 250 feet I am puzzled looking ahead in the darkness. For while the approach end of the dirt runway is marked with a flare pot on each corner, the far end is only illuminated by one. It appears from here to be on the left side.

Judging from the crab angle and the ride down final the wind isn't that bad that it should've blown one out. As I think this to myself the fourth smudge pot, marking the other corner of the runway illuminates and I realize that the village agent had only this minute lit it. He had barely beaten us to the runway which is no surprise. Morning time in the villages in winter is not exactly a hopping busy time.

We plop down within fifteen to twenty feet of the end of the runway. It is said that if you place a sheet of notebook paper on the ground and weight it with a couple of rocks, Jonesy will hit the paper on touchdown nine outta' ten times supposedly. He rolls the throttle handles forward to unlatch the reverse locks and snaps the throttles almost full aftward. This action instantly drives both propellor blades to maximum reverse angle. This literally causes the cockpit and cabin occupants (if there were any on this leg) to lurch slightly forward.

Just as quickly as the engines begin to increase to max thrust Jonesy slides the throttles forward, almost, but not quite out of reverse. The nose comes back upward off the (almost) bottom of it's strut and the remaining forty or so knots of airspeed drops away quickly. As Jonesy completes the transition from landing to rollout I watch for him to release the control wheel and grasp the nosewheel steering tiller which is quite inconveniently mounted on the left side of the yoke co-mounted with the control wheel.

I crank the control wheel hard left into the quartering crosswind holding the yoke neutral as Jonesy steers the Twatter over to the extreme right side of the dirt strip. He then has the advantage of using the whole seventy foot or so width of the runway to make our taxying course reversal. It is extremely rare outside of either Anchorage or Fairbanks to find what might be termed a taxiway anywhere in the state. You turn around and taxi back on the runways. Even in Nome, Kotzebue, and Pt. Barrow. And at one end or the other of any given runway you will find "the ramp" or what passes as one in the villages.

Sure enough, just as we begin our U-turn, our landing lights illuminate Willie Morrison, the village agent for our airline. He hurtles along on his sno-go at damn near flying speed down the trail just off the side of the runway so as to beat us back to our parking spot. Behind him his sled bounces slightly up and down in the air. It's only tied and bungeed contents it appears being a half a dozen mail sacks and three or four wrapped boxes; presumably more mail for town and points beyond.

Halfway through the turn, as the prop blast and the now becoming a quartering tailwind fight for control of the huge elevator I decide the battle in favor of down elevator with my side of the yoke. I will hold it firmly there until we again turn the aircraft into the wind on the "ramp". The ramp comfortably provides room for us to get the entire aircraft and wingspan off to the side of the runway. But it is also crowded with a dozen people and half as many snow machines and sleds this early and frosty morning. The addition of the Twin Otter literally fills it I note as I silently pray that not even half of these people want to get on. Otherwise Jonesy and I are gonna' be humpin' the whole damn load to rearrange the remaining mail and cargo to accommodate more than the three passengers whose seats will be available along the back wall after we unload the Noorvik stuff.

Jonesy shuts down the left engine immediately but leaves the right engine turning to make the heat and engine generator provided electricity last as long as possible whilst I fill out the log book and fish out the appropriate paperwork co-mail envelopes, et al that must get off here. Finally after hanging up my David Clarks on the overhead hook, unclipping my harness and zipping up my snowsuit I turn to Jonesy to tell him I'm ready and he can kill the other engine.

My mouth just hangs open as I watch Jonesy recorking his thermos and spy the styrofoam cup on the glareshield. Sliding the dented and road weary huge thermos back to it's resting place behind his seat he reaches into his breast pocket. Ten seconds later he's sucking down a good drag on his Winston and reaching for his coffee cup. Just aft and outside my door, four feet away, the right propellor continues to thrash the cold morning air in it's fully feathered position.

Jonesy has started to raise his coffee cup to his lips but has sensed a lack of movement from the right seat for some many seconds now. Turning his head to the right he lays his eyes upon my motionless countenance, mouth still dumbly hanging open. Lowering the coffee cup only slightly, the old guy finally utters his second word since first firing up the engine almost thirty minutes ago. With an accusatory tone in his voice I hear him say…. "Well?!" Now, as slow-witted as I may be sometimes, it finally dawns on me that my name for this trip is Manuel. As in Manuel labor!

Biting my tongue I reach behind me and find the door handle and hold it open as I descend quite carefully and with a good grip on the doorframe as well. The frozen snow covered ground shouldn't be slippery at this temperature. But, I am taking no chances as I step into the brisk northeast wind and the air stirred up by the propellor whishwhishwhishWHISHing the air only a couple of feet from my left shoulder now. Slamming the door shut with a good latching of the door handle I walk around the nose. Time to go to work again.

A chorus "Hi CloudDancer(s)!" erupts as I come around the nose from the gaggle of residents all standing around the right wing tip. And right hands encased in moosehide covered mittens wave their greetings to me as I holler "Morning everybody" in return before turning to unlatch the nose baggage compartment door. Willie adds his "Good morning good morning good morning!!" as he arrives bearing the ubiquitous armloads of green outgoing mailbags. We stuff them in the half empty compartment on top of the engine covers and foam air inlet plugs. Then scurrying over to his sled we each grab two more boxes of outgoing mail which just about fills the nose baggage compartment and will eliminate it's use for the remainder of the trip.

Hurrying past the now silent and cooling left engine I reach up and open the forward door of the two double doors aft the wing. The three step collapsible ladder falls to the ground at my feet having slid out from under the cargo net. Grabbing it I quickly hook it into the door ledge floor-mounted locking slots and after scramble back into the relative warmth of the cabin. I'm out of the wind anyway. Unhooking the boarding stepladder, I release it and let it drop to the ground where Willie slides it slightly off to the side with one boot as I begin to unlatch the aft door and allow it to swing open.

Only about two hundred pounds of mail (in this case canned cases of soda pop) of the almost seven hundred pounds we are carrying for Noorvik are in the cabin. The rest is in the tail compartment. Quickly throwing out the mail bags and a half a dozen parcel post packages I follow those with three "triple mailers". These are three cases of soda pop banded together as one piece. Sixty-three pounds each.

Leaping back to the ground it is now time to unload the rest of the soda pop from the tail baggage compartment which will leave it only momentarily empty. I have noted (much to my unspoken dismay) that about half a dozen people have separated from the group. Dragging their suitcases, duffel bags, cosmetic cases and Hefty bags (village Samsonite) they approach the airplane where Willie and I are now toiling. Sure enough…. there are four passengers for Kotzebue and two for Selawik, our third stop.

I climb back into the Twatters cabin, with now barely any residual warmth remaining in it. A quick glance forward though registers that JONESY appears to be quite toasty and comfortable in the cockpit as the remainder of the load in the cabin help retain heat forward. Hope his damn CUP leaks I remember thinking to myself. I now begin to roll up the aft end of the cargo net over the top of the load. In addition to the three aft bulkhead mounted seats I must access at least one right wall mounted double seat. Also the rest of the load must go far enough forward that the passengers seated there will have room for their legs too. Actually it must go forward another eight inches beyond that so that I can get to the next forward set of steel tie-down rings anchored in the Otter's floor.

Thankfully there are many cases of Pampers and a half dozen cases of potato chips for Kiana, our next stop. These are relatively light and will again fill our aft baggage compartment after the Kotzebue bags are placed in the bottom of the compartment.

It takes almost a whole twenty minutes before I rachet down the last cargo strap securing the net. I welcome our boarding passengers and then restow (securely this time) our boarding ladder and grab Willis's outbound paperwork.

Amazingly the aft passenger door handle seems somehow connected to the left engine starter. As I the snap the passenger door handle into it's closed and locked position, which extinguishes a "Door Ajar" light in the cockpit, the left propellor slowly starts rotating. Again the SNAPSNAPSNAPSNAP of the engine's ignition system reaches me over the sounds of sno-machines being started for the trip back to town.

This time I barely have my seat belts hooked up and am reaching for my David Clarks as the screeching of the propellers at full takeoff RPM hammers at my eardrums. We accelerate rapidly down the snow covered runway. As I get the headset clamped over my ears Jonesy hauls back on the yoke to launch us off to my next worksite Kiana. All of about 16NM away.

After calling the Kiana agents to tell them we are off Noorvik and will be there in about seven minutes as I reach for the logbook again. It's approaching 9:30 A.M. now and a band of grey or light blue is appearing to the southeast on the horizon. Daylight coming. I have not even finished writing all the mail numbers, times and (faked) weight and balance calculations down on the flight log when I hear the roar of the propellers being advanced to full forward for landing.

We're on short final for runway six at one of my favorite places on earth, Kiana, Alaska. Damn. What I wouldn't give for coffee and a smoke right now!

10

Share and Share Alike

Snapping the cover of the logbook shut I twist slightly left in my seat to jam it back behind my seat base while simultaneously trying to recap my Bic pen orally with my teeth and my right hand. This of course results in me stabbing my upper lip with the business end of the pen. I am trying to hurry which only further adds to the building irritation. I manage to finally cap it properly and am just sliding it into my left breast pocket about the time the Twatter's knee-high Goodyears reconnect gently with Mother Earth.

Jonesy barely cracks beta with the throttles as we have alit on what is (in those days) about the longest strip in our home region. At a substantial five thousand feet in gravel length and a good hundred feet wide Kiana is one of the smallest villages and towns in the state able to host DC-6s, Lockheed's Hercules and Argosys. It even provides them with a decent ramp so that they may park and shut down to offload while still blocking very little of the runway's available width. This being critical of course, as quite often in this state it is common to see planes landing over planes taxying the opposite way on the runway for takeoff. It is always proper etiquette however to first coordinate with and have the approval of the aircraft on the runway before "sharing".

I remember once being lined up on final for runway 26 in OTZ. I was about four miles out when the Wien 737-200 called for taxi advisories from Flight Service and upon hearing my position decided to wait for my arrival. A Noorvik born Eskimo boy inflamed with a passion for aviation was now a senior Captain for Wien and in command of the machine holding short. I recognized his voice. "Hey Bill" I sung out on 123.6 ...".Pretty good wind up here. If'n ya' wanna' go ahead 'n taxi down to the business end, go on ahead if ya' don't mind me landing acrost the toppa' ya'!"

Recognizing my voice as well, the Captain comes back with a 'Thanks. I'll just do that and hustle on down there to get out of your way." "No sweat" I respond and note the movement of the Boeing airliner as it spools up and turns out onto the runway. Still almost four miles from me Bill gooses his JT8D's and the blue, gold and white-trimmed seven-three picks up speed as it heads for the east end of the runway. Naturally me being, well…. ME, I couldn't resist the temptation to see if I could "get a rise" out of the much older, reserved and refined airline captain. I just can't help it! It's the imp in me. So I lower the nose a little more and hold off on my speed reduction until flashing across the top of the VORhouse on the hill at the east end of the runway whereupon I chop the power and get the flaps starting down.

As the big airliner was now down the runway about three-quarters of the way this would mean Bill and I should "cross paths" just before he slides off to one side of this runway so as to commence a 180 degree turn before takeoff. Perfect. Flaps extending and the nose rotates down a bit lower. And just before I reach his nose Bill has to say it. "Hey CloudDancer…." comes over my speaker oh SO quietly. "The tail on this bird is about 37 feet tall. Try to miss it."

Chuckling quietly as I keyed my microphone, I said "Sorry Bill…. somehow I just couldn't resist." And Bill came back with "'Bout what I figured from you CloudDancer" and a laugh. I musta' missed him by at least twenty feet.

So it is not unusual for small singles and light twins to go whizzing around, over, and under the motionless Herc or Argosy wings as the larger planes sit silently unloading. It's just another "50 foot obstacle" or some such that the bush pilots fit into their daily agenda.

As our Hartzell three-blades "disc" and slowly decrease the aircraft's groundspeed I lean back in my seat and glance out over the descending terrain off the south side of the runway and note three or four bouncing single headlights. Most likely headed for the airport to greet us.

Less than ninety seconds goes by before I am again crawling into the back of the Twin Otter to release the cargo net. While I throw the most of the remainder of our twenty-four hundred pounds of mail toward the back door (half-bent over or in a crouch—thirty, forty, fifty, or SIXTY pounds at a time) half of our Noorvik boarded contingent of passengers have dis-embarked. They are busy hugging and shaking hands with their up-river cousins, in-laws, and friends. The other three seated against the back wall lean out and over and exchange pleasantries as well. It is always the way it happens and is repeated every time you land at a village. Even if the villages are hundreds of miles apart.

Unload aft baggage mail. Load baggage in aft baggage. Put down more seats. And so it goes. And so it will go at Selawik as well in another thirty minutes. By the time we land and dismount in Kotzebue I will have, in the three previous hours, humped approximately five thousand pounds of cargo by hand. This includes completely or partially having loaded and unloaded the aft baggage compartment three times for another five hundred pounds or so total. I released and re-secured the cargo straps three to four more times and, cursed the seats half a dozen times at least. And … oh yeah…. fueled the airplane. And that's just the first of three trips today. I pray we don't have any extra (all cargo) sections!

Jonesy meanwhile has had three more Winstons and three more cups of coffee while maintaining a diligent watch over the continually running right engine which kept him nice and warm in the cockpit. I mean not that I got cold. Hell! I was sweating most of the trip anyway! Although the difference when looking back thirty years versus looking back at my job requirements the last dozen or so years might explain this "spare tire" around my middle. More like a spare set really.

Jonesy did give me the last portion of the last leg, indicated by waving a meaty bare bear paw in the general direction of the right wheel and quietly growling "TAKE 'er! This included the landing on runway eight as a reward for having completed the flight paperwork somewhere about the middle of Kobuk Lake on the way back in. No coffee though. That was consumed already.

After wedging our blue Otter into it's parking space and setting the brake Jonesy reaches up, grabs the prop controls and slams them aft and through the feather uplocks as if they didn't even exist and the propellers quickly rotate the blades within their hubs 90 degrees. He follows this by hooking both nickel sized red circular plastic knobs on the adjacent fuel control levers in the crook of his pointer finger and snaps those to the full aft position cutting off our PT-6s from their lifeblood Jet-A and they whine down slowly in RPM, musical pitch, and volume.

Smacking the battery/generator gangbar plunges the aircraft into lifelessness and Jonsey is already sliding wordlessly out of the left cockpit door to the ground. His cockpit door had started to shut and was then reopened with a loud grunt. The big paw reenters the cockpit to fish around under the left seat momentarily. I hear the scrape of metal against metal and then the cockpit door slams shut with a thud and click as the access handle is rotated to the closed position. Comanche Jones now walks toward the terminal's rampside entrance swaying coffee jug in his left hand shining in the morning sun.

Meanwhile our two ramp guys have begun helping the passengers alight and are removing the contents of the aft baggage compartment. The one in the cabin shouts forward at me. "Hey CloudDancer!! We got twelve outbound for upriver!!". Looking at my watch I note we have just under thirty-five minutes 'til our scheduled departure for Ambler, Shungnak and Kobuk. Passengers are supposed to be seated forward of the cargo so.... I dive through the narrow cockpit "doorway" and begin to do battle with the seats once more. I curse the seats loudly and Comanche Jones quietly. After all he's a legend (we'll get to that). I try unsuccessfully to NOT think about how damn badly I want a smoke and a cuppa' hot coffee!

The second, and for that matter, all subsequent trips for the day went exactly the same way.

About the time the last of the loading was done I would proceed into the terminal and approach "the Sphinx" as I had begun quietly calling him to myself. Always he would be found atop the same stool smoking another Winston and drinking another cup of coffee. I figured his first stop upon re-entering the terminal at the end of a trip had to be the john!

I would ask "How much motion lotion ya' want for this one Jonesy" and each and every time he'd say 'Whatcha' think?" Whereupon I would list our itinerary and say "... so I figger 'bout XXXX pounds oughta' do 'er." Pausing either for dramatic effect ... to take a drag on the ever present Winston.... or just to piss me off.... Jonesy always came back with the same one word reply. "A-A-Awwww-RIGHT!" Even so, I must admit I had high hopes for the second trip even though it was commencing before I had time to catch my breath.

As Jonesy and his thermos appeared on the ramp and the terminals front door opened I was flipping the seven or eight inch chain that attached to the fuel cap into the tank filler neck so I could clamp the fuel cap securely closed as the ticket agent escorted the passengers through the ramp access gate to our rampers. The electric take-up reel is winding the black fuel hose back into the fueling station and the last of the passengers are mounting the aluminum ladder to access the cabin as I hear the right engine begin to whine. The top of the right propeller, visible over the top of the cabin start it's slowly increasing revolutions. My watch tells me it's 11:00 A.M. straight up. Departure time.

My bladder for some reason (why I don't know, I still haven't had any COFFEE dammit!) is now sending full signals to my brain. What the hell. Unzipping my snowsuit and jeans I whip out my tallywhacker and write my initials in the snow a couple of times partially shielded from observation by the fueling station and 10,000 gallon steel cylindrical Jet-A tank. I'm fairly sure that Jonesy won't leave his auto-loading system behind. But I'm not willing to take that chance just yet.

Again I am just getting myself oriented in the cockpit in time to file a round robin flight plan with the F.S.S. as Jonesy is lining up on the runway. Then, when to my utter shock and surprise he waves the meaty paw.... (this is beginning to take on the significance of a Papal Blessing) and utters what are rapidly becoming my to most favorite if rarely heard words … "take 'er!"

This is what I LIVE for! I am in charge (sort of) of this BIG plane and I gleefully enjoy the takeoff roll and ascent into the heavens. Leveling at fifty-five hundred feet for the 93 NM leg to Ambler I trim the aircraft for hands off flight and relax. An ear to ear grin is still glued to my face. Now that the excitement level has dropped slightly the familiar coffee and smoke pangs come stabbing back at my stomach. I can only hope Jonesy will offer me some coffee and holler across the space between us "Hey Jonesy…. you mind if I smoke?"

"Go Ahead" he responds and a couple a seconds later he's fishing around in his pockets for his Winstons as he sez "Didn't know you smoked!". And of course, before my pea brain could over-ride my alligator mouth I shot back … "O-o-oH yeah! And I drink coffee TOO!" This comment, was duly noted by Jonesy according to the … LOOK … on his face as he stared at me momentarily. It did not however, as I had hoped, produce an offer to share a cup of coffee. "Well … ya' oughta' bring some then!" Discussion closed. "I got 'er" he growls. "Best try 'n stay ahead of the paperwork this time."

By six P.M. we had operated three trips, eleven legs, and been to eight different villages. I got one takeoff and two landings, one-half of one cup of luke warm coffee between trips two and three and smoked only five cigarettes all day. It was impossible I'd found to smoke while simultaneously shuffling paperwork, tickets, paper money, station manifests and flight logs as there was no ashtrays on the airplane. Jonesy went through a pack.

As one of our rampers dove into the nose baggage compartment for our winter bed-down gear (inlet plugs, engine covers, six carter heaters and wing and tail covers and extension cords) another was dragging over an A-frame work stand to aid in getting the engine wing and tail covers on. I was starving . I could eat a cow all by myself and we raced to accomplish the chores. Jonesy meanwhile proceeded to the parking lot and fired up the company pick-em-up truck to allow it's engine and cabin to warm up. The temperature had plunged precipitously with the sun over two hours ago. Ambient must be no more than twenty or so and the wind is now blowing a steady fifteen knots out of the east. It's gonna' get COLD tonight.

Ten minutes later I enter the terminal one last time for the day. Jonesy looks up from his stool and says 'Ready?" and when I respond "Let's go! I'm starved!" he hauls his bulk offa' the stool and seems to move for the door with a bit more enthusiasm in his shuffle than I've seen all day long. Like the rest of the day, the drive to the Nu-Luk-Vik Hotel, all of three minutes is conducted in complete silence. The glowing end of Jonesy's ubiquitous Winston gets brighter then fades, then grows brighter again as he puffs without removing it from between his lips. The ashes fall to his snowsuit and the glowing ember end of the cigarette dances through arcs downward, upward and side to side as the old Ford bounces in and out of the various frozen solid potholes that dot Second street. I am weary and look forward to fresh coffee. All I want. And two or three smokes not to mention a drink after dinner.

Comanche Jones practically dismounts the Ford before she stops moving and is proceeding up the cement sidewalk to the hotels front entrance at a downright spritely pace. I know neither of us has eaten since this morning and I figure Jonesy must be darn near as hungry as me, even though I did all the work. Like a horse smellin' the oats at the end of the day Jonesy is headed for the barn with a determination it seems and I hustle to keep up behind him.

To access the restaurant from the front metal dull yellow painted double doors requires an immediate (double-right) one hundred eighty degree turn after passing through the second entrance door. Now, half way through that right one-eighty U-Turn (90 degrees for you math slouches) you're facing an even wider door leading to the hotel's bar where I expect to end up after dinner.

Now truly impressed with Jonesy's increasing pace I am actually striding purposefully to keep up with him as we enter the hotel. I am therefore totally surprised when Jonesy unexpectedly comes to a complete, immediate, and sudden full stop at the ninety degree point in our turn. As close as I was tailgating I didn't even see the crash coming! I smashed into his backside at full speed. But given the girth and mass of the unmoving Comanche he barely noticed it I'm sure while I rebounded offa' him like golf ball bounced on a sidewalk!

Two staggering steps backward and I catch my balance as Jonesy turns and rivets me with the same glare with which one would regard a persistent mosquito at a summer picnic. He then growls out his longest sentence of the day thus far whilst rubbing a big paw in circles around his expansive belly. "Sure hate to EAT on an empty stomach." After which having uttered that somewhat skewed version of an old axiom (now one of CloudDancer's very favorites, of course)

Jonesy turns on his heel and marches into the bar. Only for the briefest of moments do I hesitate. Well, one or two before dinner can't hurt either I decide and I march in right behind Jonesy. With the same newly determined pace, he proceeds to the far short end of the bar by the street side exit. He mounts his bulk upon the stool having shed his snowsuit along the way and thrown it at the coat rack where it (naturally) caught an empty hook.

As if by magic the bartender is in front of us holding a bottle of Crown Royal. He asks me what I'd like to drink (I've been out of town for a while and this guy is new) while his hand snags a "bucket" (a large rocks glass) from the ice bin behind the counter.

With a flourish he inverts the glass and as it collides with the base on the bar in front of Jonesy the tip of the shiny sterling silver pouring spout lays over the edge and begins to gush an amber liquid into the icy cold tumbler. It continues to pour until a good solid three fingers is contained therein but only for a moment. For, no sooner has the pouring spout been removed, than Jonesy lifts the tumbler. He "clinks" the glass against the bottle of Crown Royal still being held in mid-air by the bartender and mutters "Here's mud in yer' eye" before raising it to his lips and draining the contents in two swift gulps. As he utters a long and hard sigh of satisfaction he sets the glass gently back in the spot from which he had lifted it. In a matter of five seconds the fluid level in the tumbler had been replenished. The bartender says he'll be right back and Jonesy and I sit there in silence for a minute or so as we watch him find some rum and concoct a decent rum and coke which he brings and deposits in my bar space.

As he sets mine down Jonesy again grabs his rocks glass and half turning in his seat, raises and extends his glass halfway toward me and mutters quietly "over the teeth 'n past the tongue … look out tummy … here it comes." And as I raise my glass in response to the toast and take a healthy swig of my drink, Jonesy takes a relatively small sip before setting the glass down. Smacking his lips he then says to me "Ya' know kid. Ya' done pretty good out there today."

Now I am stunned into silence. (A state quite unusual for me … as anyone who knows me will tell you). And while I ponder how to respond to this comment we both take another taste and I notice Jonesy again takes a small sip. As I am about to reply Jonesy lets fly with "Heardju' been around the country for a while. Kinda' nice to fly with somebody who knows what they're doin' for a change." My God! Knock me off my stool fer crissakes. He's CONTINUING! "If ya' can fly instruments pretty good you might jes' do fine around here". Another sip of Crown Royal and half the second glass has survived about two or three minutes so far.

I would come to learn that every glass lasted between five to seven minutes for Jonesy. Each and every sip also had the mysterious ability to further lubricate Jonesy's vocal chords. This a miracle in both the number of words spoken and volume as well. It was shaping up to be an interesting night.

11

"… AND If Ya' Ask Me AGAIN"

The hands moved around the face of the clock behind the bar once, twice, and then a third time. Patiently I pointed this out to Jonesy, when I could get a word in edge-wise. After my second time uh…. alert if you will, (he'd ignored my first subtle suggestion, being distracted by his thirty-fourth, fifth and SIXTH "fingers" of Crown Royal) I gave a final notice that the restaurant was about to close for the night and maybe we should get something to eat!

Again the big meaty right paw rubs circles over what could now be easily and rightfully mistaken for a keg of whiskey and he allows as how "I dunno! I'm startin' ta' get pretty full right now!" And he turns to holler at the bartender for another round before returning to the spine-chilling story he is relating to me and a half-dozen other pilots from our company. Others too have come to wash the days cares and concerns away in what is generally for most of us a nightly alcoholic group hangar-flying and girl chasing ritual.

Jonesy is ten minutes deep into his latest hair-raising story from his Air America days. He has been pretty much talking non-stop for the last hour and a half, something most folks figure I'M the king at. But I can't come near touchin' his stuff.

The story from his 'Nam days is about flying an old Curtiss C-82. Jonesy has been shot-up by small arms fire from the ground, lost engine number one…. had a fire … and gone half inverted. It seemed every horrible thing that can happen in a war zone was happening and about five minutes deep into the story as he had paused to take a sip of whiskey having finally gotten his recalcitrant number one prop to feather. I asked just outta' curiosity ya' know, "So Jonesy what wuz ya' haulin'??" And he turned to me and grunted one word. "Rice!"

He then resumes tellin' the story about how the number two and last engine starts ta' over heat from the strain of carryin' the overload an' the co-pilot has to go back an' start kickin' some of the heavier crates outta' the ass end on accounta' his regular kicker is out cold from some shrapnel that penetrated the side of the

190

cargo compartment an' DARK is comin' on an.... I interrupt again to ask. "So, what was you carryin' in the crates Jonesy?" (Even I know rice generally comes in 50 lb. Burlap sacks.) Again Jonesy turns to me and says somewhat heatedly "Ah tolja' ... RICE!"

By the time the co-pilot gets back up to the front the number two engine temps are pegged out and things are lookin' pretty grim for the good guys but we're still heading for our destination some mountainside strip by some tribal village an' maybe that ol' # 1 engine can be brought back to life and OH Lord. Now there's MORE small arms fire coming up an' the clouds are coming down an'.... "Now wait a minute Jonesy" I interrupt again. Continuing I say "Now, nobody is gonna' go to all THAT trouble for a load a' rice. (Pause is met with silence from all). So WHAT was ya' haulin' fer cryin' out loud!?"

Jonesy turned to the bar and picked up his freshly filled shot glass. For the first time since we sat down he drained it again in two gulps before turning to answer me. His coal black eyes had (I swear) flames in them as he muttered quietly, for only me to hear. "I'll tell you one.... last ... time boy. It was rice. And if ya' asks me again.... I'll be obliged ta' KILL ya. Unnerstand?" And after voicing my agreement Jonesy allowed as how I'd best be a gettin' home as we had a hangar fulla' stuff to fly tomorrow! Momma' CloudDancer didn't raise no fool. I paid my tab and left.

I arrived at the airport early the next morning. A bellyful of greasy hash browns and a huge cheddar cheese 'n ham omelet along with two biscuits slathered in butter and strawberry jam all washed down by a gallon of coffee and three glasses of orange juice had reduced the pounding in my head to a dull throbbing. This was mostly cured with some straight oxygen from the Twin Otter's on board system. I expected that last night had been a "breakthrough" of some sort for me 'n Comanche Jones and that today I would see a more talkative and "sharing" Captain Jonesy ... NOT! You know that Bill Murray movie "GroundHog Day". Run that through your mind. Day Two was identical to Day One with Jonesy. Only some of the villages were different and my hangover made the first trip rather unpleasant.

Once again at the end of the day I was following Jonesy at full speed into the hotel's front doors ostensibly to go to the restaurant again when the big damn Indian screeched to an abrupt halt in precisely the same spot halfway through the turn to the restaurant doors. Again I smacked into his backside. Rub, Rub ... growl, growl.... "Not good ... empty stomach ..." Iced rocks glass. First three fingers gone in two gulps. Second fill, small sip ... oooohhhhhh-KAY! I'm beginning to sense a pattern here. No dinner two nights in a row.

The third night I kept three paces behind Jonsey entering the hotel, avoided the rear end collision, and ordered food delivered to the bar. For me of course 'cause Jonesy ... well ...

He didn't know fer sure ... but he thought he was gettin' kinda' full already! And near as I can tell, the only cargo Jonesy ever hauled on any of his flights in Southeast Asia was ... you guessed it.... RICE!!

Now. While all this stuff might be a little funny and somewhat interesting; I've told you nothing here so far that appears to be of legendary status. So you must find yourself asking ... so what is with this legend stuff?! Well, my friends ... read on ... and you'll discover a remarkable and true tale.

12

How LONG Can You Hold YOUR Breath?

Anaktuvuk Pass. To this day, sitting in my warm home, happily enveloped in my overstuffed and sturdy, cozy, reclining and rolling high backed writing chair; those two words can bring a very slight increase of mental and muscular tension.

At an altitude of 2200 feet or so above sea level lies the village of the same name, where the pass peaks on it's (generally) north-south passage through the Brooks Range. Starting just to the immediate northeast of Bettles, the southern entrance is a comfortable distance across width wise. It would allow, for the first few miles northward anyway, for a reasonably comfortable "U-turn" even at the lowest of altitudes. But remember to slow down a lot first, hang out the flaps, and be proficient at your steep turns.

Once more than twenty miles or so deep into the pass headed north, well let me put it this way. Remember the old Gary Larson "Far Side" cartoon of the two airline pilots in their cockpit in the clouds. And they look out the windows and see a Dahl sheep standing on a rocky hillside off to the side and above them?! I'll give you five to one odds that Mr. Larson must have been riding with one of the multiple daily "scheduled airline" flight to this bustling metropolis of 280 hardy souls or so.

I can't even remember how many times I've sat, butt-cheeks clenched tighter'n the skin on a banjo, on the edge of my Cessna 207, Piper Navajo Chieftan, Cessna 402 or Bandierante's Captain's chair for what always seemed like eternity. "Cruising" anything but leisurely in slow flight northbound up the pass at anywhere from three hundred (my personal "minimum") to five hundred feet over the tundra. Ahead the pass is narrowing to maybe a mile or a little less in width. The mountain bases whizzing by a short distance to either side rise up into the clouds that are skimming just above my cockpit. And I know that the tops of the peaks are already a couple of thousand feet higher than me and growing.

More than half the time either a steady solid consistent version of precip ... either rain or snow depending on the day ... is falling. It holds the visibility down to something between two and five miles. Maybe you try to weave through or just slightly around the heavier squalls (without knocking some poor ol' sheep offa' his or her ledge with your wingtip) that reduce visibility to below a mile when you plow through them.

As I recall the pass makes about a 110 to120 degree right turn (when flying north to south) just shortly past the half-way point distance-wise. Just before the turn it gets pretty tight down low and you are COMMITTED to making the turn past a certain point. Once you negotiate it successfully however, there IS a surprisingly wide area free from rocks where you could practice slow flight steep turns. Take a few easy, deep and relaxing breathes if you don't like what you see ahead of you. For the pass narrows tight one last time before opening to all of two-and-a-half to three miles wide immediately south of the village a few miles further north.

Anywhere you are in the pass, unless there is literally no room between your airplane and the ground whizzing by you beneath your props ... you are subject to have another airplane from SuperCub size to DC-6 freighter flash by underneath you.

Once you get to Anaktuvuk there is a flat mesa type ledge of rock to the immediate (three hundred yards or so) west side of the village. It runs north-south to parallel the runway about three hundred feet or so higher than the run-way elevation. From this ledge the western walls of the pass rise steeply and immediately to something (I really can't remember exactly) at least three if not four thousands of feet above you. With the pass at the village being no more than three miles wide ... one must be EXTREMELY careful when circling or flying a left downwind for a north (the usual and slightly uphill) landing on runway 36.

From the village northward the pass gradually keeps opening slightly on a northerly heading for a few miles before making about a thirty degree left hand turn. It continues to widen and drop in elevation while now heading northwest until emptying out onto the North Slope southeast of Umiat.

On one of those very rare clear and sunny days, Anaktuvuk Pass has all the beauty of the Swiss Alps and words are totally inadequate to describe it's stunning appearance. The other 95% of the time it is one of those ... those ... PLACES. Places like Gambell or damn near anywhere on "the Chain" (the Aleutians). Also quite a few places in southeast I've heard of but never seen. (You southeast drivers get a heap of my respect too!) Places that, while they have that rare capacity to be awesomely beautiful; more often than not, are usually ugly as HELL. This was especially true in the pre-radar, pre-GPS, hell ... pre-navaid of ANY kind days. These were the places that, when you knew you had a trip or two to go there on a given day; you really dreaded even setting the alarm clock the night before.

As you might figure given the description above, it was "just one of those days" when Comanche Jones and some poor hapless youngster in the right seat (probably still in therapy) flew the leg that was destined to make the man ... a walking legend.

13

Cumulus Ganitus
INTERRUPTUS!!

Actually the weather wasn't all that bad, for Anaktuvuk that is. With the overcast slightly above the tops of the mountains and five or so miles of visibility in a steady light snow and reasonably light winds the trip IN to Anaktuvuk from the north side had been relatively easy. Approaching from the north side was always easier as the pass was noticeably wider north of the village, making it slightly easier for the Barrow based operations to get there.

Many times, when the south entry was unpassable and we had lots of go-juice in the tanks, it was standard ops for us south-side boys to punch up and fly across the Brooks Range on top. Sometimes you'd luck out and there might be a hole right over the village you could drop down through. If not, then you would motor on over to Umiat where there was a very low power (5 watt I think) NDB. I don't remember what the approach minimums were. Yes, there really was an F.A.A. approved approach procedure. But ... well ... the Minimum Descent Altitude WAS really more of a suggestion wasn't it?!

So if you could find the ground that way, then you could make a low pass over the Umiat runway to check your directional gyro setting. Then you're good to barrel off on a heading for the pass's northern entrance. But Jonesy had apparently had it fairly easy going in and expected the same coming out. Being empty to boot, except for the outgoing mail, usually a dozen or so mail bags and boxes, his Twin Otter would climb like a homesick angel. He would be above the tallest peaks again a few short minutes after liftoff.

Now, I'd been to Barrow dozens of times as well as Anaktuvuk. But I'd only been between the two a couple of times. Jonesy on the other hand had done the trip countless times out of Barrow. So on this fine morning he chose to save miles, gas and minutes by taking a direct heading for Pt. Barrow as soon as he was above the level of the closest mountains. Probably something about a forty-five degree left hand cut off the northerly running pass at that point.

This would result in Jonsey having to cut across diagonally five ... or was it SIX closely spaced "rows" of peaks that were between him and the all but sea level flat North Slope of the Great Land. Upon passing the last row he could comfortably drop down to three hundred feet if he wanted to and scare the crap outta' the caribou the rest of the two hundred nautical or so miles home.

It seems however that the weather, not unusually, had rolled in off the arctic pack ice offshore behind him and was worsening unbeknownst to him. I mean how's he supposed to know? Until he gets back within radio range of Umiat which has a sometimes operational connection to Pt. Barrow Flight Service, he's on his own. A situation with which he is quite comfortable. But as he progresses northwestward the snow intensifies dropping visibility. He then apparently somehow lost count or miscounted (by one) how many lines of peaks he had crossed. This wee but not insignificant mathematical error would shortly bring a MOST unpleasant surprise.

For now Jonesy, confident that flat land lay ahead initiated a slow (thankfully) descent toward what he figured was the flat tundra lying far below.

Sidebar—Now, for the most part dear readers ... ol' CloudDancer's testicles are ... and remain normal sized. This along with the fact that I am not sure whether it actually is five or six rows of mountains accounts for the fact that I would never even try this. So what pray tell is Jonesy doing. Is he CRAZY?! Well ... I dunno' ... weren't nobody SHOOTIN'at him at the moment, remember?! I guess now we should return to our story, and while many of you can most certainly "see" what lies ahead for the Comanche ... he can't. At least, not quite yet.

Concentrating as they must have been on their gauges, I don't even know which of the two seemingly doomed pilots first look up and outside to find their windshield rapidly filling with snow covered cumulo graniti. I don't know if there were any sheep, standing dis-interestedly off to one side; standing stock still watching as the bird metal bird came screaming out of the snow obscured arctic skies. And I really don't know ... 'cause I don't think they noted who screamed out the first response.

Only one response is appropriate. The one that is often the last two words on the cockpit voice recorder transcript before the for the fateful "sounds of impact" at the end. And as funny man Bill Cosby once said "First you SAY it, then you DO It!!" The "Oh #$%^!!" was accompanied with a simultaneous hard pitch up and Jonesy's big right paw slamming the overhead throttles forward.

I can't describe "the sound of impact" in this case and neither could the guy who told me about it and he got the story straight from the kid in the right seat. It was instantaneous and brief and they almost made it, but NO-O-O-T quite.

But they were at flying speed and they just smacked into the top of the peak. Hitting it with such forward motion that they only struck the mighty mountain a (for the mountain) glancing "blow" before careening off the top of the peak and back into the air now thousands of feet above the treeless Arctic tundra far below. (I dunno' about you guys. But personally, I think I'd rather have somebody SHOOTin' at me!)

So now … here's Jonesy and this kid. They are airborne still and descending earthward only tenuously "under control" at best. Comanche Jones struggles to keep the suddenly unstable, shaking, rattling and gyrating DeHavilland right side up with a control wheel that may or may not be having it's normal effects on the attached (we hope) control surfaces. As the altimeter slowly unwinds Jonesy's luck gets a little better as the intensity of the snow decreases and the ground appears further ahead as well, but still far below.

After several frantic long seconds turned to a couple of minutes Jonesy has now gotten a grasp on the new situation. He now has the Otter in a stabilized steady airspeed slow descent and still aimed toward the ADF needle at the top of the dial pointing to Barrow. As typical for him he has uttered not a word one on this flight so far. Okay. He did SCREAM two, but that's all. He remains silent and intensely focused as he "holds what he's got". A specific pitch attitude, power setting, and airspeed are producing a calm (for the moment) relatively relaxing period as the Twatter descends toward the earth.

Once down to around three hundred feet or so, Jonesy must decide whether to keep going to Pt. Barrow a distance of still better than two hundred nautical miles or so, or plant the thing on the frozen snow covered tundra. And while we always carried survival gear this IS the North Slope. It is colder than a well diggers ass. We are still meanwhile riding in a nice warm stable (for the moment, at least) cockpit making progress toward civilization and possible rescue if needed. And I truly have no idea how far inland polar bears like to venture. Jonesy elects to follow the course that has always worked for him in the past. Keep 'er in the air.

14

"Hey. Spill a Little of That Over Here."

As the miles slip past beneath the wounded DHC-6 Jonesy settles down. Still tensed up I'm sure but somewhat comforted with four to five good miles of visibility in the now (again) light snow and Mother Earth no more than a mere three hundred feet away. (What? Like falling from three hundred feet and ninety knots is gonna' hurt LESS than falling from three THOUSAND feet and a hundred and forty knots?!) Jonesy is now a test pilot experimenting briefly with the engines and control surfaces to discover how things work now!

He discovers that he has a five knot margin of operational airspeed. At eighty-seven knots indicated, fast even for a Twin Otter with the flaps up, particularly when EMPTY ... at eighty-seven knots he starts to get the stall warning horn. And at ninety one knots the right wing, apparently wrenched loose from it's normal position by the excessive downward forces of the impact with the offending mountaintop, begins to flap up and down slightly in a way never intended by the engineers who designed the thing. The up and down movement would normally be limited by the wing to fuselage brace strut. Unfortunately this brace now has an unintended kink/buckle in it allowing for an unwanted and undesirable freedom of movement.

So there Jonesy sits ... right arm extended upward ... his big right hand wrapped around the throttles. DAMN! It's gonna' take a LIDDLE longer to get back to base.

As they plod along in silence only the thickness of the insulation in the kid's snowsuit legs keeps the sounds of his knees knocking together in fear from sounding like a metronome at high tempo.

After LOOOOONG minutes of silence and watching the caribou scatter in every direction below as they whizz along the kid can't take it any more and has to say something. What is going on in Jonesy's mind?! Will we be alright?! Can I do anything ... and I mean anything at all to help he thinks to himself?

"Ja ... Ja ... Ja-Ja-Ja ... JONSEY!!" He finally blurts out. "Ssh ... SSH ... S ... SSH-SSh-SHOULD I go see if the WHEELS are still tha ... tha ... THA-THA ... THERE!?" he asks plaintively.

"Naw". Jonesy grunts quietly. "They're gone". He says with finality.

A couple of more minutes pass and "Ja ... Ja ... Ja-Ja ... JONEsy!! Ssh ... ssh ... should I go SEE ... if ... if ... the right ... wa-wa-wa-WINGS! O.K.?!" he utters. He is desperate to be useful, or maybe just wants to be comforted by the sight of the wing. I dunno.

"Nope". Jonsey responds. "If it ain't ... we'll know soon enough". Conversation over. And the kid knows there is no point in further trying to engage Comanche Jones in conversation this early before "dinner" time.

Spying the company provided lunch box still on the floor between the seats, and determined to do something ... anything to take his mind offa' the situation the kid digs into the box for a small can of unsweetened Dole orange juice. Now. These are the baby cans. No taller than a good sized coffee mug and made of steel (or very thick aluminum) they hold only about a half a cup of juice. And they are sealed on top with a sticky aluminum foil "pull tab". They can been a real pain in the ass to open.

Now the extra movement has attracted Jonesy's attention and he looks over his right arm at the kid. The kid's right hand, holding the small can is shaking like a leaf in gusty winds. His left hand is too, and the kid, aware that Jonesy is eyeballing him, is even more scared if that is possible. He wonders what bit of admonishment or bad news may be forthcoming from the stoic man who holds both their lives so assuredly in his two hands at the moment.

Unfortunately since the right and the left hand are not shaking at either the same speed or in unison, the kid has a quite difficult time grasping the teeny un-"gummed" portion of the peel off can top. About now, I'm sure Jonesy would normally be pouring himself a cuppa' Joe and lighting off another Winston. Unfortunately normal went out the window a few miles back.

Finally, by parking the can on his right thigh firmly, the kid is able to steady the can enough so that his shaky left hand has a shot at grasping the peel top. Which he does and then he RIPS! It off with a vengeance as if somehow IT is responsible for this mess. Of course, the instant he lifts the can from it's resting position on his thigh, the violent shaking of his right hand sends unsweetened orange juice flying everywhere about the right side of the cockpit. Finally however, he is able to locate his mouth with the can and mashes it firmly against his lip to hold it in place with his trembling right hand. He drains the remaining last small sips from the bottom of the can.

As he finishes the can he tosses it back over his shoulder into the empty cabin behind where it clangs onto the plywood floor for a couple of bounces. He then turns to look defiantly into Jonesy's eyes for a second. Jonesy grunts and looks away after a couple of seconds still silent. But as the kid turns to look forward (to the future?) again Jonesy mutters just loud enough to be heard over the sound of the engine noise. "Hey kid. Why don'tcha spill one of those over here towards ME. Mah throat's a'gettin' kinda' dry."

Well, after a couple a hours or so they finally wheel the ol' Twatter around the pattern at Barrow and line her up for what will prove to be her final landing. And as always, Jonesy sets her down on his target in the middle of the runway.

Due to the aforementioned undesigned for brief, but quite excessive downward wing loading; and the resulting effects; the impact of the belly landing was the straw that broke the camel's back … or the Twatter's back in this case. No longer needed for either thrust or lift and having hung around long enough to bring IT's side of the airplane back along with it's mate; the right wing, strut and engine now quite noisily wrench themselves free of the miracle air machine and promptly head off into the weeds and willows alongside the runway.

This leaves the now no longer asymmetrically weight-and-balanced fuselage and left wing/engine assembly to begin spinning in complete and repetitive circles. It continues down the middle of the runway until, momentum spent, the now useless pile of no longer airworthy aluminum slides to a final stop on the ice and snow packed Barrow runway.

From which emerged, literally and figuratively, a walking legend.

*What Could POSSIBLY
Go Wrong?*

Prologue

'Twas the late summer of 1981 I remember, maybe late August or early September. It's easy to remember the time frame for this Chronicle. You see, it was my very first time at the controls of any aircraft in over five months.

The extended gap in my flying career had come about as the result of another (not yet written) Alaskan Chronicle that occurred the previous March. That truly hair-raising adventure will be included someday in (the also yet to be published) Vol.III "The Tragedies". I'm thinking it will be titled either "There Are No Superheros" or "The Death of a Legend". But that is for some future date. For now all you need to know about that is this. It changed me for the better for the long term. But for the short term ... well ... for the short term let's just call it like it was. I lost my nerve. I couldn't fly. In fact, I thought I was done flying for life.

Now, on to the FUNNY stuff.

1

Washed Up at Twenty-Seven

Well, I've given up flying. Great! Now what do I do? That last thing I want to do is go back to Texas for crissake! I mean I love Alaska. All my friends are here now after making Kotzebue my home for the last eight years. Besides which I am flat broke, and to go back there would be some admission (in my mind at least) that I am a failure. Not to mention the very thought of having to ask Mom and Pop CloudDancer for sanctuary and support at the age of twenty-seven was to me completely unacceptable. Therefore I was determined to do whatever was necessary to support myself until I figured out which way I needed to go in life.

Now Koztebue, being like all rural Alaskan towns, has no secrets. It is often truly said that "If you can't remember what you did last night ; when you awake, walk to the other end of town. Two out of the three first people you ask will be happy to tell you. In detail!"

As you've gathered from other Chronicles, your CloudDancer was anything other than some "low profile" shrinking violet. While certainly not some obnoxious loudmouth braggart, ol' CD didn't have any problem with being generally "well-known" and (mostly) "well regarded", with of course the exception of SOME of my former … um … female "close acquaintances". Therefore, pretty much everyone in town, hell in all of northwest Alaska, knew of my "downfall" as well as the event from which it had resulted. Word had spread that I had quit flying. Now I was just like everybody else. So this should be interesting to watch.

Fortunately, other than the few … okay maybe a dozen or so girls that were no longer talking to me, I had managed to be pretty honorable and straight-forward in the rest of my life's dealing with people in the Arctic. So overall, I still had a pretty good reputation as an individual and luckily (for me) my friendships abounded. I now tapped them for what I could.

Swallowing a pride based on my former life as a vital part of the region's air transport system, I went seeking work. Real work. You know. The kind regular people do every day. Like with a real daily schedule. Doing the same stuff, day in and day out. Regular.

A former flying compadre' was kind enough to take me in, with his wife's permission of course. As I suspected, and he confirmed for me later, it was no easy sell on his part. For some reason beyond MY comprehension, the wives of almost all my married friends considered me to be some sort of ... I dunno' ... bad influence on their spouses. And while I freely admit to being party to some ... uh ... shall we say ... wifely unapproved activities; it seemed that I was quite often deemed by said wives to be the instigator of these episodes. This, when if fact it was their own loving husbands who initially proposed whatever it was that I was subsequently to be blamed for.

So what if one of my closest friends had disappeared to Hawaii for a week. The fact that he failed to notify his wife who had (let the record show) locked him out of his house in a howling Arctic blizzard at 3 A.M. after repeated calls to the Pondu bar failed to motivate his homing instincts; was more than offset (in our minds at least) by the fact that, had I not rescued him after the 5 A.M. bar closing and provided safe haven in my apartment ... he might well have FROZE to death!

I only went along with him to the Islands after he came up with the idea (about 7 A.M.) whilst we stood at the window of my apartment and watched the snow blow sideways for an hour and a half. (Really pie-eyed drunks are easily entertained ...) Okay granted. Not calling and saying goodbye to his three young children was a rather significant oversight. But. Here again, they weren't MY kids. Therefore the fact that he didn't call should be at least easily forgivable from the short list of MY minor transgressions in this week long incident.

In fact it was only a week long deal for me, as I had to return to work. He remained in the Islands for another eight weeks literally doing an early version of his job tele-commuting long distance from various bars around Waikiki! I returned to Kotzebue to face not just the wrath of his wife, but her parents and many siblings as well! To his adorable children I was no longer the beloved dear ol' Uncle CloudDancer. Now instead, I was the bad man who took Daddy away! Sheesh! It took me years to get past that one, but nine weeks after he left ... my buddy returns home to a "McArthur Retakes the Phillipines" WELCOME! Complete with 8MM home video footage! He was smart enough to stay gone 'til they remembered why they liked him!

Okay. Accommodations (at a good buddy bargain rate) in the spare bedroom came along with a rather clear and unambiguous set of rules provided by you-know-who. Much to my dismay rule number one was NO DRINKING! Inasmuch as I didn't have any money however, that wasn't an immediate obstacle. But I must now set about finding employment.

I short order, only a day or two, I had secured a job literally across the street at one of our town's few dry goods outlet. The store sold everything from trinkets and charm bracelets to a complete line of home furnishings and clothing for all shapes and sizes of both sexes. (Back when there WERE only two sexes.) Like my new landlord(s) the families who jointly owned this operation were friends. Their children had ridden with me across vast distances as passengers when traveling to school basketball tournaments and such. Also two of the owners were instrument rated private pilots themselves.

They were most understanding of my mental "state of affairs" and had the good grace to refrain from any embarrassing questions whilst still making it clear that if I ever needed to talk they were there. Incredibly kind and fun to work with, they set about teaching me all that there was to learn about the retail and dry goods business. Shipping, receiving and storage. Pricing and markup percentages. Inventories and display techniques. Fascinating stuff actually but not long in becoming routine and boring.

And then came the first two full-time paychecks. Holy Mother Theresa Batman! I put in 40 hours for that! Wow! I guess I forgot that $8.50 per hour instead of forty-five dollars per hour would have a large impact on the numbers to the left of the decimal. I quickly determined that I would be lucky if I could save up for one trip a year to Anchorage since I also no longer had access to reduced-rate "interline" travel discounts. I figured that my entire monthly "take home" pay from this job would be eaten up by the rent and food bills leaving little to spare for any "lifestyle". And I couldn't ask my new bosses for more as I knew they had paid me the highest prevailing wage they could just to start me.

Nothing to do but find another job to go along with this one, I guess. And fortunately for me, I heard that a job with which I had a close past relationship had opened up. The night shift bartender at the Ponderosa had just been fired. Oh boy! After a brief meeting with the owner I was hired on a probationary basis. I would work nights after my day job ended. For the next few months (as it turned out) I worked Monday thru Friday 8 A.M. thru 5 P.M. at the dry goods store. Across the street for a three hour nap before dinner and reporting for my 9:30 P.M. to 5:30 A.M. bartending shift followed by another 90 minute nap. Saturdays and Sundays were devoted to catching up on sleep during the day. The bar shift however went on ceaselessly.

I quickly learned the trade and established a reputation with both the bar owner and the clientele as a reliable and well-skilled efficient barkeep, much as I had the same reputation in my former field. The owner was very pleased that I chose to skim the customers of THEIR extra cash through "games of chance" to supplement my hourly pay rather than skimming his till as so many former employees were oft likely to do. In pre-computer days there were countless ways to rip off a bar owner. And the customers always appreciated my offer to "Flip ya' double or nothing for your order".

Starting with a 20 dollar bill every night, I'd flip for a single drink at a time. Sometimes losing my stash but four or five out of every seven nights I'd pocket a wad! As my bankroll got bigger I would flip for progressively larger and larger tabs. Many were the nights I walkedg out with an extra two or three hundred in cash. The trick was, as I had learned from reading about a study conducted by the prestigious Massachusetts Institute of Technology mathematics department, (funded no doubt by our tax $$) people have an aversion to calling "tails" on a coin toss.

The M.I.T. researchers had 1,000 people call 1,000 coin tosses each over a period of one week. That's one million coin tosses. Slightly over eighty-five percent (85%) of the time they called heads. And you and I know it can only be heads on an average of 50% of the time. The M.I.T. researchers were at a loss to explain this phenomenon until they played a little "word association" game. Their conclusion? People most frequently called "heads" dues to a deep-seated mental aversion to the negative connotations associated with "tail" such as ass. Apparently, this word "tail" could provoke thoughts of … um … alternate entry sex! Who'da thunk it! Over 85% of the world is PREVERTS! Ha! Whatever. Armed with this tidbit of knowledge and an ever-present ready to toss quarter … I made thousands! Tax free!

Also in a state where drinking is regarded as an Olympic Sport, I discovered that having a bartender for a boyfriend/playmate ranks not too far behind having a bush pilot for a boyfriend. Hence, many of my "trap line" still felt that a short term or other um … relationship with me had it's … uh … benefits! Further, as the only sober male in the entire room, I was able to watch as my competitors invested their monies and time for hours before admitting defeat and moving on. This would leave me many times with one or more of the girls competing for my attentions at closing time had I not already zeroed in on a "target".

Okay. I know (now) that such talk and behavior is reprehensible. And I herewith offer my apologies to all who might be offended. (The fact that I am now old, fat, getting grey and have little to no hope of "closing the deal" these days in no way mitigates the sincerity of or blanket-amnesty forgiveness expected as a result of this apology.) But hey … I digress.

The bar owner was also a private pilot and very interested in flying. A bit of a "peacock" in his own right he had nailed me from the get-go about my "career change" wanting to know what had happened. What caused it. And basically intimating in couched terms that I was somewhat of a PUSS if I can't get back on a bronco that's bucked me off. However, I let his comments slide. Other than that little "rub", we were becoming pretty good friends and he was giving me more and more responsibility and latitude to run the bar as our mutual trust grew. There were other comments however. Ones in particular that wasn't so easy to ignore.

2

He USED to be a PILOT

Well after a couple of months, I was into a pretty good routine. Oh, I was tired alot. But Friday and Saturday nights became my ... um ... "sleepover" nights mostly with the added benefits of me getting out from under the "no drinking" rule and out of my friend's hair for a couple of days a week so they could have some resemblance of privacy again in their lives even if only for 48 hours at most. And my income was back up to three-quarters of my flying days, mostly thanks to the fine folks at the M.I.T. math department. And of course, between the two jobs I was learning truly a wealth of knowledge that would serve me well throughout the remainder of my years.

Along with spring "breakup" came the annual influx of new faces to boost Kotzebue's population of 2700 or so souls. The migration of skilled construction workers to supplement the local workforce for the intense and short building season; the fish buyers, and of course the yearly flow of Lower 48 tourists commences every year starting May 15th. Unlike winter, no one was surprised to see someone they didn't know in any commercial establishment for four months or so. New faces, as well as some summer "regulars" would appear in both the dry goods store and the bar. Shop for souvenirs and have a drink.

Some of the summer regulars, construction workers and fish buyers with whom before I was likely to be drinking when not flying, were now being served by me. It was easier to ... well ... I guess the word is lie, isn't it. I'd just tell them that I "needed a break" from flying for a little while. Although I probably knew then that they would eventually hear the story. But most just let a sleeping dog lie, as I obviously had not wanted to talk about it. In addition of course the bar was always crowded with people from the entire Kobuk valley. Almost all of these people had been not just my passengers, but my real friends (and in some cases, lovers) for over eight years now.

You never knew who would sit next to who so of course it came to pass that someone brand new in town came to be seated next to a couple of villagers in the

211

bar. Not knowing my name of course he turned to one of my former passengers to ask my name. Like I had just learned in recent months, knowing the bartender's name, and calling it out rather than "Hey barkeep" or whistling (you whistle at a DOG bub!) or (never do this) banging your glass or an ashtray on the counter, is a much preferred way to get attention and good service. I had my back turned and did not hear the stranger ask the question. I was bending down to retrieve the 300th can of Oly beer from the cooler that night when I heard a voice behind me state in a loud and slurred voice … "Oh! CloudDancer! You don't know CLOUDDancer?! He USED to be a pilot!"

Wow! I USED to be a pilot. Damn. THAT left a sour taste in my mouth as I said it quietly back to myself. The second time I heard it a couple of weeks later was almost like the first. Still didn't taste any better. But it was the third time that did it.

3

A Day about ... NOTHING

By the end of August my "self-grounding" had lasted over five months. Probably the longest I'd ever been bound to Mother Earth since I was 15 years old. I was getting cranky and generally unpleasant to be around a lot of the time.

Trips to the airport during the day for the dry goods store were actually becoming painful. The occasional smell of burnt Jet-A as the Weinie bird taxied in or out. Maybe it was accompanied by the deep, bellowing growl of a Pratt & Whitney radial dragging ol' Bart Mason's red and white single engine deHavilland Otter into the 24 hour sunlit skies. Or I'd wind up stopping in mid-hoist on some packing crate, to try and catch a glimpse of a landing 185 or 206 that I had flown in my previous life. Of course, this resulted in the guy on the other end cussing at me and telling me to pay attention to what I was supposed to be doing!

The nights at the bar weren't much better given that all the local "drivers", some of whom I'd trained initially, now regarded me primarily as their booze or beer "gofer". "Yo, CloudDancer! Gettin' purdy DRY down on this end, ya' know!" And while almost all of them were decent if not outright very kind to me ... every now and then ... would come the thin little razor cut comment. "Hey. You remember that little strip into Utica Creek ..." or "Point Hope wuz a foggy bitch today ..." And then they'd let me listen in as they told the pilot on the barstool next to them about the day's adventure. And as someone would holler from across the bar for another Olympia and I was turning away would come the razor cut. "We-e-ell at least ya' don't have to worry about bustin' YER' sorry ol' ass everyday, eh, Cloudy?"

It wasn't hardly ever spoken with meanness or contempt. Just as a sort of closing comment. I mean, after all. Other than wrasslin' the often overly drunk patrons and minor cuts on my hand or finger from fishing the occasional broken glass out of the ice bin, I guess it's fair to say I wasn't too often exposed to any element of danger. Nor were my formerly quick wits and lightning reflexes put to much use. In general, I was becoming pretty DISsatisfied with the direction my

213

life was going. And I was thinking more and more. Wondering if and when I would ever get back on the horse that bucked me off. I was having a hard time visualizing myself doing this for much longer. And then came the day.

The Sunday morning trade was slow in the bar. It was about 11 A.M. when a group of four tourists came through the open front door doubling the size of the crowd. After a brief pause just inside the door to gawk at a couple who, by all rights, really should've been "getting a ROOM already", they strode over quickly to the far end of the bar. I guessed that their seat selection was based mostly on my ongoing debate with one very drunk and somewhat loud Vincent Tooliak at the other (and closer) end of the bar.

I'd flown Vincent down and back from his home in Noatak many, many times over the years. Drunk and sober both. And although sober was easier, at least he'd always been one of the GOOD drunk passengers when going home. Always mellow and co-operative. Totally UNlike today. Vincent was belligerent and wanted to fight today. Hell, for the last three days.

Seems he'd come home early from a hunting trip upriver due to mechanical problems with his outboard. Finding the love of his life giving HER love to Vincent's 1st cousin had sent him in a rage back out the door after demolishing the interior of his cabin . Noticing a 207 roaring across the top of town Vincent headed to the village's airstrip. And upon arriving in Kotzebue he proceeded straight to the town's one bank from which he withdrew a substantial amount of cash.

For the last seventy-two hours or so Vincent had bounced back and forth between the town's two bars, the beer and wine joint on Front Street and the hotel. Now, even the town's half-a-dozen cab drivers had had enough. Having agreed finally to "go take a nap" (somewhere OTHER than on the end of my bar please....) I was now unable to get any one of the town's three working cab drivers to come and pick Vincent up. Lord it was going to be a long day.

Disgustedly, I turned away from Vincent's angry and mostly unintelligible ranting about his love life. My sympathy had been just about completely exhausted yesterday at this time whilst listening to the story for the tenth or twelfth time already. With no little effort I tried to plaster a welcoming smile on my face and greet my new customers with some amount of genuine warmth and hospitality.

Being from New York City they appeared to be somewhat flummoxed that there was no "Bill of Fare" posted anywhere and asked me as they settled on stools if I had a WINE LIST! This was done with the straightest face I'd ever seen and I could only assume the lady was serious. So, with all the patience I had left (my well WUZ starting to run a little dry about now) I explained that wine was available by the bottle in the liquor store next door, but we did not serve wine by the glass here in the Ponderosa. We are somewhat of a more "blue collar plebeian bar" I think I replied (admittedly slightly condescendingly). Meanwhile Vincent continued loudly, head now hanging low over his folded arms on the bar. He was still alternately swearing vengeance upon, and then sobbing out his undying love for his wife with every other sentence. Add in the barely, but still audible over the juke box, slurping noises and moaning produced while the couple in the corner booth engaged in everything but the actual ACT; and the setting for an explosion was complete. All it needed was a match to be put to the fuse.

As the owner comes into the side door of the bar from the attached liquor store the four New Yorkers now conference in a scene that would have been perfect for Elaine, George, Kramer and Jerry, had Seinfeld only existed in those days. The owner was a tough and demanding boss, but was also my friend. Although ANY friendship with this man was somewhat reserved at best and had clearly defined boundaries. He had been by 30 minutes earlier and had told Vincent to leave and was now coming back to check on things yet again. The cast of the future T.V. hit meanwhile have racked their brains for what might be considered "appropriate" 11A.M. to noon beverages and begin to throw out their orders to me. After the first guy (who I thought was being funny trying to ease my obvious frustration) ordered a extremely dri-i-i-y martini shaken, with TWO olives please ... his girlfriend says as daring as it IS before noon ... she'll just have a Manhattan! Well ... flic mah' BIC!

Loudly, and barely controlling my temper, in my most condescending and expletive laden voice I interrupt. I invite the four of them to look around again and re-examine their surroundings as quite possibly they have mistaken this place for STUDIO 54! I don't have olives and Manhattan is an island as far as I know. I point out that we have a FINE selection of damn near a half dozen varieties of canned beers and for fancy drinkers I'll be happy to whip up a rum 'n coke or a screwin'driver usin' the good stuff. But if it involves more than two common ingredients (not counting ice) they shall have to wait 'til they get to a bigger village ... like Anchorage ... where they HAVE yuppie bars!

Now the boss and Vincent have gone silent at the onset of my outburst. And the biggest of the New Yorkers musters all his righteous indignation and responds loudly "Just WHAT the hell kind of bartender are you?!" And before I can open my mouth Vincent hollers down from the other end of the bar "He's not a REAL bartender. He's a pilot! At least ... he USED to be a pilot! MY pilot!" Hmmph. From the mouths of (drunken) babes.

4

An Offer I Can't Refuse

Thirty minutes later the bar is for the moment empty. Vincent has been taken to the hotel to sleep it off yet again. The boss called the owner of the cab company and convinced him it would be in his and his driver's best interests to transport Vincent. Elsewise if we couldn't rely on his company we'd have to start one of our own tomorrow. Given that my boss wasn't known to make idle threats a cab arrived within 90 seconds of the conversation's end. Likewise the two lovers in the corner both were "encouraged" to find more secluded surroundings to continue pursuing their passions. Their rate of beer consumption (revenue) was no longer deemed to be suitable for us to ignore their increasingly brazen exhibition.

The boss comes back in and sits on the end of the bar. He and I both drink coffee at the rate of two or more gallons a day so I pour him and I a fresh cup. And then, as he has so often in the past, he floors me with a one word statement out of the blue. This time it was "Find out where Hood River, Oregon is and figure out how soon you can get there if you catch the morning Wein jet tomorrow." Equally as deadpan I return with "And why would I be wanting to go to Hood River, Oregon tomorrow, if I might ask." Brantley (the boss) responds with "I'm buying a plane down there." With a little too much enthusiasm I come back with "Whoa! Al-l-lright! Whatcha' gettin'?" He tells me "A cub." "You're gettin' a SuperCub?! How many horses?"

He then explains he's got his eye on a straight Cub. A-80-8 65h.p. Continental engine and no electrical system. About as basic as it gets. Wrapped up in his detailed description about how he found it (Trade-a-Plane) and his phone conversations with the owner, it takes me a few minutes to get to the obvious question. He's buying the plane. He's a private pilot. What am I going to go there for, to inspect it first? Brantley then tells me it's all but a done deal, but he wants me, with my far greater experience with small aircraft to go inspect it. Buy it if it's good and then FLY IT HOME!

Whoops! Did you say FLY the damn thing back here from Hood River Oregon! "In case you hadn't noticed my friend ... I recently gave UP flying" I reminded him.

In essence my friend/employer Brantley had decided FOR me that it was time for me to get back on the bronc that had throwed me. He knew (I guess) better than I, that the time was right. If it wasn't done soon I might truly never be able to overcome my apprehensions. He wanted to buy a plane anyway and had been thinking about it. He was interested in becoming a more accomplished and capable pilot, even to the point of getting his instrument rating.

As a very low-time private pilot only at this point, he felt the Cub would be a good time builder and could maybe well be modified in the future to be more capable. In the meantime, buying it would enable him to force me back in the air where he was fairly sure I belonged. It wasn't the first time he had pushed me in a direction he had foreseen I needed to go, nor would it be the last. He was usually right too, which made him even that much more irritating to me from time to time.

Nonetheless I continued feeble arguments. What about my other job. Oh. He had already talked to the store owners (also pilots, remember?) and they thought it was a great idea so they would grant me the time off until I got back. Well ... I allow as how I'm still not too sure about my flying again. Brantley then tells me if I wish to remain in his employ, this was the deal. The money was XXX dollars a day cash, plus expenses, 'til I rolled back into town with his new toy. Still, I told him ... and I WAS ... genuinely unsure.

"Okay ..." he sez, and I watch the wheels turning in his head. "How about I let you take Selena along?" "Say what!" I respond incredulously. Now, knowing he's finally hooked me, he reels me in with "Yeah. Okay! I'll let you take Selena along and pay her ticket and expenses too and you go!" Damn! "No WAY I can turn that down. You got a deal!" Be on the plane in the morning was all he said to close the deal.

Think of the greatest torrid and tempestuous love affairs of history. Tony and Cleo, Liz and Dick, Ike and Tina ... then there was CloudDancer and Selena! Selena was ... a BABE. Our first meeting set the stage for the entire relationship for life. Seeing her walk into the room unexpectedly our eyes met and the earth moved. Va-VA-VOOOM! At that precise moment I knew this female was going to be among the most significant in my life. Immediately out of my mouth sprang a typical sway-vee and de-boner CloudDancer "line". These usually guarantee to overwhelm and smitten any female within hearing distance. Rather than the expected blush and swooning in response, I was told I'd stand a far better chance of performing an act I assumed was anatomically impossible. E-E-E-YOUCH!! I do admire a girl with some sass. But this girl was so-o-o fine I couldn't see nuthin'. Including the freight train that was about to run me down.

For the last four years … our relationship had been … well it alternated back and forth between a Kotzebue version of "I Love Lucy" and a fire in a munitions factory. I often described it as an amusement park carousel. Where you just go round and round … and round … and the horses they go up 'n down 'n up 'n down but never together side by side. If one's UP the other is DOWN!

Selena and CloudDancer. Boy. Did we define a love-hate relationship!

5

On Converting Kerosene to NOISE!

At this point in time it so happened that darling Selena was earning her monies cocktail waitressing at the Ponderosa as well, and was in fact due to report ro work in a couple of hours.

After making a couple of phone calls I rounded up a replacement for her and called with the exciting news. As most Kotzebue residents seldom venture beyond Fairbanks or Anchorage she was as thrilled as I was to be going to a big city "outside". Immediately she began babbling gaily about all the many things we would do (spending MY money, of course).

I interrupted her litany of sight-seeing and touristy plans to inform her that I was going for work and that she was being allowed to accompany me as an incentive. This was NOT to be viewed as an "all expenses paid free vacation". However, I did admit that we could take most likely one day in the Pacific Northwest to do touristy stuff. With her enthusiasm only slightly dampened she then began listing all the various STUFFS she would have to take. Again I had to break in to remind her of the primary purpose of this trip, and caution her to keep packing to a minimum. (Try getting that thought across to any female.) I told her whatever went south in the belly of the bg Wein jet would have to return north in the small baggage compartment of a J-3 Cub. Not to mention anything that was purchased down south.

There was a day's delay, during which Brantley and the Cub's owner haggled just a bit more over the price. I remained somewhat ambivalent while Selena chewed her nails to the quick in nervous tension that this "free trip" might slip away. But finally the next morning Selena and I climbed the rear integral folding airstairs and entered the aft end of the Wein 737-200 bound for our first stop in Anchorage. Without the slightest apprehension, from my middle seat next to her window spot, I relaxed as the familiar sounds and feelings of an airplane readying for flight surrounded me for the first time in months.

Seated on the right side just aft of the wings I clearly hear the "thunk" of the heavy plug type aft cargo door when the ramper pulls it off it's uplock and it falls snugly into position for locking. The vibration transmitted through the airframe to the soles of my boots has barely been felt when I hear the much quieter sounds of the internal mechanisms controlling the locking pins. They move into position as the handle is rotated with a muffled mechanical sound. Then there is the final "tink" as the spring loaded external access handle is retracted flush with the outer skin.

Instantly from the left side I hear the Pratt & Whitney JT8-D winding up. Less than a minute later, and much louder, the deep whine starts outside our window. It takes but a few brief seconds to accelerate the turbine wheels. I visualize in my mind the Captain's pointer finger hooked under the fuel control lever sitting at idle/cutoff. The magic number comes up on the N1 and N2 gauges and a quick upward motion by that one finger frees the fuel to flow to the combustion chamber where two huge spark plugs are doin' what they're made for. This is immediately confirmed by the resounding "THUD" of what initially is a minor explosion that grows into a spreading rage of combustion and fire. Along with the climbing musical whining tone of the engine accelerating, the combustion peaks and settles to a steady fiery stream. The aft end of the engine now pouring out hot air and noise.

A quick after start and taxi checklist are accomplished and, what with the terminal being at the departure end of the runway, we are poised just short of the runway in another two minutes. We await the landing of one of the local "bush" planes before we claim the asphalt for our takeoff roll. Ninety seconds later, having taxied practically off the damn west end of the runway to complete our turn to the east and still use every inch of runway, we sit astraddle the centerline motionless momentarily. The engines are accelerated to about 20 % thrust and allowed to stabilize before being shoved to max power for takeoff.

In the cabin the thunder from the turbojet's exhaust, no more than 15 feet from where I sit, is deafening. The vibration caused by the niagra of thrust pouring forth from the exhausts of the now SCREAMING two turbojets travels all through the airframe. It goes through the floor to the seat frames, and from there through the seats and into your butt until your inner organs can FEEL vibrations! The pavement rushes by faster and faster as I (with no jet experience) try to guess the moment of rotation. Once again I miss by at least four seconds (early).

The east end of the runway sweeps by a good six hundred feet below us as the gear "clunks" it's way into the wells, barely audible over the continued din which is now complimented by some of the inner passenger window panels vibrating in rhythm with the airframe. And then suddenly, as always, the nose pitches down somewhat and the roar of the engines lessens slightly. In a couple of decades I would come to know this as "acceleration height". And as we accelerate to a faster climb speed it again gets somewhat quieter as it now becomes harder for all the noise to "keep up with the plane". My senses are alive. I am excited! This calls for a celebration! I need a drink! Now, where is that flight attendant call button?

6

Coming to America

A brief two hour layover at Anchorage International before boarding our Western Airlines 727 flight to Portland allowed for the continued consumption of adult beverages. We chatted with friends from Kotzebue awaiting their flight north. Their envy of our great fortune was obvious and we tried to appear non-gloating, while Brantley's "expense" money disappeared at the rate of $10 (including tip) per round for the two of us. I do remember being outraged that a Bacardi and Coke ($4.75) and a Budweiser ($3.50) were priced HIGHER than at our bars in Kotzebue. And this was in 1981! But Alaska was still flowing with oil pipeline money ... and prices!

Fortunately for our trips sponsor, we were delighted to find drinks far more reasonably priced once on board the flight to Portland. At $2.50 apiece or five bucks a round with no tip allowed or required it was indeed a bargain! Selena and I worked our way through another forty bucks before the airborne "last call".

Given Selena's propensity for the outrageous occasionally; of course, I had hoped that this would be an opportunity for us to join the SIX Mile High Club. Much to my surprise (not to mention frustration) she failed to share my enthusiasm for that proposal. Worse yet, under some newly erupted outbreak of apparent prudishness, she informed me that my alternative proposal to "just mess around a little bit in our seats under the blankets", marked me as some kind of "sex maniac". Well ... harrumph! Like that's a ... BAD thing! "Oh stewardess! Two more, please!"

Giggling and stumbling out the forward exit of the trusty Boeing three-holer we bade our Western hostesses a warm good-bye and thank you. Despite their best attempts at maintaining the Stewardess Academy practiced smiles and good-bye waves I couldn't help but notice the barely disguised sighs of relief as we passed, along with a clear failure to invite us to "Come back and Fly with us again." No sweat. I got my own way home.

Much to my surprise our arrival at the Hertz counter was NOT like it shows in the T.V. commercials. Nobody was smiling at us. In fact, they refused to honor our reservation. And I had a confirmation number and everything! This apparently was overridden however by some corporate policy that dictated no car be rented to someone who appears to be "under the influence" of alcohol. I did explain that I understood that clearly and in fact I thought it was a good policy. Further, that they should have no concern as Selena (now taking a brief nap on the counter) would not be driving only ... (bu-u-u-urp hic!) Me!

At this point a Supervisor came forth from behind the counter to encourage me to stay overnight at one of the airport hotels and return in the morning. He would be happy to hold my reservation overnight without charge. Otherwise ... and he nodded behind my left shoulder. The nice policeman standing ten yards or so away leaning against the wall returned my smile with a rather curt nod. This is why some people are supervisors. They are GOOD at addressing customers problems with innovative solutions. And they know how to tell you how to get to the hotel shuttle locale.

Twenty minutes later Selena and I are checking into a nearby Holiday Inn. The distant sounds of disco music waft down a wide hall into the lobby and Selena leaves me to go find the source. Rushing back excitedly as I am concluding the room transaction she informs me that there is a live band in the lounge and we have to go upstairs to our room! Hurry! Hurry! We must change quickly and go drink and DANCE!. A live band is an extreme rarity in Kotzebue, generally only appearing once a year on New Year's Eve at the Lion's Club dance. This is of course the social event of the year in Kotzebue.

Well, two things I know. If I have any hope of engaging in sex tonight with anyone other than myself, the path to fulfillment leads through the hotel lounge. If I don't go she'll go without me and this is NOT an option. Should additional alcohol consumption and dancing "do the trick" (i.e. get her in "the mood") it would be prudent if I were nearby at the moment. Being from Alaska, one thing I know is there ain't enough good lookin' womens to go around. It is ALWAYS a good idea to keep close tabs. There is always a "claim jumper" around somewheres who'll be only too happy to take advantage of the slightest (even perceived on the girl's part) lack of attentiveness in her eyes.

The oh-eight-thirty wake-up call from the front desk just a few hours later seems to literally impact my ear drum. My hand shoots quickly out from under the covers and bounces once, twice, three times at the end of my up and down flailing arm. I blindly (my eyes are closed in pain) feel my wrist collide with what feels like a glass, knocking it off the nightstand before my right hand smacks down on one end of the phone receiver. As if the cradle were a fulcrum the receiver is launched enthusiastically upward where it collides with the lampshade and gravity takes over bringing it down on top of (eyes open now … barely) the edge of the furniture from whence it falls off. It disappears going downward and falls out of my line of sight as it passes below mattress level. This is instantly followed by the sound of breaking (cheap) glass indicating the final and complete resting stop of the receiver. I pull my head sideways off the bed to get a look. The receiver lays on it's side amidst broken glass shards and about a good 8 inch circular area of the cheap shag carpet now soaked in stale Bacardi 'n Coke.

Through the jungle of green and aqua and blue carpet fibers I can hear, as if far far away, a perky female recorded voice is inviting me to sample "our every day fresh twenty-two item breakfast buffet". Oh … GOD.

In an instant my brain spools up as I remember where I am and that I am on a mission. I have a one P.M. meeting with a Mr. Jeremy Rogers in Hood River, Oregon.… (Pause.) CAR! Dammit! I still have to go get a car too! Okay. I find my watch and see it is seven-thirty in the morning! No. Wait. I'm in Portland. Did I reset my watch? What the hell time IS it? What time did I leave a wake-up call for? Carefully I reach down and extract the phone receiver from the mess on the floor. I eyeball it closely through one squinted eye to assure there are no glass shards present before wiping it back and forth a few times on the bedsheet to sorta' dry it off.

I dial "zero" and wait it seems forever for an answer. Must've been a good ninety seconds. After ascertaining the correct time (eight-thirty) I ask the nice perky girl on the phone (could this be the same one from the wake-up recording?) if she knows how long it takes to drive to Hood River, Oregon. She said "I'm not sure. Do you know how far away it is?" I thanked her politely and said goodbye. Still grasping the phone in my left hand, I reach behind me under the covers and grab Selena firmly by the uppermost (she's sleeping on her side) naked (did we HAVE sex?) buttcheek. She is snoring and I shake her gently at first and then continually harder until the snoring stops.

As I'm doing this I move my left hand (holding the phone receiver) over the cradle and release my grip. The receiver remains firmly pasted to my open left palm by the now dried sticky Coke.

I shake my left hand gently while still shaking Selena even more insistently. Her snoring has stopped and been replaced by a moaning that sounds eerily reminiscent of some werewolf movie soundtrack. As the phone receiver finally separates from my left hand, Selena's moaning abruptly ceases. See, she's not really much of a morning person. Sober or hung over. I feel her left hand grasping mine and her nails grip the outside of my right hand brutally. JEEEEZUS! "What the ..." As she throws it as hard as she can off her body she offers her morning greeting. "KEEP your ****ing hands OFF me you son-of-a-bitch!"

Okay. I'm guessing there was no sex last nite. I sit up carefully in bed watching the placement of my feet to ensure I don't lacerate the bottom of either one. My head hurts. I think my eyelashes are actually THROBBING. Is that even possible? I have four and a half hours to rouse my "sleeping beauty" (without getting hurt in the process) and get some desperately needed breakfast. Then I need to rent a car. Figure out where the hell other than "east of here" Hood River Oregon actually is, and then find the house of one Mister Jeremy Rogers. I shake my head a little to clear it. Bad idea. I rise slowly and carefully to my feet noting that I have a morning woodie. Briefly I toy with the idea of sliding back under the covers and trying to awaken Selena by poking her in a different manner. Still not to clear on the events of the latter part of the evening, and given the ferocity of her morning greeting (two small droplets of blood are leaking out of the top of my right hand) I choose to retreat to the bathroom. I turn the shower on full cold.

7

A Place For Everything

Three hours later (the majority of which was spent motivating Selena to face the day) I am cruising eastward on I-84 in my rented Chrysler LeBaron. What. You think I'd rent a Chevy Geo on somebody else's tab?

After enduring the 20 minute long ordeal of first rousting my traveling companion I then suffered through the agonizingly drawn out period required for her to "get ready" (1:10). The productive portion of the day started off with a great breakfast at Elmers. Following that I dropped Selena (who had absolutely NO interest in airplanes) at the largest closeby shopping mall. My initial offer of two hundred dollars to "shop with" was met by a lukewarm and tepid response, with no indication of even a forthcoming kiss. I immediately kicked in another C-note. After all, I still had hopes that we might overcome last night's disagreement (whatever it might have been) and resume our normal "can't keep our hands OFF each other" relationship sometime soon. Very soon. That produced a nice smile, a kiss (no tongue though), and a caution to drive carefully.

Now with the cruise control set, and my seat slightly reclined, I gaze to the left and enjoy the view of beauty and splendor that is the Columbia Gorge. Once east (upwind) of Camas, Wa. I leave the putrid smell of the papermill behind. Now a sweet scent of clean air roars through the cabin of the LeBaron as I choose 4-60 fresh air conditioning over the manufactured breeze of the car's system. And for the first time in many months I cast my gaze upward with a real genuine interest.

The sky cover is scattered to broken at what I guess to be three to four thousand feet above the ground. I feel my airman senses trying to awaken. What are the trees beside the road saying about the winds close to the ground. I try to judge the movement of a cloud nearby the sun to compare to what the trees are telling me. There is the possibility I may actually fly a plane again today. Am I UP to it?

The miles roll by effortlessly under the big Chrysler's chassis and I revel in the feel of being in command of the big machine on such a pleasant stretch of road. The feeling is a surreal and mostly unattainable one where I come from. If you added all the gravel "roads" end to end in Kotzebue, including the one out to the old Air Force site, they might total ten miles. I doubt it. The only chance to experience such a feeling in Kotzebue would be to take a new car straight off the airplane from Anchorage. And for about 15 seconds after reaching 65 miles per hour you could set the cruise control and enjoy the ride. It would then be necessary to quickly apply the brakes so as not to run off the other end … of the RUNWAY! I know. We've been known to do it many a time in both our cars and with our dirt bikes in days gone by.

Bridal Veil passes by and then the town of Dodson. A cautious "position check" on the Texaco map and I come to a quick agreement with the sign ahead to the right. Hood River—25 miles.

I will be well early. My plan. In the days before "MapQuest" and Google Earth I always allowed extra time to "temporarily misplace myself". This, even though Mr. Rogers had supplied me with explicit and very clear directions to his house, which I had copied as carefully as any airborne clearance. We (Jeremy and I) had engaged in a most enjoyable "get acquainted" conversation over the phone earlier whilst my darling had conducted her morning rituals.

Jeremy's accurate directions brought me a couple of miles south of I-84 and directly to a mailbox marked "Rogers" at the end on a long gravel drive where I stopped and consulted my watch to find I was 20 minutes early. A glance up the long and curved gravel drive revealed just a glimpse of the corner of one building that appeared from this distance (about 200 yards) to be a house.

Not wishing to be too early I decided to cruise a little down the road and drink in the rare and enjoyable wooded scenery. I let the car idle along at six or seven miles an hour and looked ahead where the redwood pole fence bordering his property seemed to stretch for miles ahead into the distance. Brief partial flashes of buildings, a tractor and a couple of horses peep in and out of view for the first 100 yards or so. Then it seemed that a cleared area was just thirty or forty yards on the other side of the trees for quite some time.

The odometer said I'd rolled closed to three/tenths of a mile when a larger gap in the trees revealed a cleared area and … a windsock! I looked ahead and still the fence ran on at least as far as I had idled along so far. Wow! His own airstrip! This dude must be rice! The fence ended another 4/10th of a mile down the road. Ni-i-ice joint. Reversing course I idled back to the driveway to find my watch now reading about 11 'til the hour so I turned in. I figured if I hit the front porch at nine 'til that would be pretty respectable.

The slam of my car door must have been heard inside for before I could cover the ten yards to the front door of the sprawling ranch house the screen door opened. A nice stoutly built fella' emerged with a welcoming smile and said 'Mr. CloudDancer, I presume" sticking out a right hand in friendly greeting. "Jus' call me Cloudy" was my reply as I stuck my hand into a calloused and working man's firm grip. I liked his handshake. Firm with a look straight in my eye and a smile in his. Refusing his offer of lunch leftovers, I accepted a glass of homemade lemonade from his wife as we sat for a few minutes inside his cavernous living room making our acquaintance. I explained my relationship with Brantley and how I'd come to be here while omitting the details of what had led to my flying hiatus. And Jeremy told me a little bit about himself and the history of the J-3.

Seems Mr. Rogers, among a few other business interests, operated an aerial photography service. The J-3 had been the initial platform for his photographic missions but had since been replaced by a Cessna 185. What with the J-3 not getting the use needed to pay it's own way anymore it was deemed to be "surplus" so to speak. It was apparent from the way he spoke of it that he truly loved it and was going to miss it. He loved to fly, and there was no purer flight than in the J-3. But I could tell Jeremy Rogers was also a practical sort who insisted that things be useful as well.

Fifteen minutes into the conversation, wherein I'm quite sure he was evaluating ME as well, he extended the invitation. "Well, whaddaya' think? Shall we go have a look a 'er?" I took a last sip from my lemonade and jumped up excitedly. "You BET!"

Heading out the back kitchen door revealed a view of two buildings. A separate two car garage and a much larger structure, obviously a hangar. We walked the ten intervening yards or a dirt and gravel pathway. Stopping on the concrete pad outside the entry door, as he wiped his feet, he turned to me and said "'Preciate you doin' the same if you don't mind. I try to keep it neat in here." And as he swung the white aluminum sided door inward and stepped in I looked down to do same.

Then I looked up as I stepped inside. Whoa. At probably thirty by fifty and a good ten feet tall inside, this was SOME spread. Sunlight streaming through the many windows reflected off a gleaming dull very light grey concrete hangar floor. It was immaculate. There wasn't even an OIL stain that I could see. Coiled yellow electric extension cords hung in formation on pegboards along with air hose lines and garden hoses. On another wall hung tools, equally symmetrically placed. A place for everything and everything in it's place. Only the wooden work tables under the tool pegboards showed signs of actual use. Everything else was pristine.

Including the two airplanes in the center of the arena.

8

Back in the Saddle ... Almost

A J-3 and a 185. Does life GET any better? The two air machines sat tail by tail. Both were at first glance spotless, "And I'll be close to flawless, as well" I think to myself. Obviously this Rogers fella' has the dough. Obviously he has attention to detail. I expect I am going to be impressed with a closer inspection as well.

Jeremy walks over to the nose of the J-3 and pulls the two copper cotter keys holding the cowling bottom secure and gently and gingerly opens the left side of the cowling. "Come have a close looks at 'er" he invites. Ten minutes later I have poked and peered in every available orifice and portal of the airplane. There is not a spot of grease or grime anywhere. Not on the mag wiring. Not on the wheel assemblies. Not even on the floorboards in the airplane. They gleam in freshly painted glossy black paint. You can SEE yourself in the polished wooden propellor. As I lay under the tail of the airplane inspecting the underside of the tailfeathers I hear a metallic rattling sound begin and sunlight begins to pour in the hangar as Jeremy pushes first one then the second rolling hangar door to it's open limits.

He opines that I ought to hear the engine run to which I agree, hoping he'll offer more. And of course he does. Telling me he never runs his engines indoors we'll have to roll her out. And since we're gonna' go to all that trouble (as a slight smile begins to crease his weathered features) he continues with "after we listen to her run, since it's so nice and all today, maybe we should take her up." My grin goes ear to ear at this point, as I slowly and very gently resecure the open cowling.

Rolling the Cub out the hangar door gives me my first clear view of Jeremy's home airstrip. My guess of 3,000 feet was off by only 200 as the strip measured 2800 by 60 feet bordered on all sides by trees ranging as high as 30 feet. We brought the Cub to a halt alongside an old but gleaming green and yellow John Deere tractor with a towing mower latched onto it's rear. Jeremy said it was the one with which he had cleared the strip and uprooted the over 250 tree trunks necessary to provide the clearing.

Standing forward of the struts as he prepared to help me fold my 6' 3" frame into the front seat we both suddenly realized that we were still one control stick short of a full set of controls! Mr. Rogers, like so many other aerial photographers had removed the extra stick as a safety precaution long ago. Unfortunately after searching for 20 minutes or so, of all things, this was ONE item which seemed to be misplaced. And a somewhat chagrined Jeremy asked me if I still wanted to go up. I said yes immediately. I liked the man. My gut told me he knew what he was doing. But mostly, it was a perfect day, and I wanted to FLY again. Besides, if I was gonna' buy the thing I needed to see her put through her paces in some form or another.

Strapping in to the front seat, I manned the brakes and the mag switch and throttle. Jeremy had assured me however that I would not need to move it. With his left hand grasping the inner cockpit window frame he reached forward with his right hand and smoothly pulled downward on the propellor. Instantly the little Continental caught and burst into song. I watched the skinny black needle rise on the oil pressure gauge as Jeremy turned to me with a big grin saying "First time, EVERY time!"

I hunched forward as he climbed in the aft seat and secured himself. Feeling his feet join mine on the brakes I heard him say 'I got 'er' and slid my boot heels backwards off the small brake pedals. Jeremy let her idle for another two or three minutes, using the time to check the controls and get the door buttoned up. Like everything else on this airplane the door mechanism worked smoothly without any sign of friction or binding. A small burst of throttle and we pulled away from the buildings. The runup produced exactly the expected results and shortly we were lined up facing the far end of the strip.

The flight was … incredible. Thirty minutes flew by as if five. We opened the door and flew with the breeze for a while blasting into the plane. No surprise the engine purred like a Singer sewing machine. She was "equipped" with the bare essentials of flight. Just a needle-ball, an altimeter, vertical speed indicator, and oil pressure and temperature gauges peered back from the dark black face of the instrument panel two feet ahead of my face. A whiskey compass hung overhead. A visual "instrument sweep" was accomplished in one glance. Your eyes needn't hardly move to take them all in at once. Even with no control stick of my own I felt fully ALIVE for the first time in months. I marveled at the precision of Jeremy's flying as the sideslip on short final slowly and smoothly transitioned to straight as an arrow and perfectly level just as the wee black tires with their cub yellow "hub caps" again rolled onto the grass.

Spinning around he taxied back to the hangar slowly. Very slowly I thought. And I suspect he was thinking about his relationship with this inanimate object which he obviously loved, and how it may be coming to an end.

9

It's a Done Deal

We sat in silence for just a moment after the propellor ticked over the last compression stroke. Then as Jeremy reached for the door handle he broke the silence with "Well. What do you think of her Cloudy?" I replied with "I think I need to look at the logbooks and decide if we got ourselves a deal here." And he came back with "let's go get some more lemonade and some cookies then."

Over the kitchen table we sat perusing the biography of an old airplanes life. Faded ink written decades earlier right up to the last annual done three months ago. The last three logbooks unlike those previous that documented the plane's early life, were absolutely spotless. Not a smudge, fingerprint, nor one faint minuscule oil stain marred any page in the logbooks that Jeremy Rogers had kept. It was then that I learned that he was an A & P as well. Almost all the work except the annual signoffs were accompanied by his signature and license number. All in all I had never seen a more impressive (albeit simple) combo of airplane and logbook. I was sold. BUT! This was not my deal to make nor my money to spend.

Now Jeremy was selling this plane at a very fair price upon which he had finally come to agreement with Brantley. A VERY fair price. But my boss/friend Brantley does not trust hardly anybody. I won't debate whether I thought it was a character flaw of his or not. It was the way he was, and nothing I was going to say or do was going to change it. But, outside his blood family, I WAS one of an extremely small group of people in who he placed some degree of faith and trust based on long association. I asked Jeremy if I might have a private phone conversation and he led me into his den and indicated the phone on his desk with a "Help yourself. I'll be in the kitchen."

Brantley had been anxiously awaiting this call and was on the line within two seconds of his secretary saying "Oh Hi Cloudy!" at her desk four feet from his. Never one to waste words he says "O.K.Cat. What you got?" Upon hearing my full detailed report he then instructs me to make the deal contingent upon an inspection by a mechanic of our choice. He instructs me to go to a couple of nearby airports immediately and try to arrange an inspection for the following day. "Get back to me when it's set up" he says in closing as he hangs up the phone.

Jeremy seems troubled after I relay the information to him. The reason is immediately apparent. "I gotta' tell ya' Cloudy. I can respect his position and feelings. But here's MY dilemma." And Jeremy proceeds to tell me about a fella' in California who is prepared to fly up tonight to buy the airplane. He had tried to wire Jeremy his asking price PLUS an extra thousand bucks to lock up the deal sight unseen two days earlier as I was traveling down from Kotzebue. Jeremy, being apparently a man of his word, had concluded a contingent deal with Brantley. He would not dishonor his word even for an extra grand. But. He said he HAD told the California fella' if we didn't close a deal this afternoon that he (the California fella') could come get the airplane tonight. It was just a matter of a phone call.

Was this a "bargaining tactic"? I don't think so. The price was settled. My gut told me this was real. He seemed almost sad that he had to tell me that. Seems another phone call north was in order and I returned to Jeremy's den and again closed the door. I dreaded making this call. I had observed my friend and employer Brantley conduct many business deals for his various companies over the years. He's a tough, extremely tough negotiator and never likes it when "glitches" crop up unexpectedly. But I also know he really WANTS this airplane. I answer all his terse questions directly. "No. I don't think it's a tactic. I believe him." I say in response to the obvious question. And we go over every minute since my arrival at the Roger's house in detail again. Then Brantley asked me the most critical question he ever could. "What does your GUT tell you Cloudman" (He almost always called me Cloudman. That or "cat".)

I then told him about the QUALITY of all I'd seen. The order and neatness in everything I'd seen. An overall positive perception. I closed with "Brantley. I think you'd like the guy. He looks you in the eye, has a good handshake, and a hearty laugh. I think the man is honorable and there is a good deal to be had here." Then I reminded him that tomorrow was Labor Day and that I'd likely not be able to get any inspection for at least 48 hours. We could lose the deal.

With his full reliance based on my gut feelings he made his decision. "O.K. Make the deal. Call me and let me know when you're gonna' get out of there." Click. I returned to the kitchen with a grin on my face and said "O.K. Jer. Let's cut some paperwork here. It's a done deal! But I want another control stick too!" and Jeremy's face broke into a grin. He said "Wait a minute. I gotta' make a call first." He reached into the front pocket of his Pendleton shirt extracted a small notebook. Flipping it open he reached for the phone hanging on the wall and dialed as he read the number silently to himself. I listened as he told the man in California that there would be no use in coming. The plane had been sold. I walked out to the car to get the briefcase with the dough out of the trunk.

As we filled out the necessary paperwork Jeremy and I discussed my plans for heading north. Upon learning that I would have Selena and god knows HOW much STUFFS with me we concluded that departing off his strip might not be the smartest option. I hadn't flown a Cub since I was 14 (13 years ago). I hadn't flown a taildragger in three or four years. And I hadn't flown anything in over five months. I really need a "check-out" in this airplane with someone who knows it well.

We come up with a plan. Jeremy will find the other control stick and re-install it in the Cub. Either late today or early tomorrow he will move it over to the public field at The Dalles a little further east down I-84. And as he has long-laid plans with family for Labor Day we decide to meet early Tuesday morning at the airport where he will first check me out around the patch. Then after I shoot a few landings I can gas up, load up Selena (and god knows HOW much STUFFS) and depart for the Great Land. Well. You know what they say. The best laid plans …

10

RIDE That Bronc Cowboy!

We were up quite early to see the Tuesday morning dawn grey and rainy and windy in Portland. Not a good sign. Selena and I had both refrained from any alcohol consumption the previous 24 hours. For me, a precaution to ensure that my "flying senses" would not be compromised. And I had insisted she abstain until after at least her first ride in the Cub. Given that on a few occasions when she had accompanied me in a various assortment of airplanes over the years, the only time she got sick was after being out with me the night before. This resulted in no SMALL argument. She got no booze. You KNOW what I didn't get!

But we did have fun playing (sober) tourists on Monday, spending more of Brantley's "expense" money on good dining and souvenirs for our friends and a drive westward see the Pacific Ocean.

Upon arriving at The Dalles airport much of my apprehension had vanished along with half the cloud cover and almost all of the rain. Conditions gradually improved the further we put Portland behind us during the cab ride eastward. Unfortunately, so did the wind speed. By the time the cab driver had finished unloading us in front of the FBO where I was to meet Jeremy the wind had become the primary remaining concern. It was gusty out of the northeast. The kid behind the counter in the FBO said he'd seen the anemometer hit 28 knots at one point although the gusts seemed to regularly peak at 25 now and the steady breeze was down to 17 or 18 knots. Interesting enough had it been straight DOWN the runway, this wind was some 25 to 30 degrees off the runway center-line from the left. Not exactly the best conditions for an initial Cub checkout.

Jeremy showed up on the dot at seven A.M., and after making some small talk with Selena for a moment he looked at me and said decisively that he felt we should hang out for an hour or so in hope that the wind would continue to decrease in velocity as it had over the last couple of hours. Selena dug out some People, or US, or some such magazine (they're ALL "Twinkies for the Brain" in my opinion) and proceed to get lost in it as Jeremy and I had our first cup of airport coffee.

An hour later the only change had been in my bladder pressure. The Cub rocked gently (it seemed) it her tiedowns. I had pre-flighted the hell out of it. The wind speeds and directions had held steady although even more clouds had disappeared and there was no rain to be sen anywhere. After the fifth cup of coffee and the tenth personal visual inspection of the wind indicator by me I was getting antsy. The impatience of youth. Selena was no help either. For the last half hour she had been whining that she either wanted to "get this show on the road" or ... go SHOPPING somewhere closeby until I figure it out. It was at this point I began to despair of ever getting laid again. A lot of the small details of the following thirty or so minutes escape me. But those of you with light plane flying experience in and around the Columbia Gorge can see what's coming by now.

I honestly can't remember if I did the run-up in the tie-down spot while still tied down. I think I might have. I honestly can't remember clearly the taxi route I took once the plane was unchained from the ground. I remember it was very, VERY slow. I could have WALKED to the runway threshold in under half the time I am sure. My focus was as intense as it ever had been as I manipulated the stick to keep all the controls surfaces where they needed to be. Downwind. Crosswind. Quartering from the front, the rear. I must be nuts! I tell myself.

Jeremy's quite intelligent refusal to fly and Selena's goading along with my impatience to be underway allowed my alligator ego to override my pea brain. Now a tiger is trying to get MY tail it seems as I creep to the runways edge. I sit there repeating the same stupid four word phrase in my mind that got me (myself) into this mess to begin with. "It's JUST an airplane!!" And using those four words I had convinced myself that I could check myself out if Jeremy didn't want to go.

I didn't know it yet, but by the time I had managed to reach the end of the runway half the airport had assembled in front of the FBO. Faster than the crack of a lightning bolt, word had spread around this intimately small aviation facility of an impending disaster to be witnessed! As the hotshot Alaskan "Bush Pilot" sat, legs braced against the brake pedals and shaking like a set of maracas in a Mexican cantina on a Friday night; I'm sure money was being wagered left and right among the onlookers. I can only imagine what the odds were being bandied about. And now I sat pointed directly into the wind at about a thirty degree angle to the runway centerline. I need to know. Can I still fly. Do I still have the kahunas when I need to? Only one way to find out I finally convince myself.

I release the right brake and suck the stick all the way into my gut and full hard right 'til it stops. I feed in the power gradually trying to force the tail starboard far enough to check for traffic on final. Satisfied that there is none, I chop the throttle and let the wind weathervane the airplane back the other way.

Many is the time in Kotzebue when you return from a trip to find the winds straight down the runway from the east at forty to fifty or fifty-five knots and relatively steady. In the winter it was impossible under those conditions to use either of the two taxiways leading to the ramp. One was 90 degrees to the ramp and runway and the one on the west end was forty-five. So landing, (sometimes HOVERING in an empty Islander or single or Twin Otter) in on the ramp was, while not standard practice, an infrequently used but not unknown semi-official "procedure". Hence I had no qualms about taking off directly into the wind at a diagonal to the runway centerline. And even without a history in this airplane, I knew I would be airborne long before I hit the end of the asphalt on the other side. Hell. I was struggling to keep from going airborne (or ass over teakettle) since I left the tie down spot. SCREW it! Time to FLY, and I shove the throttle smoothly forward and release the brakes.

As the wheels begin to turn I release the back pressure on the stick to neutral just momentarily before pushing slightly forward. The tail LEAPS into the air. My eyes are riveted forward and fixed on the far side of the runway now slowly coming nearer. Before I can consciously even think the thought (uh ... WHAT's my airspeed?) The plane practically STOPS forward motion (it seems) and jumps vertically with no further control input from me! In an instant the runway has dropped twenty feet below the plane as if somehow the earth had mysteriously collapsed from beneath me.

Holy CRAP! I quickly ease the stick aftward and get the nose off level and pointed up! I don't think we rolled three plane lengths. I had barely reached the centerline! WHAM!! Upward we jolt another two hundred feet or so in the blink of an EYE! JEEZUS! I bank slightly right and begin to track parallel to the runway now visible out my right side and almost five hundred feet below me. About a 15 degree left crab keeps the runway in the same lateral position from the airplane. WHHOOOF! The bottom falls out and I am jerked hard upward against my seatbelt as the altimeter records a 100 foot drop with the nose practically pointed at the sun and the little Continental still hammering away at full power.

I have been "flying" alongside the runway now for ... oh ... I'd say about TWO DAYS! My eighty year old Gramma CloudDancer would make better forward progress with her walker! I raise the nose in an attempt to climb to pattern altitude and every time I do, I am literally in a hover! I have enough thrust to either climb or fly forward in this wind. But it is simply that. A choice for now. Both are not possible simultaneously it seems. I settle for a "climb in position" mode until reaching what the altimeter tells me is 1000 feet AGL. I believe I am losing ground now.

I lower the nose to level and ease the power back some what. At a groundspeed that even a self respecting snail would be ashamed of, I now churn forward through the air hoping the east end of the runway is within my fuel range. The BAM! turbulence is atrocious and I wince slightly as some of the worsts gusts strain Mr. Pipers trusty creation. I hope the bolts holding these wings on are big mothers! And TIGHT!

Initially I had thought I'd go out to the practice area. Do a couple of stalls, a couple of steep turns … you know … yada … yada!! Now? No way was I gonna' be able to keep my buttcheecks clenched this tight much longer. I want back on the ground and am relieved as I see the east end of the runway finally slide aftward out of my line of sight.

My finely honed recently reawakened "pilot sense" intuitively tells me that my downwind leg will be … short! I expect it to be (if I ever get this airsheen turned around) all of about 2.8 seconds in duration, as I plan to start my turn to "base leg" at midfield. I have targeted the "upriver" (upwind) end of the runway as what we will call my "landing zone". I just seem to remember that it presented the shortest and least risky route back to the FBO assuming I still had anything left to taxi after arrival. I decided this would have to suffice as my "checkout" and the fact that I didn't have three landing s in the last 90 days was no longer looming as such an important issue. Besides. It appeared I had a great chance of "getting current" in just one circuit around the pattern here.

I don't remember the landing(s) either. Other than to say I made it, much to the disappointment and financial detriment of many, I'm sure. And I somehow returned the aircraft to it's tie-down spot without flipping it over taxying in either. Thank You Lord Jesus.

11

Over or Under

By the time Jeremy had re-anchored the Cub to Mother Earth and I crawled out, the majority of the crowd had dispersed. A few however remained, either to see what shade of white I had turned, or to check out if I had custom fit blue jeans with extra room in the crotch. However, one Levi overall wearing elder pelican, complete with a piece of straw protruding from the corner of his mouth apparently spoke for them all. As I approached the group standing with arms folded and leaning against the white walled building I glanced his way. The straw stopped wiggling up 'n down in his mouth as he raised his voice to be heard above the still blowing winds. "I heard summa' you fellers were half a bubble off alright. But I never knowed ya'll were plumb CRAZY!" To a man, the other three remaining men in the group nodded silently in agreement. I couldn't have said it better myself and no response other than a slight shake of my head in concurrence was possible.

Selena rose as I came inside, came over and said. "How was it? Are you done? Can we GO now?" She hadn't even gone outside to watch! Go? Or no-go. What the hell. With more weight in her she'll be easier to taxi I try to convince myself. The real reason I want to go though is I've spent just about enough time in America. I'm used to Alaska now. Way too many people here all hustling about like it's important. It's time to go home already.

Again Jeremy tries to present what is obviously the common sense viewpoint and again I ignore him. With great reluctance he helps carry all our assorted STUFFS out to the airplane as the lineboy pulls up with the 80 octane truck to the nose of the pretty little ship. As we get to the tail of the airplane with our arms full of belongings, Selena comes to an abrupt halt right next to the right horizontal stabilizer and freezes. I stop after a couple more steps and turn to find her still standing, mouth now slightly agape. She looks first left to the top of the rudder and then her gaze follows the plane's lines forward 'til she is staring intently at the visible portion of the propellor.

I believe I remember her exact words as being "CLOUDY! What the hell is THIS!?" or some such. I said "Babe. This is our plane." "Uh-uh." she sez. "No way in HELL am I riding in this ... this thing! It's a TOY!" I sigh heavily. "Selena this is exactly the same size as the Cubs on the ice in front of town at home in the winter. You've seen these all your life!" I replied. I knew she had ridden by dozens and dozens of SuperCubs parked on skis on the ice of Kotzebue Sound all winter. I had told her what kind of plane we were flying back in. I don't need any more static today.

"No way" she says again. "You can fly back in this thing if you want to but I'm taking a real airplane! BUY ME A TICKET!". Jeremy meanwhile has set his armload of stuff by the right wheel. Clearing his throat somewhat self-consciously and wishing to spare me as much embarrassment as possible he says quietly "I'll check to make sure we didn't leave anything inside" before departing the scene quickly.

It takes ten minutes of talking to get Selena to even come look inside the plane. Only by telling her there is not enough money left to buy her a full fare ticket home, and that Brantley will not pay for it as it is not part of the deal, am I able to convince her that this Cub is her ride home. She finally acquiesces and begins to hand me things as I start packing the baggage area. We fill it top to bottom and from the aft wall to jammed against the back of the rear seat. It all fits. Just barely.

Jeremy now emerges again from the FBO and tells me he's paid for my fuel fill-up as a "parting gift". Selena and I return to the building for a last minute "pit stop" as Jeremy stays with the plane. Selena and I clamber in on our return and Jeremy stands beside the open door as I secure myself in the front seat. Finally situated I turn and stick out my right hand. He again grasps it firmly. He says "Happy flying, and you come back by and visit me again if you're ever down this way. Tell Brantley the invitation is good for him too!" I told him he'd been a wonderful host. What a great guy. With that he again reached forward and prepared to prop the little bird one last time. Standing by until I gave him a thumbs up from inside the cabin, he first untied my right wing and then scampered around the front of the airplane giving the idling prop a wide arc of clearance. Untying the left wing he looked up at me with a last smile. I slid open the small window to my left and hollered "Take care Jeremy" over the engine's clattering. With a "thumbs up" back at me he ducked down and disappeared behind the left wing.

Again I goosed the throttle with my left arm now resting comfortably against the window. Time to focus intently again on my taxying procedures. About 1500 miles away lies our destination. And the longest journey begins with … just the first rotation of the little tires.

The wind hasn't let up even a little bit. Again it takes long and careful minutes to reach the end of the runway. Again I stop short of the runway by mashing on the left brake to swing my nose and try to "clear" as much of the airspace on final as I can. Yep. I'm STILL the only yo-yo in the area it appears. Once again the tail slides to the left as the plane lives up into the wind freely.

It seem not that I might have gained a five degree or so advantage in wind direction over my last takeoff. I sit rooted to the same piece of asphalt but my plane is at a lesser angle to the runway. The nose now point a good 100 feet or so further down the far (north) edge of the runway. And for this I am grateful. I consider all I am asking of these wings and the little Continental engine now ticking over slowly and (relatively) quietly for the moment.

Back in those days I was about 180 lbs and Selena barely broke 100. But directly ahead of my eyes the coat-hangar—like metal wire fuel "gauge" jutted upward full range; the cork on the bottom of the indicator floating on top of a full twelve gallons of red-dyed 80/87 octane avgas. I knew our survival gear weighed in at 30 pounds. Add in all the "STUFFS" Selena had packed and purchased (mostly clothes, thank goodness) and I well knew we were at or over gross weight for takeoff. And although operating over gross was standard operating procedure back home, I knew I had never done it in anything smaller than a Skyhawk. And THAT was hairy enough sometimes!

Very intently I focused on the areas within a twenty or thirty degree wide swath of airspace directly ahead of the longitudinal axis of the airplane. Where in that area was the LOWEST possible path of clearance if I needed it? Trees? Power lines? Over or under? (UNger!. Definately Under!) I was quite unsure just how much altitude I was going to be able to acquire for every horizontal mile traveled. Although my initial flight indicated I wouldn't be progressing forward any too quickly and I felt comfortable that I would be able to attain a reasonable four or five hundred feet after a few minutes.

There appeared to be no significant obstacles in my projected path for the first couple of miles straight ahead and to the right. A short time over some flat farmlands would get me out over the great Columbia River. That'd be good for an extra 140 feet or so of air beneath the wings.

I turned to look at Selena and smiled at her reassuringly. I said "Well babe. This will be a bit of a roller coaster for a couple of minutes, but don't worry. We're safe, okay?" Her grim and silent look back at me showed a lack of complete faith in my statement.

This time we used the entire diagonal width of the runway and about five hundred feet in length before I hauled back on the stick just as the left wheel was short of the runway's edge. The plane immediately was lifted by a strong gust to seventy-five feet or so where she continued to chew the air with her little wooden prop providing enough thrust to keep us moving forward at a slightly better clip than the first flight. And although the turbulence was still quite jolting the worst of the it failed to produce any equally devastating downward thrusts. Even with Selena's constant screaming and dire threats regarding my manhood (when and if we ever "survive this and LAND" to quote her) I was encouraged enough to level off at five hundred feet and throttle back slightly for a period of level flight.

The little Yellow Cub now bounces and rocks back and forth as we slowly crawl across the farm fields headed for the Columbia Gorge. Selena's continual shrieking has subsided to just momentary spasmodic screams that erupt with each of the heavier jolts. She questions whether the wings can hold on. She questions how long it will be before we land (we've been UP all of five minutes now); she questions whether planes are supposed to fly SIDEways and finally questions whether my parents were EVER married! This is followed by immediate further threats to my future hopes of fathering children as we reach the edge of the gorge. The ground drops away beneath as I lay the Cub into a twenty-five to thirty degree right bank hoping to scare her into silence. In mid turn the worst jolt of the flight thus far finally accomplishes THAT job and simultaneously had me wishing I was wearing Depends for men. Quickly I snatch the stick and rudder hard left to recover from what HAD to have been at least an (unplanned) 45 degree bank!

The controls response is swift and sure and the wings snap immediately level. This airplane is pure response to the stick. No slop. It's a GOOD feeling. I give thanks silently for the meticulous care Jeremy has lavished on her as Selena resumes her verbal assault on my character and heritage.

We now crawl generally eastward along the Columbia as I peer ahead intently watching for other traffic in the air. A dot in the distance above us at 11 o'clock grows swiftly into a Cessna 172 or 182 and just as quickly passes on the other side of the river. Heading downriver and downwind he passes as what seems to be just short of supersonic speed. I return his (or her) wing-waggled "Hello" with my big fat left hand in the windshield hoping they will see it and not think I am stuck up. Selena has been silent for almost a full minute now and I do not wish to set her off again with a wing-waggle greeting in return. Up ahead I begin to see The Dalles, Oregon coming into view and decide to resume my efforts to climb as the turbulence continues a slight but noticeable reduction in intensity. I am headed for higher ground and will need more altitude eventually. May as well try and get some now.

12

What Could POSSIBLY Go Wrong?

The heavily loaded machine struggles valiantly upward averaging a solid two hundred feet per minute. I'm actually getting about 260 feet per minute on the vertical speed indicator, but the downdrafts exceed the updrafts or so it seems. As the altitude increases it appears that the cars eastbound on I-84 seem to be passing me at a somewhat slower rate than before. I'm not sure if this indicates a real reduction in the headwind or is simply one of those visual distortions caused by an increase in the distance between me and them.

Passing over The Dalles I keep a sharp eye out for air traffic in the pattern, which of course means I'm still looking ABOVE me to see "pattern altitude"! I have managed to nurse the Cub all the way up to about thirteen hundred feet as the airport passes off to my right. With the oil temp approaching the yellow I again lower the nose for increased airflow. A rough Timex—eyeball—mental math calculation gives me an average forward progress of something just under 3/4's of a mile per minute or about 45 M.P.H. groundspeed. Although the "coat hangar" fuel guage still indicates close to full I begin to wonder that, if this keeps up, can I even make my 1st planned destination. Still about ninety miles away, I've planned a stop at Sunnyside, southeast of Yakima, Washington.

Selena has finally settled down somewhat and only the now increasingly rare strong jolts rate a surprised gasp or comment. Airborne all of about 25 minutes now she already asks "How long 'til we land this thing.?" Lord, this is gonna' be a long trip (or so I THINK).

Speaking of the Diety, I also about this time began to wonder about other things. I had not flown in many months prior to today because I had lost my nerve after a frightening episode that had occurred the previous March. (You'll have to wait to read Volume III, the Tragedies, to find out about that one.) And although it would be two years yet before Dennis Quaid and Ed Harris would make the Mecury Seven astronauts and the term "The Right Stuff" household names, I was aware (like all serious pilots) of it's existence.

I had it. Had it? Hell, I wuz full of it! Even my friends knew, for yheu often told me I was "full of it". But then ... after that fateful day in March of 1981 ... I LOST it. I didn't come apart at the seams. But it leaked out. And it leaked out quickly. The "Right Stuff" was nowhere to be found within me. There was none left when I went looking for it a mere week later. Gone. So I made the hardest decision I ever made in my life and grounded myself. But now, thanks to Brantley, here I was back in the air. An innocent person's life was once again in my hands alone.

But I was feeling pretty good all in all. My pilot senses were sharpening again. My pilot brain seemed to be functioning on all cylinders smoothly. And certainly my pilot ego had returned intact. Still a little bruised, but intact none the less.

Today's flying efforts thus far had definitely been demanding. No doubt about that. But in no way had I felt it was high pressure or potentially fatal if I screwed up! So what would happen when and if the "chips were down" and I was "all in". How do I KNOW if I am really okay to fly again? How WILL I know until and if that "something" happens again. Obviously I would never find out for sure unless some small at least, but demanding situation arose? As Selena I meandered slowly up the gore I uttered a silent prayer in my mind to the Lord. "Please God. Give me some sign to answer and quell my doubts." People. Be DARN careful that you want and what you PRAY for. HE listens!

Sidebar Now, the many passengers who have been with me during my other ... um MISadventures, along with the Captains and First Officers who have flown with me in the dozens and dozens of simulator sessions in my airline career already know this. It seems that when things go wrong or my airplane misbehaves I have a SLIGHT tendency to cuss at it. Well. Sometimes it's a slight tendency. When only minor stuff is failing or going awry. Apparently the intensity of my cursing, and the vulgarity of the (feminine gender) names with which I may address my airplane varies in direct proportion to the degree of calamity and confusion involved.

I do this completely unconsciously with absolutely no forethought and definitely with no malice intended, other than at the offending system(s). I have always done this as long as I can remember. It is my standard, conventional, and routine response to what airline pilots refer to as "Non-Normals". It's reflexive.

The Master Caution yellow flashing light illuminates along with a single chime in my Airbus cockpit. I am trained to say "ECAM Condition" (meaning "what's the problem") and most times in the simulator I do! In an airborne real airplane though ... I can practically guarantee you the first words out of my mouth will be "Well kiss my ASS!" followed by the required response. And of course, should it be more serious, resulting in a Master WARNING red flashing light with a repetitive chime dinging ... well. Who DOESN'T start with "Holy S**T!"?? Add in some airplane undirected aerodynamic misbehavior (like heading for the weeds in the middle of a high speed takeoff roll or airborne uncommanded flight gyrations) and apparently I'll start to outcuss a barful of drunken sailors!

The one or two times this happened in the simulator when my flying partner was female damn near got me sentenced to three days of sensitivity training by Human Resources! (But I made the landing!) I only told you all this so in a couple of pages I can save myself a lot of @&#$@!(s), %*&$#@ %^#*&#@!(s), and &*^^#$%@!(s). Now back to our story.

Up ahead to the south I catch sight of Biggs, Oregon and glimpse sections of Highway 97 approaching from the south. Sure enough there is a bridge right where my Texaco map says it should be. I begin a gradual ten to fifteen degree bank to the left after warning Selena what I was about to do and aim for the far north and east side of the bridge. Halfway across the great Columbia river I holler over my right shoulder "Say goodbye to Oregon and hello to Washington babe. We're on our way home now!"

As the dry land of Washington slides beneath our wings I again increase power and ease back on the stick. I am heartened to see the vertical speed needle creep slowly upward to rest on the 300 foot per minute "up" marking. I know I need at least another 1500 feet of altitude and would prefer to gain another two thousand. My goal is 3500 feet. It will be enough to see me through the hills to the northeast comfortably as I follow the highway. I could do it at 3000 feet, but that would not leave a lot to spare for "contingencies", you know.

The clouds rise higher and disperse more and the wind is shifting directions. Under what is now "guesstimated" by me as 5000 foot scattered to broken clouds it appears the wind has shifted to a more northerly direction. (Naturally. That's the way I need to go!) On the plus side, about 1800 feet below us now it appears that we are staying about even with almost ALL the cars now so I can make the assumption that the velocity has died down somewhat. And conditions seem to improve the further north we go.

There is only continuous light turbulence now and Selena is even starting to enjoy the ride a little and relax back into her seat. Big bumps are now almost non-existent. And finally halfway between the river crossing and the hills I have attained three thousand feet. I will level here and allow the engine to cool a little more before trying for five hundred more feet of altitude. Our climb rate was down to 125 to 150 feet per minute and the oil temp pushing the yellow again. I am pleased and contented in my little aerial world again. It feels GOOD I'm thinking.

Below us the ground gradually rises up to steal our altitude very slowly away. A sharp poke in the right shoulder and I here Selena's excited voice. "Cloudy! Lookit all the COWS! Wow!"

She leans with her forehead pressed against the plexiglass of the right window just behind my right shoulder. The is the slightest smile on her face as I turn to catch her taking in the view. I am very pleased that my sweetie is now relaxing and starting to enjoy this flight as she had so many in the past in larger airframes with me. I reply to her with a question. "So Whaddaya' think? Pretty cool after all, eh?" As she opens her mouth to reply, before she can get a word out ... someone else has to get his two cents in. You know. MURPHY!

Sidebar (again)—Go down to Ace Hardware or Home Depot and get one of the BIG aluminum garbage cans like we all used to have outside our house when we were kids. Obtain a large metal serving spoon like the cafeteria lady used to use in the kitchen to serve the green beans. Set the garbage can on a bare (preferably) cement floor and station a small child on each side of it by the fold down handles. Now. Take the serving spoon and hold it inside the can placing against the inside wall of the can. As quickly and FURIOUSLY as humanly possible, now "stir" the spoon clockwise (or counter-clockwise, it doesn't matter) around the inside of the can and, for good measure every few circles change to a back and forth sideways motion (again as fast as you can). Have the two children take the handles repeatedly to their fully extended limit before smartly smacking them down back flush with the outsides of the can. This should be done as fast as the kids can do it too. You are now hearing a VERY close approximation of what I am about to hear. Read on. Sidebar ended.

I am twisted half around in my seat to the right. As Selena gazes out the window I am admiring the cuteness of her upturned nose and the beauty of her lips and just beginning to think of tonight's possi ... WHA-A-AN-N-NGG!! And NOISE!! And in just a microsecond I sense the feeling of my seat falling away from me! In another microsecond I have whipped around to facing fully forward in my seat just in time to see the nose slide downward through the horizon.

Out of my peripherical vision I note the vertical speed needle begin IT's downward arc confirming we are beginning to fall! As I YANK! back on the stick with my left hand, my right hand balls instantly into a fist which I first raise up to eye level in front of me. I bring it SMASHING down on the curved upper por-

tion of the Cub's black metal instrument panel ahead of me. The NOISE is
HORRIFIC and I specifically remember as the bottom of my right hand collided
painfully hard with the panel SCREAMING at the plane. You miserable
BITCH! Every time! ... I crawl IN! to one of you F***ers! ... You're trying to
KILL ME!! You *&%$!! And the noise continues unabated. But I have restricted
our rate of altitude loss and now hold best glide speed reducing our rate of sink to
about 500 feet per minute. MAGS! Mixture! THROTTLE! DAMMIT! Nothing
halts our fall! I have about four minutes between me and Terra Firma.

As I begin to look for a landing spot the string of invectives continues to pour
forth. I won't write it because it's too profane and would offend many of either
sex to have to read it. Just, every third word or so, insert one of George Carlin's
"Seven Dirty Words You Can't Say on the Radio." For good measure throw in
one every other sentence from Eddie Murphy's "Raw" HBO Special as well.
That'll about cover it.

Of course, I look at the bordering farm fields with renewed interest now.
Cows. LOTS of cows, fallen tree trunks, and a few ditches and ravines thrown in
for good measure. DAMN! I am already pointed into the wind and wish to stay
that way. The land is climbing slowly uphill beneath me. The dadgum fields
would've been perfect! Okay. No sweat. We got the Highway just below us to the
... JEEEEZUZ CHRIST!! WHAT the hell is going ON?

A look now to the left and down to Hwy 97's two northbound lanes now
reveals that we are WHIZZING by the cars! What the ...! DAMN! The cars!
The cars are not MOVING! Distracted by Selena and the cows for over a minute
and a half I had been looking out the right side or backwards. I had not SEEN
the cars slowing to a stop. Now as far as I could see ahead, the two right lanes are
packed bumper-to-bumper with motionless metal rectangles of all colors. But I
need to LAND! NORTH DAMMIT!

We've lost another five hundred feet and are now down to somewhere around
1000 to 1200 feet above the ground. I must make a decision. I can even more
clearly now discern the complete LACK of suitability of the bordering farm fields
along the highway. The tree trunks or logs or whatever the hell they are that litter
the pastures are HUGE. Gullies mar the land as well. Again I glance at the highway ahead. East (northbound) lanes are unusable. Out of the equation. The
southbound lanes however are flowing uninterrupted and there are many large
gaps in the traffic. No time to think or wonder. I commit and haul the airplane
around to the left. Immediately the groundspeed increases at a notable rate! We
are still falling at about five hundred feet a minute. But now, the ground instead

of rising to meet us is ALSO falling away allowing me a few more precious seconds of time to consider the impending reunion of airplane and earth.

Great. This is JUST great I think to myself. My second landing in SIX months. Haven't been in a damn tailwheel airplane in a couple of years or more. Haven't been in a Cub since whenever. Suddenly the thought intrudes and I hear Brantley's voice ringing in my ears "What does your GUT tell you Cloudy?" GREAT! Right now my gut tells me that if by some chance I live through this, I can look forward to YOU killing me! (We have no insurance on this machine because no one would sell us "trip" insurance for a Hood River to Kotzebue sojourn.) Yeah, I made a GOOD deal here for ol' Brantley, I think as I continue to cuss the airplane.

Oh boy. Downhill. Downwind. A quartering tailwind from the left. The ground is rising up to meet us and with five or six hundred feet left I start the little machine sliding sideways toward the asphalt ribbon looking over my left shoulder. We move at a slightly greater speed than most of the traffic but the is a Kenworth haulin' logs comin' downhill at a pretty good clip. That sum'bitch better not mess up my hole …

The altimeter now unwinds all too quickly through one thousand feet indicated still going down at the rate of five hundred feet per minute or so. I am sure I have less than six hundred feet left between the Cub's small tires and the farm fields now WHIZZING by underneath. I notice two or three things with my attention now over my left shoulder. The northbound (uphill/upwind) lanes are now open. Apparently the southern end of the traffic jam is now behind me and for just an instant I consider trying to haul her around in another left one-eighty. I look at the airspeed sitting at 50 MPH. I have NO idea what a Cub stalls at straight ahead … much less in a bank, and we're heavily loaded. And the altimeter has passed 800 feet. I am committed to a southbound landing.

Also there is a good half mile gap in the southbound lane between two clusters of automobiles. I am squarely alone in the middle of the gap with one small exception. If you call a Kenworth pulled 18 wheeler loaded with HUMONGOUS LOGS a small exception! This guy is just aft of me about two hundred yards and closing the gap between us noticeably. But there is no way in hell he is ever going to get past me before I run out of altitude and airspeed. I'm a now fresh out of ideas!

I figure I'm doing a groundspeed of somewhere about sixty-five miles per hour and he's gotta' be knocking off a good eighty. My eyeball estimate is that given no change to any of the factors, the truck and I should arrive at my landing spot at about the same time. The altimeter has just passed six hundred feet and the ground can't be more than three hundred feet below me. Thank GOD (I THINK) that it is still sloping gently downhill. I begin slipping the airplane to the left slowly toward the black asphalt ribbon no more than forty yards or so to my left.

I've always had a great "eye" for estimates. It's what made me an All-Star outfielder on my schools baseball team. It's why I played free safety in football. Somehow, I always knew in the first couple of seconds of a ball's upward trajectory exactly WHERE it would come to earth. Seems I hadn't lost the "eye" for estimates. The Kenworth, at more than twice my size and weighing loaded I imagine twenty-five times what I do barrels along seemingly destined to occupy my space. Dammit.

With my free left hand I slide open the side window and stick my left arm out. I wave it madly in the wind fore and aft. Fore and aft. "Get outta' the way!" I shout. (Inject invectives.) In response, the driver, who has now braked and taken up station as … as … my left WINGMAN! now happily toots his horn in … what … greeting!? With only a hundred feet and a few seconds of aviating left I am enraged!

Again I wave my arm out the left window forward and aft. You dummy! I hurl new and previously unheard combinations of curse words across the few remaining yards of empty air that remain between me and this … this IDIOT! He is now using his right hand to alternately give me two blasts on his air horn interspersed with frantic waving vigorously back at me! Honkhonk!! WAVEWAVE! HonkHonk! WAVEWAVE! My dear JESUS! This rolling BOZO thinks we're … WHAT?! Has he listened to too many C.W. McCall songs?! This fool thinks I wanna' play CONVOY!

My head flips forward-left-forward-left-forward so damn fast I must look like I'm a spectator sitting ringside at a damn table tennis match. Altitude and airspeed are now all but spent. Numb—nuts is at eight o'clock low and about twenty-five yards now and intent apparently that we shall mate. I have no choices left. The ground and I are about to meet once again momentarily. I can see the sun glint of his gold capped tooth as he grins broadly up at me from under his straw cowboy hat. I am now that close. The double toots from the air horn and waving go on unabated. Suddenly a large bloodhound dog leaps up in the right seat and lunges at the cabs right front window. Planting his paws he looks up at me and I can SEE the damn thing barking with meaning. Good Lord! I'm in a scene straight outta' Smokey and the Bandit!

It's TIME! "Get the HELL outta' my way you DUMBASS!" I scream! At the same time I change from my frantic fore and aft waving to a new signal. For just two or three seconds I hold my arm completely still out the left window and pointed slightly aft directly at his cab. At the end of my left arm is (quite naturally) my left hand. My left hand now conveys, in an instant, what all my obscenity-laden screaming could not. Yes, the internationally recognized one-digit universally understood sign worked it's magic.

The last thing I saw with my last leftward glance was the trucker's wave frozen in mid-air. His mouth had fallen open, and the bloodhound barked silently on. Only when my left wingtip had practically crossed over the asphalt at what now was an altitude of less than twenty-five feet, did the moron ever figure it out. My peripheral vision just caught the beginning of the smoke that poured off the fast rolling truck's tires as he jammed on the brakes to avoid my tailfeathers. He exited my line of sight aftward in a millisecond.

Now I could concentrate on the landing. Wheel it or full stall? There was NO way I wanted that little tail wheel on the ground any earlier that absolutely necessary. Thank the Good Lord the wind was STEADY, even if quartering from the left rear. I was steady on the rudder pedals for now but I was working the stick like Gramma CloudDancer churning butter. WHERE was the Aspha ... chirp-chirp! And I quickly move the stick half forward to pin the tiny tires to the roadway. My size 13EEE boots dance lightly and quickly on the ruder pedals as I take extra caution to make sure I DON'T hit either brake pedal.

The airspeed indicates now forty or so with the tail still high up in the air. I focus on trying to track the center white stripes. Keep them under the belly center as best I can do. And as the airspeed slowly bleeds off I keep adding forward stick. As soon as the stick touches the forward stop I hold it and wait for the tail to settle. It does with a light thunk and rhumbling sound. Right away I suck the stick back full into my gut. We are still doing a good thirty miles per hour groundspeed. I ease on the brakes gently and evenly being extremely careful to hold my track.

And as the groundspeed drops away I brake harder and harder. I want this show OVER! And in a few more seconds it is. I guess somewhere shortly after the tail touched down, I must've stopped my continual verbal abuse of the airplane. For as we came to a complete and final stop, I heard only the sound of a deep DEEP sigh being released and the now much, much slower WHANGWHANG-WHANGWHANGWHANGWHANG of the engine as the prop barely turns over at a low idle. This sound too finally ceases as I whack the mixture control to idle cutoff.

13

When Good Guys Wore White Hats

Having exhausted every possible combination of curse words, like the engine, I too finally fall silent. After the horribly loud and continual metallic banging sounds of the last three to four minutes, I discover that silence can indeed can deafening. It lasts for all of ten seconds before being broken by two other sounds that drift in through the open side window. The sound of a car horn honking as it passes northbound with arms waving out the front and back left windows combines with the sound of pneumatic truck airbrakes as the big rig now arrives behind my forlorn little Piper machine. Toot! Toot!

With a final muttered "damn!" I suddenly think of Selena and whip around in my seat. Of course, she is still there! But the girl is as white as a ghost and her hands still grip the back of my seat tightly. She does not look well. "Are you okay babe?" I ask. "Get me OUT of this GODDAM machine right NOW!" she practically screams at me. "I don't FEEL good."

Quickly I wrench the door handle and swiftly lower the bottom half flush with the side of the plane before reaching up to secure the window portion. I hurry to try and extract my lanky frame from the cramped confines of the front seat. I nearly dislocate my left foot, which has failed to follow the rest of my body in a spectacularly uncoordinated and graceless attempt at a rapid egress. My boot is now wedged between the control stick and the bottom of the front chair as I hop up and down on the right foot again cursing in frustration. And now Selena throws in a few choice words of her own as she struggles with a seat belt that is totally unlike the ones she knows from the airliners.

Barging into the middle of this apparent Chinese fire drill comes the trucker around the right rear of the airplane with a "Hey Thar' good buddy. How yew Doin'?" And I, having finally gained my balance on my right leg alone by grasping the strut respond "How the %*&$ you THINK I'm doing you DUMBASS!"

252

At which point HE has finished passing under the wing and has turned around to face me and straightened up. I now look at him approximately eye-to-navel. Oops!

DAH-um!

I look up to his face a good foot or more above mine. If he was smiling before … he's not now. At this point Selena chimes in with another screaming "Goddam you CloudDancer! Get me OUTTA' here you sonofabitch!" Which disrupts the trucker's thought process (thank you Lord). And looking back over my left shoulder at Selena I see her continuing to claw at the canvas and leather seat belt assembly. "I'm coming dammit! Can't you see that I'm stuck you …" and I let THAT one trail off. No point in having everybody mad at me, although it appears I may be having that thought a little too late.

Looking up again at the giant before me I say quite apologetically, "Heh, heh. Sorry about that sir. I'm jus' a might overwrought at the moment." And I now manage to twist my leg free and pull it out with my left hand. "'SCUSE me just a second there bud while I rescue my Princess here." I say as I turn to help Selena. Fifteen seconds later I have extracted her from the little plane and she dashes off to the side of the roadway.

I straighten up in the corner where the trailing edge of the right wing meets the fuselage and look up again to my new friend and begin to apologize some more. He responds with a "Heck. Doan' worry about it son. You two alright?" Whereupon I take a glance over at Selena. She is well clear of the roadway, actually in the drainage ditch by the side I think. Doubled in half, she is now doing a great job of blowing beets. "Yeah. We'll be fine." I reply. "I just gotta' get this broke airsheen offa' the road." I thank him but decline the big cowboy's offer to help fearing his big hands will either break the plane into pieces or punch a whole through the fabric. I tell him "It's a real light .machine. Dudn't take nuthin' to move this old girl" I said as I turned and walked toward the tailfeathers.

I had spied a graveled in portion of the culvert that led to chained gate in the barb wire and post fence that ran as far as the eye could see in both directions. It being a few yards forward of the airplane a slight sideways push on the rudder castered the tailwheel and started to swing the nose to the right as I hollered "Watch up front!" at the trucker and he dodged the blade of the prop. With still the very slightest downhill slope in my lanes the plane rolled almost freely backward after I straightened the tail wheel on my "runway centerline stripes". I glanced across the plane now to see Selena now sitting in the tall grass. "I'll be there in just a couple of minutes babe." I hollered. "Are you okay now?" from me got only a one (freshly manicured) finger in a non-verbal reply which elicited a hearty laugh from my new friend. I reached down and lifted the tail of the airplane as she started to roll a little faster. Turning to my right I went tail first across the compacted gravel over the driveway across the culvert. The Cub's wheels had a good two feet to spare on either side.

In the last few minutes quite a crowd had gathered on both sides of the road. The southbound side stopped because they had to, and a couple on the northbound side stopped for the entertainment value of it all. Thank GOD there were no picture phones in those days! Horns had been honking in friendly greeting from the northbound lanes as cars passed. Now as I cleared the southbound two lanes of Washington State Highway 97 and cars began streaming past, there were honks and shouts of Good Luck from the southbounders as well. One even hollered "Nice landing!"

Jerry Jeff or Billy Bob or whoever he was remained at the nose of the airplane, now at rest. I ducked back under the right wing and stuck out my right hand and said "Howdy. CloudDancer!"

My big hand was drowned in his football sized hand and I winced as he pumped my hand and said "Nice tuh MEETcha' CloudWrangler good buddy. Ah'm Red! Ya'll gonna' be alright? Ya'll wanna' ride?"

Cars now fifty yards back up the road parked behind the motionless 18 wheeler were now starting to honk their horns as well as I replied. "Well. Thanks a lot Red, but you're headed south and believe it or not, I was going north. So I think I'll catch a ride to Yakima instead, but I sure appreciate the offer. He says "Wa-a-a-ll, alright then ... an' Hey! I'm sure a'sorry 'bout that ... well ... I mean ... I didn't KNOW ... you ..." "Yeah. No sweat there Red. We made it." He comes back with "Well. I'd best git along CloudDicer. I hate it when people hold me up you know." and he turned to leave.

Passing Selena a few yards back toward his truck he makes a slight left turn and the slightest of bows with his upper body with a small tug down on the brim of his cowboy hat. He waves a big hand and a station wagon brakes to a swift stop in the right lane to let Red cross over to his idling Kenworth. Watching him clamber up into his cab reminded me of the Lone Ranger mounting Silver in one fluid motion. The door to the cab was barely closed before the WHOOSH of the brakes being released was followed by the first motion of the tires. Two more toots on the air horn could've just as easily been heard as Hi Ho SILVER! AWAY!

I quickly dash over to Selena who is now in conversation with a much older couple. I mean like, these people are in their fifties at least. They had stopped going northbound to gawk and saw her sitting in the grass. Two very, very nice people whose names I can't remember. But they were kind enough to offer us a ride to the next phone north. Selena was being charming and so I said I'd go secure the airplane for the time being.

The gate to the pasture(s) was held closed by an old well rusted lock and chain that looked as if they hadn't been touched for twenty years or so. I therefore assumed that no one would need to use it for at least another 24 hours. I was carrying over a hundred yards of 1/4 in. white nylon rope in my survival gear. And this was fortunate, for there were no real large rocks to be found that I felt would make good chocks for the main gear.

I had to turn the plane around. But by doing so I was able to tie the wings to the road level cattle guard just outside the closed gate. This put the tail instead over the metal pipe drain culvert buried under the driveway for runoff water to flow through. The tailfeathers were thusly really tied to the ground. No more than 15 minutes after landing Selena and I were again making a groundspeed of about fifty-five knots toward Yakima. Only now, we were quite comfortably ensconced in the rear seat of a white '75 Caddy.

14

You In a Heap o' Trouble Boy

As only Muphy himself could arrange it the northbound traffic was now flowing uphill quite smoothly as Selena and I got somewhat acquainted with our hosts. They were fascinated, as so many from the Lower 48 are, by all things Alaskan. So it was one question after another. Was Selena an Eskimo then? Was I born in Kotzebue too? Isn't flying in small planes SCARY? (Selena and I disagreed on that answer!) How do you stand six months of nighttime?

But the conversation was pleasant and helped pass the time. So much so that I paid hardly NO attention to the first ambulance that I saw across the median. It was racing southbound with lights and siren on and we passed it about fifteen miles north of our landing site. Selena was having the driver's wife name the best places to shop in Yakima since it appeared we might be there a day or two. Then, having traveled no more than another five miles north, the second set of flashing red lights appeared in the distant north coming towards us. As we had all see the first one pass just a minute or two earlier, like lookie-lous everywhere we stopped talking to gawk as we drove.

I expected … I don't know what I expected. But the rotating reds soon developed into another ambulance that again tore past us in the southbound lanes goin' like greased lightnin'. Can't remember who broke the silence after it passed, but how clearly I remember someone uttered "Hmmmm. Musta' had a bad accident back there somewhere." No sooner than those words have been spoken and all eyes are front again (mostly) and two more sets of lights appear in the distance. We wait and sit in silence closing the distance with the flashing lights at what has to be a combined groundspeed closure rate of oh, 190 MPH. These flashing lights however were blue! Two Washington State Troopers, one seemingly in hot pursuit of the other, are barreling down the south side going flat out it appears to me in formation. These guys are hauling ASS man!

Thinking out loud I say "I wonder wha … oh … NO!" and Selena says "What. What's wrong?" I replied "You don't THINK … I mean do you think

256

somebody called in a PLANE CRASH!?" The ensuing short silence confirmed for me the others in the car also thought it might be a possibility. I ended it with a statement to our hosts that I thought it would be best if we stopped at the next available roadside oasis of some sort. I figured I'd better get on the phone pretty quick and talk to somebody? Although I sure wasn't certain who I should make the first phone call to. In NO case, was Brantley my FIRST choice. I wanted to put that one off until I had something at least remotely positive to add to my report of events.

The drive north continued with me now silent and brooding as Selena continued to chatter away with our hosts. Well, brooding may be the wrong word. I was trying to decide whether I should even bother trying to call Jeremy up. After all. It WAS a DONE deal. I mean, he's got Brantley's cash, and I, or to be more precise Brantley (shudder) now had ownership of one obviously very ill, not to mention unflyable airplane. I was only grateful for one thing. I'll get to make the report to Brantley over the phone. At least out of physical distance of his no doubt furious reaction if not out of hearing.

I fully expected whatever phone receiver I was holding at the time to first overheat and blister the palm of my hand. This would result in my dropping the receiver only to watch it first begin to steam before melting completely into a puddle of liquid plastic. The sound of Brantley's inflamed and passionate description of what he is going to do to me when I get back would gradually grow weaker until finally being drowned out totally in the puddle of now molten and bubbling plastic. Kinda' like that scene in the Wizard of Oz. You know, where the witch melts and screams "I'm melting! I'm melting!"

Go with your gut instinct, or something like that. That's what Brantley had said. Well. We did. And I'm pretty damn sure that my gut instinct has lost some of it's "value" in Brantley's eyes for sure and maybe mine as well. My deep thought is broken by the elderly gentleman behind the driver's wheel as he calls my attention forward. Here, about thirty-five miles or so south of Yakima we have come across a combination truck stop and large family style restaurant. I decide that Selena and I will dismount the Caddy here and I will get on the phone. It has been no more that 45 minutes since the Cub's tiny wheels squeaked onto the highway.

Profusely thanking our hosts, we gather our meager overnight bags from the cavernous trunk of the car and wave goodbye before turning to go inside. We were in the middle of the Yakima Indian reservation and it was approaching noon. There were three or four other white guys in the joint. All sitting around the counter in a gaggle and exchanging tales of 18 wheeling cross-country "road warriors", they obviously belonged to the big rigs in the parking lot. Many native brown eyes of both sexes turned to stare at us. A white guy with some BABE of an "Indian" chick that nobody recognized as local. I told Selena to get us a both and order me some food as I went to make a phone call or two.

A bank of pay phones hung on the wall close to the front swinging glass doors and I turned to face them. Like I would a bank of slot machines, I regarded them, wondering if any one was any more or less likely to ... MELT! With a reluctant soft sigh I picked the one in the corner next to the wall. This so I could have something to lean on as I stood and took the verbal beating I was now resigned to. In desperation I decided I would call Jeremy first and see if there was any help he was willing to provide. I prayed silently that his emotional attachment to the plane was not completely severed.

I was in luck. It wasn't. He answered on the second ring and, upon recognizing my voice, broke in excitedly with "Hey! Landed already? Where you at? How you doin'? How's my old girl treating you?" And I responded with "Well ... Jeremy . You're NOT going to believe this, but ..." And then I gave him the whole story. His initial shock was apparent enough by his choice of words. I hadn't heard the man utter so much as a mild oath in the entire time I'd ever talked to him over the last few days. He came out with two "Holy Shit!"s and a "goddam" as he listened. I ended the tale with "Look Jeremy. I know we got a done deal and all and you don't ...". Before I could get the word "owe" outta' my mouth he came back with a "Bullshit son. Don't worry about that. Where are you at right now".

I relayed our progress to this point and he responded. He said there was a particular motel or roadside inn on the south side of Yakima. He asked if I could get there and I allowed as how I figured I could and would head that way after eating a bite. He said he'd leave his place after lunch and drive north to pick me up and would stop to check the plane along the way. After picking me up we'd head down together and figure out what was wrong with the plane. I heaved a HUGE sigh of relief after hanging up. I had figured him for a decent straight sort of fellow. He was certainly measuring up to that rating so far.

Returning to the booth, again followed by the silent stares of most of the patrons, I began to relay the contents of the conversation to Selena. She asked if I'd also called Brantley. And I was in the midst of explaining how I figured I might as well wait 'til this evening when I might have a more complete picture of WHAT to report, when Jackie Gleason walked in the door. I mean. It wasn't REALLY Jackie Gleason. But if you saw the "Smokey and the Bandit" movie (starring Gleason and Burt Reynolds) I referred to earlier, it looked like another scene from the movie comin'. With a paunch belly that would make a department store Santa proud and mirrored Ray Ban sunglasses resting on a nose that would've made Rudolph (the reindeer) proud, the law had arrived on the scene. I immediately suspected this to be the occupant of one of the two State Trooper vehicles I had seen racing southbound no more than a half hour ago.

The large man stood two steps inside the glass double entry doors and turned his head slowly to the left then back through a right swivel stopping only momentarily on the four truckers. Not for nothing was this guy in law enforcement. He turned around and looking out in the parking lot counted one, two, three ... yep. Four "big rigs". Turning back to the counter he begins to resume his visual sweep of the room. I turn to my double bacon cheeseburger immediately and attack it with vigor putting on what I hope is a convincing show of "being normal" whilst trying to do what almost no one else in the room was doing ... IGNORING the man. In my mind I rapidly run through all possible scenarios that I can foresee. I fail to come up with even ONE hope for a positive outcome resulting from a conversation with this man.

I feel his gaze stop upon me and settle. I'm too scrawny to be a trucker. And I'm too white to belong here for any other reason. Like a yard square block of dry ice under the assault of Superman's heat vision I feel as if I am about to EXPLODE under his stare. My peripheral vision begins to detect his movement as I continue to turn beef into mush in my mouth. I wish I could just keep chewing for the next oh ... five minutes or so. But having pretty much liquified (except for the "bacon bits") this mouthful I have no choice but to swallow. I follow quickly with a mouthful of Coke from the oversized red plastic tumbler glass on the table in front of me. He's getting closer only two tables away as I start a sentence to Selena.

By mid-sentence he has stopped at the table and now looks down at Selena and I both sitting with overnight bags beside us in the booth. I stop and look up. I see myself, the table and the damned overnight bag in the right lens of his mirrored shades, while the left lens offers a distorted reflection of my darling Selena. The big man hooks his thumbs in his gunbelt as he speaks. "How ya'll DEWin' tuh-day boy?"

"Uh ... just fine sir. Just fine. What can I do for you officer?" I respond. And he says "You flyin' that liddle aeroplane back down the road aways south mister?" And I sez "Airplane? No, no. I don't know nuthin' about no airplane sir. Why's that?" "Oh" he relies. "Somebody landed an aeroplane back south down the road a bit and it's a bit of a problem, but obviously not YOURS". As he finishes this sentence the right hand leaves the gunbelt and goes upward to remove the Ray Bans as the left fishes in a side pocket coming out with a men's hankie.

As he polishes the lenses with apparent indifference he asks "So where YOU two from?" Afraid that he'll ask for my I.D. I answer only partially truthfully "We're hitch-hiking home to Alaska" I say. "UH-LAS-ka ya' don't say. What a co-incidence. That aeroplane was going to Uh-LAS-ka!." Quickly, a little too quickly I come back with "No kidding. Yes. That is QUITE a coincidence." "W-e-e-e-ll...." comes from him in a slow drawl. "I guess I'd best be gettin' along" he continues "gotta' figure out what we're gonna' do with that aeroplane down there".

I'm now fidgeting quite uncomfortably in my seat and my mind races. But all the gears, wheels and pointers inside my head crash to and immediate halt when I hear him utter as he replaces the Ray Bans on his nose slowly. 'Guess we'll just hafta' figger out how to cut the damn WHANGS offa' the thing an...."

Involuntarily and instantly, in a microsecond in my brain I can envision Brantley ending my LIFE in the MOST hideous and cruel manner immediately after I report that! It resulted in a quite audible and startled gasp as the lawman continues to rest his gaze on my head which is in severe danger of exploding right now! Almost unconsciously my mouth opens and blurts out "Whoawhoa ... WHOA! GeeZus man. You don't CUT the wings offa' ... uh ... oh"

Needless to say, this led to a full confession on my part. But it wasn't as bad as I thought. After I brought him up to speed on my plan, he actually turned out to be helpful. He gave us a ride to the motel where I was to meet Jeremy. And after we registered and settled into the room, he and I sat at the small circular table by the window in the motel room and filled out his necessary (multiple) reports while Selena lay on the bed watching television. The big trooper was still somewhat wary that I was being completely forthright with everything, but that ended when Jeremy showed up.

After talking to Lord knows who, he was able to assure us that the airplane could remain in it's present position for 48 more hours only. He also assured the there were frequent passages of Trooper vehicles that would eyeball it regular like. Jeremy and I both heaved a BIG sigh of relief as the Troopers car rolled out of the motel parking lot.

Jeremy and I took Selena to the closest mall and I parted with another substantial chunk of "expense" money and cab fare to get her back to the motel. Jeremy pointed his pickup truck south and we were off to the airplane.

15

Carmel Sue Somebody....

The plane was intact and appeared to have been untouched when we arrived. The first thing Jeremy wanted to do was to try and fire 'er up so we did. She caught on the first pull and the din and racket was immediate and resulted in Jeremy whacking the mixture knob closed immediately with a loud "DANG!" coming out as an accompaniment.

He clambered out of the machine and walked over to the back of his truck. He dropped the tailgate and slid a huge Craftsman brilliant and spotless red toolbox out and carried it over to the nose of the Cub. And after opening the cowlings said "I'll break the nuts and plugs loose and you talk 'em off for me, okay?" And in a couple of minutes that was accomplished. The plugs and cylinders were barely even warm to the touch the engine having only fired on each no more than a dozen times before he had shut it down.

I then watched with great interest as Jeremy went from cylinder to cylinder. He'd have me slowly rotate the prop as he placed the handle end of his socket wrench through the spark plug hole and rested it against the unseen piston head. He'd find top dead-center on each piston, then give a hard push against it. On the forward right cylinder as he pushed he gave a surprised grunt and said "Well ah'll be SWITCHED." And I said "What." He said "Wait a minnit ... les' do that one again." We did. And he said "Damn Cloudy. I don't believe it." I just looked at him puzzled and he gave his verdict. "The durn crankhaft is broke! I've never seen that happen!"

Well. I'd never heard of it either. But I knew is was damn bad and most likely expensive.

Three hours later we were back at the motel and it was approaching six o'clock. As soon as the door was even halfway open I spied Selena and she JUMPED off the bed hollering "You were on Tee-VEE! You were on the NEWS ... I mean ... the PLANE! The PLANE was on the news!" "Oh God" I groaned as Jeremy tried to hold back a laugh. "What did it say" I asked thinking to myself this must be a slow day. Couldn't President Reagan have gotten a damn cold or something??

"It just said the plane was from Alaska and landed because of engine trouble. I just saw the end of it. But there's news again at six o'clock and it might be on again you think?" see seemed eager to see it once more. I muttered quietly "Only if I'm really lucky today."

Well. The time had come. It was time to call Brantley. I steeled myself and dialed the numbers and talked to the operator asking her to reverse the charges. Brantley's secretary answered on the first ring and asked me to hold. Before I could hope for a long hold it was over and I heard Brantley's voice "Where you at cat?"

The conversation from there actually went FAR better than I ever could have hoped. He actually asked first if both Selena and I were okay. Then he asked about the airplane and was happy in his approval of my landing. He listened quietly to my post landing report right up to the "cut the wings" comment of the State Trooper where he finally started to explode as I had expected. I cut him off quickly and got the story back on track and he listened quietly as I brought him up to the minute. When I ended I waited for another explosion, but none was forthcoming. Upon my telling him that Jeremy was with us still in the room and was waiting to talk to him, Brantley was QUITE surprised and grunted "Okay. Put him on."

I listened intently as Jeremy gave Brantley a concise summary of his mechanical analysis. Then much to my surprise (I could only imagine Brantley's surprise on the other end) I continued to listen as Jeremy spelled out his offer to help us. In the background the television was playing the introduction to the six o'clock news. The first story was something about the local apple crop. This was in Yakima, after all. I hardly noticed it. And I was far more interested in Jeremy and Brantley's conversation anyway. "CLOUDY! CLOUDY!" Selena screamed! And I turned to see the full screen on the T.V display a black silhouette picture of a jetliner "broken" in half with the words "PLANE CRASH" emblazoned across the screen! I'm sure it was the only time in my life I momentarily prayed that there had been a plane crash somewhere else.

But of course, it was not to be. Jeremy had interrupted his conversation with Brantley momentarily and seeing a full screen shot of his former Cub on the television said to Brantley "Wait a minute. I got to watch this with CloudDancer. My pla ... er ... YOUR plane is on the evening news." Then a moment later said "Okay" before turning to me and saying "Brantley says turn it UP. He wants to hear it too!" "Yeah. Why nott!" I replied grabbing the remote as Jeremy held the phone receiver out in the direction of the television.

Switching from a distant shot that encompassed the entire plane, fence, cattle grate, and securing ropes the next shot was of the right side of the tail. The view moves progressively sideways to the right (forward) and continues around the nose of the airplane as the reporter states the few details known which must have been gleaned from the trooper's report. I prayed that the Trooper's had some provision against releasing names. But it didn't matter. I had forgotten.

As the cameraman continued now around the left side of the airplane still moving slowly sideways he arrives at the left wingtip. The camera is now squarely focused on the left windows. There is a very small little white square barely visible in the left bottom forward portion of the side window. The camera very, VERY slowly centers the white square in the lens and then slowly zooms in on it as I hear the reporter saying these words. "And just in case anyone stopped by and got nosy … the pilot left a note." The white speck has now grown into a recognizable full sheet of shirt-pocket notebook sized paper. It alone now fills the screen. I remember each word I wrote as we all read them on the screen together with the reporter.

"To Whom it may NOT Concern. Yes. This is a REAL airplane. No. It is NOT a toy. So please DON'T **** WITH IT! I will be back tomorrow to get it. Signed...." And then. Like a dumbass I printed my full and correct name (with middle initial) and the words "Kotzebue, Alaska" underneath. Clearly visible on the screen. My name! Oh. They BLURRED OUT the **** word so you couldn't read that! But not my name. NO! That was there in clear view on the screen bottom. And in my mind's eyes I could see half a dozen F.A.A. inspectors all over eastern Washington dropping their dinner forks to reach for THEIR pocket notebooks and a PEN!

That ended the report and I sat there dumbfounded as Jeremy laughed and renewed the conversation with Brantley. A short few minutes later they had come to terms on how Jeremy would assist me getting back on the road with a working plane (assuming of course, I was able to stay out of the FED's gunsights long enough). Jeremy said he'd be back in the morning to pick me up around eight o'clock and departed once again for Oregon.

After waving goodbye at the motel room door I flopped on the bed just as Selena bounced up and said "Let's go across the highway and eat!" Oh God. I was exhausted. My adrenal glands had worked overtime at least 50% of the day today. They must've hit redline at least twice! But I had noted as we pulled back in to the motel this evening that the large restaurant across the street had a cocktail lounge sign with the half-tipped and tilted neon martini glasses. And I definitely need a drink tonight!

We devoured a good prime rib dinner before adjourning to the cocktail lounge next door. And over MANY drinks Selena and I speculated on the various possibilities for the next few days. I was fairly sure they would be immediately decided by Brantley whose last words to Jeremy over the phone were to tell me to call him back before going to bed for the night.

After two and a half hours in the bar I insisted to Selena that we return to the room as I knew for sure at least I was going to have a busy day tomorrow, if not her. But the truth was, like a moth drawn to the flame I had to see if I made the 10 o'clock news as well. I prayed that some mayhem … a damn kidnapping … anything had occurred in this sleepy Yakima valley since six P.M. that might knock me outta' the news lineup. But it was not to be (again). And I stripped off my clothes as I sat on the end of the bed again watching the exact same report I had seen four hours earlier. Damn!

Selena emerged from the bathroom and took the remote from beside me on the bed and turned and clicked off the television. I started to look up half irritated ready to say something about how I was watching that when … instead I found myself face to bared nipples. With my mouth hanging open (I'm sure) I raised my stunned gaze upward as Selena swung her left bare leg over my legs to stand astraddle of me and placed her hands on both my shoulders. As my eyes met hers I saw a … smouldering look. Her eyes seemed ready to break out in a wildfire. I started to say something. I don't remember what, for at that instant she SHOVED me back with both hands and leaped on my prone form.

Somewhere after 1 A.M. (No. I'm not kidding you.) Somewhere AFTER 1 A.M. I finally finished what she started. This … this had been building up (in ME at least) for over five days since the night before we left. (She was busy packing you see.) And today had been an emotional rushing roller coaster for us both at times. And that's what it took apparently to break the logjam. And I'm here to TELL ya'. I mean. We did some things that … MAN! I mean I didn't KNOW there were so many different uh, … I mean … uh … summa' the positions that girl got us into! Damn! I mean every five minutes. JEEZ! And I was kinda' proud of my uh … abilities before! DAY-UM!

I was exhausted to the point of collapse after almost three hours of non-stop gymnastic performances that would have made an Olympic contender proud. With what little energy I had left I rolled over and looked at the clock. And with the last bit of energy I rolled back over and draped my arm around Selena's still rapidly rising and falling stomach and groped for one of my all time favorite play toys. Quietly I asked as I nuzzled the back of her left shoulder blade how in the hell she had come up with the ideas for some of these physically astounding positions we had so recently perfected.

I was too tired to even stay awake for the entire explanation. I just remember it was something about a picture book with cartoons done in pencil written by some Asian lady named Carmel Sue Something. I remember wondering as I feel asleep how anybody could name a kid, particularly some Asian chick Carmel Sue. Boy. Now that's dumb! (Z-z-z-z-z)

Epilogue

I've always been very fortunate and mostly accurate with my "gut instinct". And although I only had the privilege of knowing Jeremy Rogers for a very short time he is one of the most standout memorable individuals of my life.

The following morning he picked up Selena and I and drove us to the Yakima airport where Selena boarded a Horizon Airlines F-27 for Seattle to transfer to an Eskimo Airline smoker for Alaska. Brantley (wisely) decided the sooner he had her back cocktail waitressing in the Pondu the better for his "expense account". The airfare was cheaper by comparison, I'm sure.

Then Jeremy and I proceeded southbound to the airplane where, upon arrival, I met his entire extended family including his son-in-law who had arrived with a large towing trailer with a picnic table attached to it. I learned how the wings come off a Cub while the rest of the family played and read books. At midday Jeremy's daughter and wife broke out a full blown hot meal and we had a picnic by the roadside.

The original plan hatched by Jeremy and Brantley was this. The plane would be disassembled and towed back to Jeremy's place where he would crack open the engine and install a new crankshaft. Then along with a friend of his who was an AI we would quickly reassemble the airplane and with a fresh brand new annual sign off I would restart the long trip northward.

Jeremy agreed that if Brantley would pay for the parts, that he and his friend would provide the labor (along with MY assistance of course) and the annual sign-off for free. Unbelieveable.

This man had every right to tell my to go fly a kite. But he sold me this airplane. No. He really SOLD it to me. As the best. And he felt he had let us down in some way. In his eyes at least, this was not a done deal quite yet. A remarkable human being. So I could only be absolutely FURIOUS at that bastige MURPHY when he raised his ugly head yet one more time.

See, we were southbound and preparing to cross the Columbia gorge. And the wind was howling again. Jeremy, his wife and I in his pickup with the picnic table and toolboxes in back were following his son-in-law as our trucks rolled onto the bridge. We proceeded slowly across at no more that 35 MPH or so. I don't know if going any faster or slower would have changed what was coming. But halfway across we winced and both uttered the same curse as we saw the tail of the airplane break it's restraints and instantly jump about a foot and a half sideways to slam into the side rail of the trailer 20 yards ahead of us.

His son-in-law knew what had happened of course as we could see his wife and kids looking backward out of their cab. But stopping on the bridge was FAR to dangerous for all involved. And although he knew nothing about flying he was smart enough to turn east coming off the bridge so that when we stopped the fuselage was nosed into the wind.

Jeremy and I inspected the new damage in silence. We found even more ropes and tied the tail much more securely before turning westward for the short remaining distance to Hood River and Jeremy's home. I listened in awe as Jeremy called Brantley, informed him and took full responsibility as he and he alone had initially secured the plane to the trailer.

I think it took three more weeks to get all the work done. And then about another week and a half to finally make it back to Kotzebue with the airplane. I finally arrived back in Kotzebue after a final stop to show the plane off to my friends in Kiana. I thought that everything that had possibly gone wrong could have. For a while at least. But, of course I was wrong.

Four and a half weeks is far ... FAR too long to leave a BABE of a girl un ... um ... unattended in Kotzebeu. Hell. Four and a half DAYS is too long to leave most any decent looking chick unattended anywhere in Alaska. It appeared I was a bachelor again as Selena had uh, moved on in my absence. (Something she had failed to tell me in the two or three times I'd managed to catch up to her by phone since we last saw each other.) Of course Brantley, not wishing to distract me from the focus of my mission, didn't deem it important enough to relay to me either in our almost DAILY update conversations.

Whatever. I was a PILOT again. In search of a new flying job.

In the Beginning

Many of you have written or Emailed or even called to ask a common question. "CloudDancer. How did you wind up in Alaska in the first place?" So I thought it appropriate to put in Volume II . Might save you a stamp or your long distance money.

I've spent countless dozens of hour pondering it. I believe it changed the entirety of my being. I changed who I was and what kind of man I was to become. I saw wonders undreamt or even unheard of before in my life. The formerly significant now became meaningless and the trivial became treasured. Was the genesis of the "Chronicles" an intervention of Fate, a stroke of luck, or just good Karma? I've always felt it was more than just a "chance" encounter between a teen-aged CloudDancer with "Dan Gunderson" of Kotzebue.

It was in 1973 and Dan was in Fort Worth Texas at Meacham to earn his Air Transport license. He had come all the way from Alaska lured by the old Ed Boardman's ad in Flying magazine.

This meeting occurred when Dan, tired of dining at the café at Fort Worth's Meacham Airport, rented a car and got on the nearest freeway. After over a week in the airport motel and terminal coffee shop he was restless and bored. He was determined to find a different restaurant in which to dine. He found the nearest freeway and proceeded to timidly entered the traffic. Coming from an Eskimo village of 2600 people in the arctic Dan was a little short of freeway driving experience. He found the traffic to be very intense and much to his dislike. He therefore determined that the would exit the madness at the first sign of a decent restaurant.

It so happened at that very moment, young CloudDancer was sitting in a restaurant of a well-known national chain having a last cup of joe. He was on his was to make a fourth and final visit to the army recruiter's office. He fully expected he'd be signing enlistment papers in the next couple of hours.

This particular restaurant had played an extremely significant role in young CloudDancer's life since it opened in early 1970. CD had wiled away hundreds of hour as a customer swilling iced tea after Civil Air Patrol meetings, search and rescue missions, and weekend bivouacs where we honed our skills. Hours were spent antagonizing the poor waitresses while I and my fellow cadets discussed our dreams of future flying and fame and glory. And sometimes we'd just talk airplanes in general.

Indeed it was in this very same building in which a young CloudDancer bussed tables, swept floors and washed dishes for many months. The meager dollars and pennies earned were poured into my first flight ratings. Why one Christmas Eve, when all the waitresses except one failed to show up for work, it was our young protagonist who came to the rescue. On his night off, he went home and donned clean black pants and a white shirt. Then he returned to the restaurant to don a waitress apron.

The customers laughed and enjoyed the spectacle of our bewildered young airman-to-be giving his all for the cause. Their patience was remarkable as was their generosity. My "shift" lasted for four-and-a-half hours, until the 10P.M. girls came to work. And the customer's $57.43 in tips bought another four hours of dual for my commercial. But of course we're talking about meeting "Dan Gundersen", which was the second most life-impacting significant event associated with that dining establishment.

The manager of this place owned a Cessna 172. He an I would quite often spend some of his slow time in flying discussions and we were doing so this day. You see, I had decided to enlist for the V.A. benefits as I saw no other way to effectively achieve my career goals in a timely fashion. However enlisting in the Army was a big step that I must admit I was somewhat unsettled about given the time-frame in our country's history. It was into this moment, having spotted the large sign visible from the freeway blundered Dan Gunderson.

As I had cup after cup of coffee and chatted about flying Cessna 172's with Steve the manager, Dan Gunderson sat a few feet away. He was faced 90 degrees to me and Steve at the other counter. We both noticed that he was listening intently but remained completely silent as the thirty minutes passed in which he consumed his meal. Then standing next to me only a couple of feet away as he paid his bill at the register, I could feel his stare as I knew he was taking glances at me.

After he walked out, we watched him climb into his brand new Yellow, brown, and cream Plymouth Omega and drive away. We both thought the guy was a little *weird* ya' know? I mean, he was really paying attention to our conversation. *Weird*. Huh. Oh well. He's gone.

I decide to have a procrastinating seventh and final cup of coffee and talk my decision over with Steve one last time. Unbeknownst to us meanwhile, Dan Gunderson has gone down the street where, spotting a Dairy Queen sign, gives in to his ice cream craving. And as he sits inside the DQ methodically destroying a banana split with extra whipped cream and nuts he is mulling not only his future, but the future of his family's flying service back home in Kotzebue.

He and brother Rod have been mulling over the idea in recent weeks of hiring a pilot as they quite often lose trips for lack of help. They had just yesterday decided over the phone that Dan should look for a suitable candidate while down south. This, despite the fact that the first and only other pilot they had hired just the previous week was from Texas and had just quit after three days with no notice in a dispute over "maintenance procedures". (See "If You EVER Do THAT Again".) Dan was truly at a loss as to how to hire someone and what he was looking for.

He kept thinking back to the kid he had listened to talking in the restaurant. Maybe he might be okay. Maybe inexperience was a good thing. We could teach him RIGHT. He didn't really sound like he was too convinced about that Army thing. But would he want to go to Alaska?

This and a hundred other thoughts raced through his mind as the three piles of soft ice cream and their toppings of chocolate, pineapple, and strawberries began to mingle and melt into a cold, sweet soup in the red plastic "boat" serving dish.

Unable to reach a LOGICAL conclusion "Dan" decided to rely on FATE. As he slurped the last of the ice cream down he made a decision. He would drive the two blocks back to the dining establishment where he had seen the kid. If the kid was still there he would talk to him, and if he liked what he heard he would offer him a job. If the kid was gone … well … then, he must not have been the guy they needed.

Meanwhile (back at the ranch) CloudDancer has had all the coffee he wants at this sitting, knowing full well the last two cups were pure procrastination. Four years as an Army Warrant Officer in return for the V.A. benefits that would pay for all his ratings and college. Then … look out American, Delta, Braniff, TWA, Eastern, PanAm, Western and all. Here comes

CLOUDDANCER! Who will be the lucky airline that gets him!

The nagging thought that somehow he might actually have to spend the whole four years flying them damn fling-wing UH-1's or Chinooks bothered him only a little. After all, the recruiting officer had repeatedly *assured* him that the TOP 2% of each class was guaranteed fixed wing assignments. And with your fixed wing experience "you should be a shoe-in". And of course, our Cloudy, with his vast experience of all of 243 hours at the time, not to mention all the cockiness of youth figures he is in the top 2% of all pilots anywhere anyway. So. Should be no PROOOOblem. Right!?

With a sigh of resignation our fledgling aviator slides his empty cup across the counter. Arising from the stool he slides his hand into his pocket fishing for his wallet. The manager straightens up, unfolds his arms and extends his right hand. He says "No. This cup is on me, my friend, and best of luck" as a firm handshake is exchanged. At the swinging glass door CloudDancer stops for a moment and turns around and looks about the restaurant, empty but for a couple of other mid-afternoon coffee drinkers and two waitresses.

Steve looks at him, not having moved from the spot where they shook hands. As CloudDancer's glance comes to Steve he says "Boy ... I've had a lot of history here ... See ya." and walks out the door.

The parking lot all but empty, I walk the twenty or so paces to my car door in deep reflection of my life thus far. My left hand grasps the car door handle to yank upward and release the door and at that exact moment behind me I hear HONK! HONK! HONK! I stop and look over my right shoulder to see what the hell all the honking is about! I am flabbergastered to see that same weird guy from in the restaurant a while ago sitting out in traffic honking his horn. He stops doing it when he sees me turn around and look at him. Wha ... the HELL??

He is sitting awaiting the opportunity to make a left turn back into the parking lot where I stand now puzzled as heck. Holding his left arm out the window, it seems as if he is pointing at me! His hand is out palm flat up and forward like a traffic cop. I look curiously around me and, as I knew, I am alone with my car in the parking lot. So across the some twenty-five of thirty yard distance I put the most quizzical look on my face. I poke myself in the chest with my right index finger and mouth the word "me?" The old guy in the Omega, glancing repeatedly forward looking for a break in the oncoming cars so he can turn in now nods his head rapidly up and down and turns forward again.

Now, I know Momma CloudDancer always told me not to talk to strangers. So far this guy certainly qualifies. But, I can't help it (sorry Ma) ... I gotta' get this guy' story I lean against my closed car door and fold my arms across my chest. He pulls in three spots over and gets out and I study him walking around the back of his car toward me. A good six inches shorter than I and slightly roly-poly I look him down and up.

As my eyes rise to his face again I lean forward off my car as he sticks his hand out in greeting. His eyes dance in amusement at my look of obvious bewilderment, but his goofy grin is almost immediately infectious. "Hiya" he says quite calmly. "My name is Dan."

"Hey Dan. My name is CloudDancer. What can I do ya' for?" which gets a chuckle from him.

And he says ... "So. You're a PILOT, huh?" And now Chronicle readers, as one of my all-time favorite story-tellers is wont to say ... "And NOW ... you know the REST of the story"

(credit: Paul Harvey)

Closing Comments

Once more we reach the end of another
collection of CloudDancer memories.

Again it is most important to me to offer you my
deepest thanks and appreciation for the precious time
you have spent sharing these true stories of my younger
days. It is a great privilege and honor for me that remains
the real highlight of the later decades of my life.

In 2009 I will release "CloudDancer's Alaskan Chronicles"
Volume III, the Tragedies. Unlike the first two books, it
will provide little, if any laughter. Because quite often there
were true stories that weren't funny. But they were as much
a part of the arctic flying experience as the humorous ones were
I hope in telling them, that quite possibly I might exorcize
some of the demons that I have lived with for the last thirty years.

Meanwhile as always, you're invited to stop by my
website at www.clouddancer.org. You'll find there an
easy link to Email me your thoughts and feedback. I
really love hearing from you guys, even when you feel
the need to throw a raspberry or two.

As before, the Chronicles remain a true labor of
love written for the common man in common language.
It never was, nor is my intent to be anything other than who
and what I truly am. I'm just a regular pilot who, after repeated
prodding from my internet readers, decided to create this series.

CloudDancer

978-0-595-48770-7
0-595-48770-X

CPSIA information can be obtained at www.ICGtesting.com
Printed in the USA
LVOW12s2031010615

440733LV00001B/139/P